FRENCH VINEYARDS

French Vineyards

The Complete Guide and Companion

Michael Busselle

PAVILION

To Pat

First published in Great Britain in 1998 by
PAVILION BOOKS LIMITED
London House, Great Eastern Wharf, Parkgate Road, London SW11 4NQ

Text © Michael Busselle 1998
Photographs © Michael Busselle 1998
Maps © ML Design 1998

Designed by Andrew Barron and Collis Clements Associates

The moral right of the author has been asserted.

A CIP catalogue record for this book is available from the British Library

ISBN 1 85793 598 5

Typeset in 10/13 Berkeley OS Book
Printed and bound in Spain by Bookprint
Colour reproduction by Anglia Graphics

2 4 6 8 10 9 7 5 3 1

This book may be ordered by post direct from the publisher.
Please contact the Marketing Department
but try your bookshop first.

Distributed in the U.S. by Trafalgar Square Publishing,
North Pomfret, Vermont.

FRONTISPIECE:
THE CHATEAU OF ALOXE CORTON IN THE CÔTES DES NUITS.

CONTENTS

ACKNOWLEDGEMENTS

I would like to thank Catherine Manac'h of Sopexa for her invaluable help in researching the book and to Gillian Green of Air France Holidays for arranging my trip to Corsica. I would also like to thank the countless kindly French vignerons I've encountered in the course of my travels, who have patiently answered my questions and spent time showing me their vineyards and caves. Last, but not least, I'd like to thank my wife Pat for keeping me company, acting as unpaid photographer's assistant and becoming, if only in self defence, a pretty good navigator.

INTRODUCTION

M Y OBSESSION WITH vineyards began a long time ago, on one of my very first visits to France, 39 years ago, when I saw a road sign pointing towards a village which had the same name as one of my favourite wines. Since then I've followed countless such signs and a consuming ambition was born to visit every wine-growing area in France, from the smallest plantings of *vin de pays* to the biggest of the great and famous vineyards.

After very many years of travelling through the French countryside, I have now achieved this aim, completing my travels even with a tour of the Corsican vineyards. However, the task can never be truly complete, as in recent decades there has been a revival of many vineyards which were destroyed during the phylloxera blight, and new, small vineyards are being planted as I write.

To make the book easy to use as a reference for those travelling through a particular part of France I have arranged this book in regional sections which are further sub-divided into the individual *départements*. In the larger wine-growing areas, and those with a signposted *route des vins*, I have listed details of the individual *appellations*, grape varieties and style of wine separately from the descriptions of the tour, but not in the smaller vineyard areas, such as some of the Vin de Pays and VDQS *appellations* where there is often just one or two wine villages and a limited range of wines and grape varieties.

The large-scale Michelin maps, or the Michelin atlas, are essential to locate many of the places I describe. The key wine towns and villages of each region are indicated on the regional maps and by referring to these in the Michelin index an appropriate page or sheet number can be readily found.

Along with descriptions of regional food and local specialities I have also, in the end section of the book, included a glossary of the principal grape varieties used in making French wines to help provide a guide to the type and style of wine produced in each vineyard.

Mike Busselle

PAYS DE LA LOIRE

THE REGION OF Pays de la Loire encompasses the *départements* of Mayenne, Maine-et-Loire, Loire-Atlantique and Vendée. To the north lie Normandy and Brittany, to the south Poitou-Charentes, while the region of Centre lies to the east and to the west is the Atlantic. Many rivers criss-cross this mostly flat landscape, which has large open spaces of water meadows, orchards, fields of grain and vineyards. The most important vineyards are planted close to the River Loire in the *départements* of Loire-Atlantique and Maine-et-Loire, but there are also some to be found in Vendée.

LOIRE-ATLANTIQUE
THE WINES

THE APPELLATIONS TO which the *département* is entitled are: AOC – Muscadet, Muscadet des Coteaux de la Loire, Muscadet de Sèvre-et-Maine and Muscadet Côtes de Grand Lieu; VDQS – Coteaux d'Ancenis and Gros Plant du Pays Nantais; and Vins de Pays – Marches de Bretagne and Pays de Retz.

During the seventeenth century the Dutch were enthusiastic consumers of the wines of Nantes; they were exacting too, always wanting more and better quality wines. Much of the wine made here was red, and it was not until a catastrophic winter in 1709, when the sea itself froze and most of the vines were destroyed, that white wine began to be made in any quantity.

The disaster was a blessing in disguise. The *vignerons* decided to replant their vineyards with a white grape that was more frost resistant than the black they had

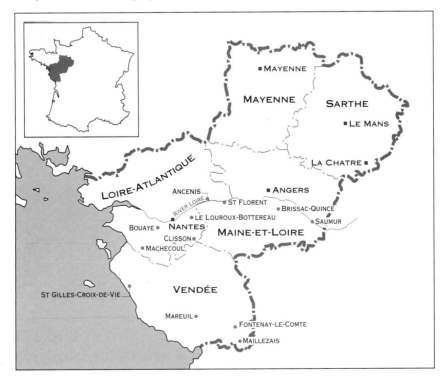

ABOVE TOP: VILLAGE HOUSES NEAR ANCENIS.
ABOVE: MUSCADET VINEYARDS NEAR LA VARENNE.
OPPOSITE: VINEYARDS OF THE COTEAUX D'ANCENIS OVERLOOKING THE LOIRE.

been using. The grape, Melon de Bourgogne, became known locally as the Muscadet; the wine made from it, although generally inexpensive, is recognized as one of the classic whites of France. Muscadet de Sèvre-et-Maine was awarded an Appellation Contrôlée in 1926. It is a crisp, dry wine, and is the perfect accompaniment to the seafood and shellfish found in the region.

The vineyards of Muscadet extend south and east of Nantes, but the most highly acclaimed wines are made around the villages to the south-east of the city. They take their name from the two rivers that traverse this countryside – the Sèvre and the Maine. The best Muscadet de Sèvre-et-Maine comes from the regions of the towns of Vallet, St-Fiacre and Maisdon-sur-Sèvre.

Muscadet des Coteaux de la Loire is produced in vineyards on both banks of the Loire, while Muscadet Côtes de Grand Lieu is produced from nine communes to the south east of Nantes, near the lake of that name. Much of the Muscadet you will experience is called Muscadet-sur-Lie; this is very slightly *pétillant*, a mere tingle on the palate. The term '*sur lie*' means that the wine is left to drain naturally after fermentation while still in contact with the lees (the sediment of the must), rather than being racked off and filtered into a fresh cask or container; this causes a small amount of carbon dioxide to be retained after bottling, creating the very slight fizz.

Another notably dry white wine is produced in the Pays Nantais region. Gros Plant, which has the designation VDQS, is made from the Folle Blanche grape, and the area of production is much wider than that of Muscadet, extending from the Atlantic coast to the south of the Loire estuary. It is also made '*sur lie*'.

Coteaux d'Ancenis wines are produced in the vineyards around the town of Ancenis, on the north bank of the Loire. They are mainly red or rosé, with some white, and are also classified VDQS. In addition, some Vins de Pays are made in the region: Vin de Pays des Marches de Bretagne is produced in Sèvre-et-Maine and is a red wine made from Gamay or Cabernet Franc. Vin de Pays de Retz is produced in the triangle of countryside between the Loire Estuary, Bourgneuf-en-Retz and Pont-St-Martin, using a range of grape varieties. Red and rosé wines are made from Cabernet Franc and Gamay as well as Grolleau Gris, a variety which is seldom found elsewhere in France under its own name.

THE VINEYARDS

Ancenis, situated on the north bank of the Loire, and boasting a tenth-century château which was partly destroyed in 1624, is a good place to start exploring the vineyards of Loire-Atlantique. The town was a busy port during the eighteenth century but is now known for its pig market and its wine trade. It is worth visiting the *cave co-opérative* situated on the main road just to the east of Ancenis.

The Route des Vins begins by crossing the suspension bridge to the village of Liré, where there is a museum dedicated to Joachim du Bellay, the sixteenth-century poet who was born in Liré. Continue westwards along the D 751 to the small wine village of Drain and then to Champtoceaux, an attractive town set high up on the hillside above the Loire. Along the edge of the hill behind the church, there is a small park with inspiring views over the river below. From Champtoceaux the road winds down to the riverside, a pleasant spot for a picnic or a stroll. The road climbs again, providing some sweeping views over the vineyards to the Loire and the northern bank of the river, and then continues to the village of La Varenne. The Château de la Varenne, a large elegant mansion set in a wooded park, has a *caveau* where visitors are welcome to taste the wine.

The route continues through the village of La Chapelle-Basse-Mer, notable for its lofty church spire, to the important wine town of Le Loroux-Botterau. From here the wine route continues along the D 307, past Moulin-du-Pré, where a number of ancient windmills are to be seen on the top of the vine-clad hill. Drive up to the oldest one – which has a cross mounted on it – where the views over the vineyards are breathtaking.

The route continues through the small wine villages of Le Landreau and La Chapelle-Heulin to Vallet, which is known for its wine market, held each year in March. There is a Maison du Vin here where you can taste and buy wines from more than 40 different *vignerons*, and a lively market takes place in the church square on Sundays. The route follows the D 763 to the small but important wine village of Mouzillon, distinguished by its Gallo-Roman bridge, and then on to Clisson, a very picturesque little town with a ruined château, an ancient covered market that is still in use, narrow streets lined with old houses, a fourteenth-century church and an impressive viaduct spanning the River Maine. There is a tasting cellar next to the covered market.

A few kilometres north of Clisson, on the N 149, is Pallet, an important wine town where a number of *vignerons* and *négociants* invite visitors to sample their wines. There was a fortress erected by the dukes of Brittany here once; now you will have to content yourself with a picnic on the gentle banks of the River Sèvre. Crossing the river just beyond Pallet you come to the village of Monnières. Nearby is the old mill of La Minière, surrounded by vineyards. The view is superb – it is claimed that ten church steeples can be seen from here. One of these is in the next small village, St-Fiacre-sur-Main, where the Byzantine-style church tower soars up high above the vineyards. This is one of the most highly reputed wine communities in the Pay Nantais, and there is a greater proportion of land given over to vines than anywhere else in France. If you are in the area at the end of September then a short detour to la Haie-Fouassière will reveal a convivial wine fair at this time every year.

The next wine town, Vertou, on the outskirts of Nantes, is a lively, medium-sized place; there is an attractive riverside promenade and plenty of opportunities to taste and buy the wines of the region. From Vertou you take the D 74 towards the village of Haute-Goulaine. On the outskirts is the magnificent Château de Goulaine, which dates from the fifteenth century. You can taste the château's own wine and take a guided tour of the building. Cross over the Loire to Thouaré-sur-Loire and continue through the wine villages of Mauves and Le Cellier (which has an annual wine fair at the end of September) to the riverside town of Oudon, dominated by an enormous medieval keep – if you brave the climb to the top you'll be rewarded with a panoramic view of the Loire valley. The wine villages of Couffé and St-Géréon complete the circuit back to Ancenis.

Pays de Retz

Although the vineyards are much smaller and more widely distributed than in the Pays Nantais, those of the Pays de Retz provide a valuable diversion for those seeking the lesser-known wines of France as well as an insight into a peaceful countryside of water meadows, marshes and lonely beaches. A tour can be made by beginning in the village of Pont-St-Martin, about 10 kilometres south-west of Nantes.

A few kilometres west of Pont-St-Martin is a silent and rather mysterious lake, Le Lac de Grand Lieu. Surrounded by reedy fringes and marshy terrain, it is the

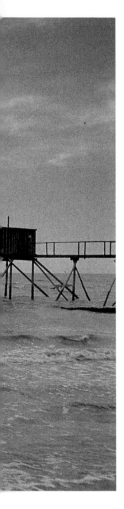

ABOVE: A VIGNERON OF THE MUSCADET REGION.
OPPOSITE TOP: FISHING PLATFORMS NEAR BOURGNEUF-EN-RETZ.
OPPOSITE BELOW: THE HARBOUR OF PORT-DU-BEC NEAR EPOIDS.

haunt of freshwater fishermen who paddle across it in flat-bottomed boats to catch eels, pike, tench and zander. I watched a fisherman unload two enormous zanders, 10 or 12 kilos each, and a basket of plump bream into a perforated keeping-box half-submerged in the water before punting his small craft out on to the lake for another sortie. The lake can be approached from the village of Passay where there is a viewing platform from which to observe the abundant birdlife.

The nearby town of St-Philbert-de-Grand-Lieu is an important production area for Gros Plant, and there is a tasting kiosk on the edge of the town. The abbey church of St-Philbert-de-Grand-Lieu at the southern edge of the lake is one of the oldest in France, founded by monks from the island of Noirmoutier in AD 815. It contains the sarcophagus of St Philbert, who was born in Gascony at the beginning of the seventh century. Machecoul, 15 kilometres to the west, was the historic capital of the Pays de Retz. Here stand the ruins of the four-teenth-century castle of Gilles de Retz, who fought alongside Joan of Arc. He later became a notorious criminal and the model for writer Charles Perrault's character Bluebeard in the story first published in 1697.

At Bourgneuf-en-Retz, near the coast, there is a small museum displaying the history and culture of the Pays de Retz, set in a charming seventeenth-century house. The rather bleak, muddy coastline to the west harbours the oyster beds of the Bay of Bourgneuf; the shoreline is covered feet-deep in old shells, and numerous rickety wooden fishing platforms jut out towards the sea. To the north is Pornic, a pretty fishing port at the head of a deep inlet where sailing boats are moored at the foot of a thirteenth-century castle.

MAINE-ET-LOIRE

THE MAIN WINE-GROWING region lies to the south of the Loire between Angers and Saumur. Vines have been grown here for well over a thousand years and the wine was widely exported, much of it to London, especially after Henry Plantagenet, Count of Anjou, succeeded to the English throne in 1154. From the Middle Ages right up until last century, the Loire was an important waterway and the export trade continued to flourish; again the Dutch were major customers for the wine and to some extent controlled its production.

THE WINES

This relatively small area produces a considerable variety of wines. The most widely known are the rosés, most particularly the sweetish Rosé d'Anjou, made mainly from the Grolleau grape variety: its popularity has declined somewhat recently because of the general trend away from rosés to dry wines. Cabernet d'Anjou, another rosé made here, is generally considered to be superior; it can be either semi-sweet or dry. Rosé de Loire is quite a dry wine; Gamay and Pinot Noir grapes are used in its production. Finally, there is Cabernet de Saumur, a rosé similar to Cabernet d'Anjou but a little drier and paler in colour.

Méthode champenoise wines – Saumur Mousseux or Saumur d'Origine and Anjou Mousseux – are also made in this region, those of Saumur being particu-larly well known. Much of the wine is stored in vast caverns and tunnels carved into the tufa (coarse rock) cliffs near Saumur, very much like those of Champagne itself. These wines are made from a variety of grapes, including the Chenin Blanc, Chardonnay, Sauvignon, Grolleau, Pinot Noir and Gamay. Another sparkling wine found in the region is Crémant de Loire, and *pétillant* wines are also made.

The region's white wines also offer some interesting varieties, such as those from Savennières, produced in a few vineyards on the north bank of the Loire just to the west of Angers. Highly alcoholic, the wines are dry and fresh with a lovely bouquet reminiscent of honeysuckle. There are two additional separate appellations within this tiny region: Coulée de Serrant and La Roche-aux-Moines, both capable of considerable ageing.

White wines are also made in the Layon valley, south of the Loire. The appellation is Coteaux du Layon; it is a sweet wine made from the Chenin Blanc grape, often served chilled as an aperitif. Within this region are two individual appellations, Quarts de Chaume and Bonnezeaux, both sweet, fruity, white wines. An appellation from the region around the small River Aubance is Coteaux de l'Aubance; these wines are mainly white, but reds and rosés are also made here. Anjou-Coteaux de la Loire, from vineyards to the north of the river, is a white wine, either dry or semi-dry. There are also dry white wines produced under the appellations Anjou Blanc and Saumur Blanc.

Red wines are also made in the Anjou-Saumur region from the Cabernet Franc, Cabernet Sauvignon and Pineau d'Aunis grapes. The appellations are Saumur Rouge, Anjou Rouge and Saumur-Champigny, the latter being a particularly appealing red wine with a rich ruby colour and a bouquet reminiscent of violets.

THE VINEYARDS

The vineyards of Anjou-Saumur are separated from those of Touraine by only a few kilometres. The wine route is signposted, but fairly convoluted, and I have suggested a simplified circuit, which can easily be extended or modified as time allows.

The little village of Montsoreau is the starting place; it lies beside the Loire, and has an imposing fifteenth-century château with a fortress-like exterior looming high above the houses. There are hotels and restaurants, and a well-positioned campsite by the riverside. It is also a good spot for angling. A small road climbs the hill behind the village and you can follow a track up through the vineyards for a magnificent panorama of the château and river.

A short detour to the south along the D 147 leads to Fontevraud l'Abbaye with its famous abbey founded in the eleventh century and containing the bones of four, possibly eight, Plantagenet kings and queens. This was no ordinary abbey – it was made up of communities of monks, nuns, repentant prostitutes and lepers, under the control of a woman. Fontevraud is particularly fine architecturally, because the medieval monastery buildings survive in their entirety. The kitchens are especially interesting; set in a huge octagonal tower, they have an ingenious ventilation system, the smoke from the five fireplaces being removed by a cluster of twenty chimneys.

Returning to the D 751 (which becomes the D 947 after Fontevraud), continue towards Saumur. The road runs between the tufa cliffs (formed from porous calcium carbonate rock) and the riverbank, passing the small wine villages of Turquant, Parnay and Souzay-Champigny. Some of the small roads which wind up into the vineyards behind these villages are well worth a detour, as the countryside is both pleasing and peaceful. The nearby town of St-Cyr-en-Bourg has an excellent *cave co-opérative* where you can buy a good Saumur-Champigny.

The town of Saumur is about 5 kilometres north. This was a Huguenot stronghold in the sixteenth and seventeenth centuries. Like every self-respecting

THE CHATEAU OF SAUMUR OVERLOOKING THE LOIRE.

town in the Loire region, it has a spectacular château; here, it is perched high up above the blue-grey slate roofs of the town. The Château de Saumur was built by Louis X at the end of the fourteenth century and in its time has been a prison and a barracks as well as a fort. It now houses two museums, including one of the history of the horse – Saumur is now famed for the Cadre Noir, the national riding school.

A kilometre or so west are the twin towns of St-Hilaire and St-Florent, where most of the sparkling Saumur wines are made and stored in huge tufa caves; here the *vignerons* vie for space with the flourishing mushroom-growing trade, and you can sample the wines and visit a mushroom museum.

A short drive to the south of Saumur along the N 147 leads to the hill town of Montreuil-Bellay, set on the left bank of the River Thouet. From here you take the D 88 and the D 31 to the village of Bouillé-Loretz and then follow the D 159 to the village of Passavant-sur-Layon, where a small peaceful lake is overlooked by a ruined château. The Layon valley leads northwards through a succession of quiet and pretty little villages set amid gently undulating countryside where the vineyards that produce the wonderful sweet white wines of the Coteaux du Layon are mingled with meadows and vast fields of sunflowers and maize.

The wine village of Martigné-Briand is dominated by the ruins of a château destroyed in the war between the republicans and royalists in 1793. Continuing through the villages of Aubigné and Rablay-sur-Layon, you come to Beaulieu-sur-Layon. Here there is a Cave des Vignerons, where you can sample and buy the local wines and admire an impressive collection of ancient Angevin wine bottles and glasses.

A little to the south-west the N 160 crosses the Layon to the wine village of St-Lambert-du-Lattay. From here a small road winds through the hillsides where the Quarts de Chaumes grapes are grown to the village of St-Aubin-de-Luigné; nearby is the ruined Château de la Haute Guerche. Drive down to the riverside town of Rochefort-sur-Loire, which declares itself a capital of wine; it has a tasting chalet just outside the town. Rochefort also boasts a Romanesque church built of granite, and a fine campsite.

Crossing the Loire, or rather its several 'arms', you come to Savennières, famed for its dry white wine. Between two bridges a road on the right leads to Béhuard, an island on which there is an ancient village of stone houses; in the centre is a tiny chapel built on a rock. From Savennières it is only a short detour to St-Georges-sur-Loire, where you can see the remains of an ancient priory, part of which is used as the town hall. Close by is the grandiose, moated Château de Serrant, which was designed by Philibert Delorme, the architect of the Tuileries gardens in Paris (the chapel is by Jules Hardouin-Mansart, whose most famous works are the Invalides Chapel and the Place Vendôme in Paris). The château is surrounded by a well-tended park and is magnificently furnished.

Returning to Savennieres and taking the riverside road, the D 111, turn right into a small lane about 1 kilometre before Epiré and you will come to the Château de la Roche-aux-Moines, where the famous Coulée de Serrant wine is produced from the vineyards high on the hill above the river; visitors are welcome both to taste the wine and to visit the château and gardens.

The village of Epiré is the home of a number of growers producing Savennières wines as well as Coulée de Serrant and la Roche-aux-Moines. It was in these prize vineyards that I saw a machine being used to harvest the grapes. No, this wasn't mechanization at the cost of quality, I was told. On the contrary, the machines allow the grapes to be harvested in a fraction of the time taken by hand picking and therefore the level of ripeness is more constant – which must improve quality. Another advantage is that harvesting can be continued at night, when the temperatures are lower, causing less oxidation and spoilage of the juice.

Along this riverside road to the east is Angers. Recross the Loire here and follow the D 761 south for about 12 kilometres to the town of Brissac-Quincé, with its elegant, seven-storey château dating from the seventeenth century; it was built by the second Duc de Brissac and, uniquely, was returned to the family after the Revolution. You can complete the wine circuit by going back to the Loire along the D 55 to St-Rémy-la-Varenne, with the nearby ruined Abbaye de Sainte Maure, and then following the very attractive riverside road through the villages of le Thoureil and Gennes back to Saumur.

VENDÉE

THE VINEYARDS

TO THE SOUTH of Bourgneuf-en-Retz is the Marais de Machecoul, a marshy landscape of reed-fringed dikes, streams and muddy creeks threading their way through moist meadows. Here, between Bourgneuf and the island of Noirmoutier, are the borders of the Vendée and a coastline which is almost completely dedicated to the cultivation of oysters.

At Epoids, to the west of Beauvoir-sur-Mer, is a wide, muddy inlet lined by moored fishing boats around which a fisherman's village has developed, with wooden shacks, rickety jetties and shops which sell everything from anglers' tackle to boats and outboard motors. There are places, too, where you can buy a dozen of the freshest oysters you're ever likely to taste, with a bottle of Pays de Retz or Fiefs Vendéens to wash them down.

Fiefs Vendéens is a VDQS appellation which was granted in 1984 to the vineyards of the Vendée. These, as in many other French wine-growing regions, were much more extensive during the Middle Ages. Planted initially by the Romans, the vineyards were taken under the wing of the many abbeys which were constructed during the tenth and eleventh centuries, and this has led to the appellation being given the appendage of Fiefs. Both Rabelais and Cardinal Richelieu were admirers of the Vendée wines, which at one time were given the name of Anciens Fiefs du Cardinal.

Today there are about 340 hectares of vines in all, farmed by 130 *vignerons* who belong to the Syndicat des Fiefs Vendéens. The vineyards are cultivated in four quite separate areas, each producing wines with a distinctive character. More than 60 per cent of the production is sold directly to the public by the *vignerons*, and although there is no *cave co-opérative* there are numerous opportunities to taste and buy the wines.

Brem-sur-Mer

The most northerly of the Vendée vineyards are those around the village of Brem-sur-Mer, just south of St-Gilles-Croix-de-Vie. Brem-sur-Mer consists, in fact, of two villages, St-Martin-de-Brem and St-Nicholas-de-Brem, the latter of which was burnt by pirates in the ninth century and reconstructed in 1020. The little church of Brem dates from this period in the eleventh century and was dedicated to Saint Nicholas, the patron saint of sailors. The vineyards extend around the neighbouring villages of Brétignolles-sur-Mer, Landeveille, L'Île d'Olonne and Olonne-sur-Mer.

The Domaine de St Nicholas at Brem is one of the leading producers in this region and has an extensive modern winery and *caveau*. Red, white and rosé wines are made here by Patrice Michon and his sons, using Chardonnay, Gamay and Pinot Noir from their vineyards around L'Île d'Olonne, a nearby village marooned within a curious marshy region of muddy creeks and dikes.

From St-Martin a road leads along a creek to a gloriously wide sandy beach, backed by dunes, which extends for many miles to the north and south. Access to the beach is also possible from St-Nicholas which is busier and more of a resort than the quiet fishing hamlet of St-Martin.

Further north, at Brétignolles-sur-Mer, a small road loops off from the D 38 and follows the wide sandy beach for several kilometres. One of the finest beaches in this region is at the busy seaside resort of St-Jean-de-Monts, about 20 kilometres to the north, where a wide boulevard runs alongside the seashore. To the south, along the sand dunes backing the Atlantic ocean, is Les Sables-d'Olonne, an elegant town which was custom-built during the last century as the Vendée's first seaside resort.

Mareuil-sur-Lay

About 50 kilometres east of Les Sables-d'Olonne is the little town of Mareuil-sur-Lay, where a lovely twelfth-century church and the remains of a feudal château complete an attractive waterside scene.

The countryside around Mareuil contains the largest section of the Vendée vineyards. They extend to the villages of Bessay, Château-Guibert, Chaille-sous-les-Ormeaux, Le Champ-St-Père, Corpe, La Couture, Dissais, Rosnay, St-Florent-des-Bois and Le Tablier. Mareuil is known primarily for its rosé, but red and white wines are also made from the permitted grape varieties of Chardonnay, Chenin Blanc, Sauvignon Blanc, Colombard, Pinot Blanc, Cabernet Franc/Sauvignon, Pinot Noir, Cot and Gamay.

There is a small outpost of the Mareuil vineyards to the north-east, around the town of Chantonnay, but these are beyond the boundaries of the VDQS appellation and are sold as Vins de Pays de la Vendée or Jardin de la France. Philippe Orion, based at the village of St-Philbert-du-Pont-Charrault, is one producer making red, white and rosé wines from varieties similar to those used for Fiefs Vendéens.

Vix

The third small area of Fiefs Vendéens wines can be found around the village of Vix, 30 kilometres or so to the south-east of Mareuil. There is just one producer, the Domaine de la Chaignée, with a total vineyard area of about 25 hectares. A white wine is made here with a base of Sauvignon Blanc with some Chardonnay and Chenin Blanc. A rosé is made from a blend of Gamay, Pinot Noir and Cabernet, and a red from Cabernet Franc and Sauvignon. They are proud of the fact that their wines were chosen by Henri Gault, of Gault-Millau fame, for his daughter's wedding reception.

Vix lies at the northern edge of one of the most interesting regions of western France, the Marais Poitevin. It is made up of a complex maze of rivers, dikes and shady canals bordered by meadows and fields of grain and pulses. All this was once sea, the Gulf of Poitou, which was subjected to an extensive programme of land reclamation by five powerful abbeys in the region. The work began with the Canal des Cinq Abbés in 1218, but was not completed until after the Wars of

Religion, which ended in 1598. Between 1607 and 1658 Henri IV employed Dutch engineers to develop the elaborate drainage system which still operates.

The attractive village of Coulon, just west of Niort, is one of the places where boats can be hired to explore the many miles of waterways. The picturesque village of Arcais, further west, also has a small 'port' with boats for hire, and a network of country lanes running alongside the canals also enables the motorist to explore the region. The Auberge de la Rivière on the banks of the River Vendée, near the village of Velluire north of Vix, offers stylish and comfortable accommodation and excellent food in a tranquil waterside setting.

Pissotte

The village of Pissotte a few kilometres to the north of Fontenay-le-Comte is the location of the fourth and final area of Fiefs Vendéens vineyards. Here too is just one producer, M. Xavier Coirier, with around 12 hectares of vines. He makes a highly-regarded white wine using a blend of Chardonnay, Melon de Bourgogne (Muscadet) and Chenin Blanc, together with an excellent red and rosé.

About 10 kilometres north of Pissotte, beyond the Forêt de Mervant, is Vouvant, a village built on a rocky knoll overlooking the green valley of the River Mère. It has retained parts of its ancient walls, an old stone bridge, the keep of the feudal castle and a Romanesque church with a beautiful portal.

The Château de Terre Neuve at Fontenay-le-Comte is well worth visiting. It was built in the sixteenth century and has a number of outstanding architectural features including two monumental fireplaces and a magnificent dining hall with a sculpted stone ceiling.

THE CUISINE

One of the impressive dishes that you will find on most menus as you approach the Atlantic is also one of the most simple: *plateau de fruits de mer*, a succulent selection of shellfish fresh from the sea – winkles, mussels, oysters, crabs, langoustines, tiny brown shrimps and clams – served on ice with wedges of lemon and freshly ground black pepper. A glass of chilled Muscadet or Gros Plant superbly complements the *plateau*. On Sundays at lunchtime you will see restaurants full of French families consuming dishes of *fruits de mer*. Usually it will be well into the afternoon before they are ready for the next course.

Inland there is an abundance of freshwater fish: *alose* (shad), trout, salmon, *brochet* (pike), *sandre* (zander, rather like a large perch) and *anguilles* (eels) are found on most menus in the region, usually grilled or poached with a white wine and cream sauce, or made into a *bouilleture*, a stew with eels, which are also used to make pâtés and terrines. *Ecrevisses à la nage* are freshwater crayfish in the shell cooked in a *court-bouillon* flavoured with tarragon and usually served cold with mayonnaise. There is here a wonderful light, creamy soup called *veloutée d'ecrevisses*, delicately flavoured with crayfish and saffron, which will be found in one of the many riverside restaurants along the banks of the Loire.

The area is also renowned for its excellent poultry, beef and, most notably, pork, which is made into *charcuterie* such as *rillettes* and *andouilles*. Familiar recipes are frequently given a local flavour – *fricassée de volaille au vin d'Anjou*, sautéed chicken simmered in dry white Anjou wine, for instance. The most famous cheeses from the region are the *crémets* (soft fresh cream cheeses) made in Saumur and Angers. The brioches of the Vendée are renowned and even the smallest village has its specialist baker producing delicious buttery, golden loaves.

POITOU-CHARENTES

T HE REGION OF Poitou-Charentes encompasses four *départements*: Vienne, Deux-Sèvres, Charente and Charente-Maritime. Although largely flat, the landscape is extremely varied, ranging from the fertile farmland of Vienne to the marshy hinterland of La Rochelle, the estuaries of the Seudre and Gironde and the peaceful, shady water meadows beside the River Charente. Vineyards can be found throughout the region, but the most densely cultivated area is in the Charente where Cognac is produced.

VIENNE

Haut-Poitou

IN THE FARMLAND to the north-west of the city, scattered among fields of maize, sunflowers and wheat, are the vineyards of Haut-Poitou which were granted a VDQS appellation in 1976. The vineyards were established by the Gallo-Romans in the end of the third century and, from the port of La Rochelle, wine became a leading export to places like Hamburg, Amsterdam and London.

The vines are planted on the gently rising slopes, called *groies*, which are covered with a chalky soil. The white grapes, principally Chardonnay and Sauvignon, are grown on the higher terrain where the chalk deposits are thicker, while the black grapes, Gamay and Cabernet, are grown on the lower rises.

In 1865, before phylloxera, Dr Guyot reported that there were 33,560 hectares of vines in Poitou, but today there are only about 1,000. The little market town of Neuville-de-Poitou is the centre of the region's wine industry and

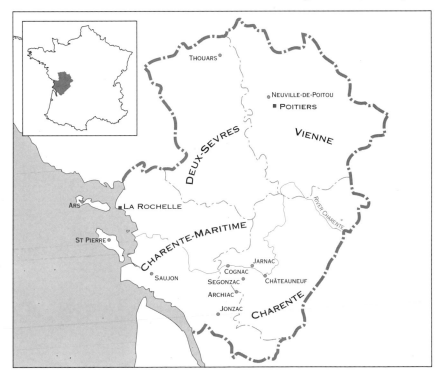

ABOVE TOP: COGNAC VINEYARDS NEAR ARCHIAC.
ABOVE: VINEYARDS NEAR SEGONZAC.
OPPOSITE: FISHING BOATS ON THE ILE D'OLERON.

the location of the *cave co-opérative*. It has become one of the most successful in the country with a very active export market. The co-operative is supported by 450 *vignerons* with 820 hectares of vines, which represents about 95 per cent of the total production.

The most prestigious of its wines are produced from three individual *domaines*. The Château de Logis has 20 hectares of Chardonnay vines, most of which have at least 15 years of growth. The wine is fermented for up to 15 days at a low temperature and bottled in the spring. It also has 11 hectares of Sauvignon Blanc, with vines of a similar age.

The Château la Fuye has 9 hectares of Cabernet Franc and Cabernet Sauvignon, with some vines exceeding 20 years of growth. The wines are given a traditional long period of fermentation and blended in the proportion of 80 per cent Cabernet Franc and 20 per cent Cabernet Sauvignon. They are bottled after being aged for nine months in oak barrels. A rosé is made from Cabernet with just 'one night' skin contact, and lighter, young-drinking reds are also produced from Gamay and Cabernet. *Méthode champenoise* wines are made, as well as a Blanc de Blancs Brut from 100 per cent Chardonnay, and a Brut rosé.

A drive through the vineyards can be made by following the D 990 and D 91 to the pretty village of Blaslay, in the valley of the River Palu, and then heading eastwards along the D 15 to Cheneché and Vendouvre-du-Poitou. From here the D 21 leads to the attractive old village of Marigny-Brizay.

I visited M. Descoux at the Domaine de la Rôtisserie, one of the half-dozen or so independent producers. He farms about 11 hectares of vines, of which a third are Sauvignon Blanc, producing a wine which has brought him considerable acclaim along with his red Cabernet and Gamay. His *caveau* is situated in a large 200-year old troglodyte dwelling, complete with a kitchen and chimney, which was once the family home.

DEUX-SÈVRES
Vins du Thouarsais

JUST BEYOND THE southern limits of the Touraine vineyards is one of France's least-known appellations, the VDQS Vins du Thouarsais. The town of Thouars lies about 40 kilometres south-west of Saumur and is set on a rocky bluff beside the River Thouet. There is an impressive view of the town and its château from the Chemin de Panorama which leads along the riverbank from the D 759 towards Cholet.

The village of Oiron, together with its neighbour Bilazais, about 10 kilometres south-west of Thouars, is the focal point of the vineyards and the home of the appellation's leading producer, Michel Gigon, who farms about 7 hectares. He produces both *sec* and *demi-sec* white wines from Chenin Blanc, a rosé from Cabernet Franc and a Gamay red. M. Gigon also makes *brut* and *demi-sec* sparkling wines from Chenin Blanc, produced by the *méthode champenoise* in the caves at Saumur.

Oiron is an attractive little village with a fine Renaissance château and a seventeenth-century collegiate church. A dozen kilometres or so to the north of Oiron is a troglodyte village, Tourtenay, where there is an extraordinary subterranean *pigeonnier*. Some Vin de Pays is also produced in the *département* around St-Pierre-à-Champ, just beyond the limits of the Coteaux de Layon.

Once described as the finest village in the universe, Richelieu lies about 45 kilometres due east of Thouars. In 1621 Richelieu was bought by Armand du

Plessis, who a decade later celebrated his elevation to the post of Cardinal de Richelieu by building a grand château and enclosing the village behind walls.

Entered by fortified gateways, it has many fine houses around its perfect central square. The town hall contains a museum of art, documents and objects associated with the Richelieu family and the château, which was demolished after the Revolution. To the south of the village is the large park which belonged to the château, criss-crossed by tree-lined avenues, and a number of pavilions and an orangery survive as a reminder of its former glorious days.

CHARENTE & CHARENTE-MARITIME
THE WINES

IF CHAMPAGNE IS the king of wines, then Cognac is certainly the emperor of *eau de vie*. It is more than just a type of brandy – it is the yardstick by which all others are measured. Brandy is simply a concentrated form of wine: when wine reaches an alcohol level of about 16 to 18 per cent during the fermentation process, the yeasts that transform the sugar into alcohol are killed off. For wine to be of greater strength than this, either pure alcohol must be added – as it is with port, for example – or it must be distilled to remove some of the water. This is how brandy is made – by heating wine to boiling point, then condensing the steam it gives off.

In the Middle Ages the major exports from the Charente region were salt and wheat; the region's white wine was often only included in a shipment to complete the load. Later, in the seventeenth century, the wine-growers of Cognac began distilling their wines, partly in competition with growers closer to the coast, who had something of a monopoly on undistilled wine, and partly so that, in their more concentrated state, the wines could be shipped more economically. On arrival in London or Amsterdam they were diluted with water before consumption. At this time brandy (from the Dutch *brandewijn*, or burnt wine) was not the choise of the gentry but a cheap, rough wine drunk by the proletariat as an alternative to beer.

The grape types used to make the wines from which Cognac is distilled include the St-Emilion, a variety of Ugni Blanc, Folle Blanche, Colombard, Sauvignon and Semillon. The process of distillation is quite complex and is carried on even today on small farms in the traditional copper stills. The thin and acidic white wines used for Cognac are often little more than 8 or 10 per cent alcohol, but are subsequently distilled in two stages to a strength of about 70 per cent alcohol. This is too strong and, immediately after distillation, too harsh to be drunk as it is, and the fiery spirit is put into oak casks to mellow for at least two years – more for the finer cognacs. Its warm golden colour is a result of this process and of the tannin which it draws from the oak. Caramel may be added for colour, and, finally, distilled water is used to dilute the spirit to its final strength of 40 per cent alcohol.

As well as Cognac, this area produces Pineau des Charentes, which has its own appellation. This is an aperitif wine made by adding *eau de vie* to the white wine of the region; it is customarily served chilled. The Charente region is also an important producer of Vin de Pays; the two *départements* possess no other appellations for table wines, and the output is considerable. For the production of Vins de Pays de la Charente an increasing number of black-skinned varieties, like Cabernet Sauvignon, Cabernet Franc and Merlot, are being grown to make both red and rosé wines as well as white.

ABOVE: A LOG PILE THATCHED WITH VINE PRUNINGS
IN THE COGNAC REGION.
OPPOSITE TOP: THE CHATEAU OF OIRON.
OPPOSITE BELOW: VINEYARDS NEAR COGNAC.

THE VINEYARDS

The finest brandies are made from grapes grown on the chalky hillsides around the town of Cognac in regions known as Grande Champagne and Petite Champagne – the two most prestigious *crus*. The vineyards which produce the lesser *crus* – Borderies, Fins Bois, Bons Bois and Bois Ordinaries – as well as Pineau and Vins de Pays extend over a much wider area, including the coast near La Rochelle, the Île d'Oléron, the Île de Ré. The suggested tour of the Cognac region is not signposted but is easy to follow with the use of a map; it includes the most significant of the Cognac vineyards, villages and countryside.

The ideal introduction to the region is a visit to Cognac, even though it is a rather grey, grim-looking town, its roofs blackened by a fungus which thrives on the fumes emanating from the casks of maturing brandy. These casks are stored in the old part of the town, in riverside *chais* which you can visit; there is a regional museum here too, with a section on the making of Cognac. Nearby are the Château de Valois, where François I was born in 1494, and the twelfth-century church of Saint-Léger with its impressive Romanesque façade.

From the centre of Cognac take the N 141 towards Angoulême for a short distance and then turn left on to the D 15. Cross the river to St-Brice, a village with a sixteenth-century château set in a park. Nearby, close to Châtre, is the ruined twelfth-century Abbaye de Nôtre-Dame de Châtre, standing in isolation in the middle of a wood, surrounded by meadows and vineyards. Here you are close to the lazy waters of the Charente, in a land of lush green water meadows, woods and rolling hills of vineyards. You get a real sense of being far away from the bustle of the twentieth century, particularly when you come to a town like Bourg-sur-Charente, set beside an enchanting stretch of the river and dignified by a beautiful twelfth-century church and sixteenth-century château.

Jarnac, the next town on the circuit, is considered to be the second home of Cognac; several important shippers have their bases here in riverside ware-houses. The town has a broad, tree-lined main street and immaculate public gardens which stretch down to the river, as well as the Château de Chabannes. The peaceful little village of Triac also has a private château. From here cross the Charente and take the D 90 to St-Même-les-Carrières, which is a good place for a relaxing walk by the river. In Bassac the Benedictine abbey, built in the twelfth century, has an unusual four-storey Romanesque bell tower and a fortified church. There are some handsome stone houses lining the narrow streets of the town. Another peaceful riverside spot lies at the point where the small road crosses the river at St-Amant-de-Graves. The nearby village of Graves boasts an exquisite little Romanesque church.

Everywhere you travel in the Cognac region you will see producers' farms. These are usually contained within high stone walls behind large closed doors, giving them a rather forbidding look. However, you will invariably be welcomed to taste the locally made Cognac.

Châteauneuf-sur-Charente, further along the river, is somewhat larger than many of the other villages but quite similar in character, with a twelfth-century Romanesque church. The route now turns away from the river to head back westward and begins to climb up into the chalky, domed hills where the vine-yards are more densely cultivated. Between the small grey-stone village of Bouteville and its neighbour St-Preuil, whose church is surrounded by vines, the road reaches the highest point of the undulating landscape, giving some fine views of the surrounding countryside. Nearby Lignières is a particularly charming village with a lovely Romanesque church and two châteaux: the moated, seventeenth-century one is used as the town hall; the other is nineteenth-century.

Beyond the tiny hamlets of Touzac and St-Médard-de-Barbezieux, which has a quaint little church in its centre, is Barbezieux, capital of the Petite Champagne region. This mellow old town is full of narrow winding streets and old houses, overlooked by a fine church and an imposing Renaissance château perched up above. There is yet another twelfth-century Romanesque church in Barret, the next village along the route. These churches are often quite tiny and have sometimes been so heavily restored that little of their original character remains. It is not uncommon to see fifteenth-century ribbed vaulting, a cloister that was added 200 years later and nineteenth-century marble cladding in a church dating from the Middle Ages. Beyond the town of Archiac, near St-Fort-de-Né on the D 731, is a fine example of the region's dolmens (megalithic tombs), their mysterious stone formation looking rather incongruous in the middle of a vineyard.

From Archiac the route turns eastwards to Ambleville, then north to Juillac-le-Coq, with its twelfth-century church, crossing open countryside that is a mixture of meadows, farmland, woods and vineyards. Around Segonzac, the capital of the Grande Champagne region, the rounded chalk hills are completely covered in neatly patterned vineyards, reminiscent of the landscape in the Marne valley where its aristocratic namesake is produced.

From here, you return towards Cognac through several small villages, Genté, Gimeux and Ars, where there is a twelfth-century church and a Renaissance château. The final part of the route leads through the villages of Merpins (where you can visit the remains of the Roman town of Condate and the mound of a feudal castle), Jarnouzeau, Javrezac on the River Antenne and Richemont (where there are two châteaux, one seventeenth-century, the other eleventh).

Before going back into Cognac it is worth travelling a little further north to visit the twelfth-century Abbaye de Fontdouce near Burie on the D 731. On the way, just outside Cherves, is the fortified Château de Chesnel, the domain of the Comtes de Rouffignac, where you can sample and buy both Cognac and Pineau des Charentes.

Île de Ré and Ile d'Oléron

The furthest reaches of the Cognac vineyards, and those of the Vins de Pays, can be found on the islands off La Rochelle, the Île de Ré and the Île d'Oléron. These should not be missed. La Rochelle, an old port, is the point of access to the Île de Ré, via an impressive toll bridge built in 1988. The island is an especially important production area for the Vins de Pays Charentais as well as Cognac and Pineau. The *cave co-opérative*, Les Vignerons de l'Île de Ré, at Le Bois-Plage-en-Ré, has a sound reputation and produces a Vin de Pays rosé, a Blanc de Blanc, primarily from Colombard, and a 'Réserve du Gouverneur', a particularly good red made from a blend of Merlot and Cabernet Franc.

The island has wide sandy beaches washed by the Atlantic tides and backed by sand dunes. There is an extensive network of small roads kept exclusively for cyclists and, with many places hiring bikes, this makes a very enjoyable and relaxing way to explore the island – especially as there are very few hills.

St-Martin-en-Ré is an enchanting harbour town, with quayside cafés and shops creating an atmosphere which is a happy blend of fishing-port character and pleasure-port prettiness. Further to the west, the village of Ars-en-Ré, if rather more self-conscious, also has a great deal of charm.

ABOVE TOP: A SUMMER LANDSCAPE NEAR POITIERS.
ABOVE: VINEYARDS NEAR NEUVILLE-DE-POITOU.
OPPOSITE: A HOUSE IN THE MARAIS POITEVIN NEAR THE VILLAGE OF ARCAIS.

To the south, the Île d'Oleron is reached by a long viaduct from Le Chapus. It, too, has extensive vineyards and is an important producer of Vins de Pays, with a large *cave co-opérative* at St-Pierre-d'Oléron. There are some fine beaches here as well, but the island does not have quite the same appeal as the Île de Ré.

Back on the mainland, don't miss seeing the nearby village of Brouage, stranded like an island itself in the midst of the marshy hinterland to the south of Rochefort, and completely surrounded by walls and fortified gateways. During the Middle Ages it was the centre for an important and flourishing export of salt. It was first fortified in the sixteenth century, and became a base for the King's troops during the Wars of Religion; during the seige of La Rochelle in 1628 the fortifications were strengthened and extended by Cardinal Richelieu.

The oyster-beds of Marennes lie to the south of Brouage around the estuary of the River Seudre. Another interesting village, Mornac-sur-Seudre, is to be found on the left bank near St-Sulpice-de-Royan. A cluster of low white-washed cottages with a small port beside a muddy creek, the village somehow has an atmosphere more Mediterranean than Atlantic.

About 20 kilometres south-east of Mornac on the right bank of the Gironde estuary beyond Royan is another curious little village, Talmont. Set on a small promontary, it consists of a single street lined by flower-decked cottages. At the end, on the edge of a cliff, is Sainte Radegonde, a tiny twelfth-century church. It was from here that many pilgrims embarked on their sea voyage to the shrine at Santiago de Compostela.

THE CUISINE

The region has an extensive coastline, and the benefit of some of France's finest shellfish beds, so good seafood features on most menus. Two dishes to look out for are *mouclade*, in which mussels are prepared with egg yolks, white wine and cream, and *chaudrée*, a fish stew in which a variety of fish and shellfish are cooked in a *court bouillon* with white wine and shallots.

While the ham of Poitou is famous, its poultry is also excellent and often used to make galantines, stuffed with *foie gras* or herbs. This is also good dairy country, the butter of Deux-Sèvres rivalling that of Normandy, and cheese like Caillebotte d'Aunis (made from sheep's milk), Jonche Niortasie (goat's milk) and Caillebotte Caille (cow's milk) are worth looking out for.

Charentais melons are famous, with their firm, orangey-pink flesh and sweet, honey flavour. Here they are often prepared by slicing off the top, pouring in a good measure of Pineau des Charentes and leaving to chill slightly for a few hours before serving – they are wonderful!

CENTRE

T HE CENTRE REGION comprises seven *départements*: Eure-et-Loire (which has no vineyards with an appellation), Sarthe, Indre-et-Loire, Loir-et-Cher, Loiret, Cher and Indre. It encompasses the Touraine, the heartland of the Loire valley, and is also a region of many other rivers, such as the Loir, Cher, Indre and Vienne. Great châteaux, historic towns, picturesque villages, rich farmland and numerous vineyards combine to create a land of plenty which was succinctly described by a well-known resident, Rabelais, as the 'Garden of France'.

LOIRET
Vins d'Orléannais

A SHORT DISTANCE to the south of Orléans is the source of France's shortest river, the Loiret, which after just a few kilometres joins the Loire at St-Hilaire-St-Mesmin. Within this small pocket of countryside are the vineyards of the VDQS appellation Vins d'Orléannais, which are planted around the hamlets of Les Muids, Fleury, La Grange, Le Buisson and Le Bréau, while Mareau-aux-Prés is the main wine village of the region.

Vines have been cultivated here for more than two thousand years, and the wines were appreciated by Charlemagne, Louis XI and François I, who ordered part of the forest of Orléans to be cleared in order to extend the vineyards. Today they are of a much more modest extent, about 160 hectares, and there are only a handful of producers.

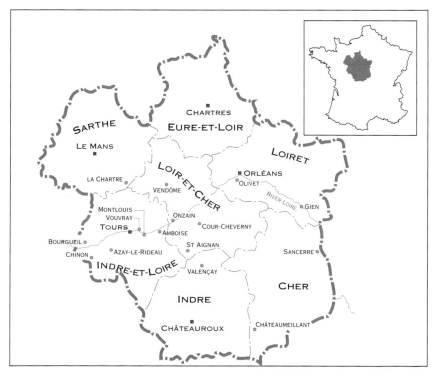

THE CHATEAU OF CHAMBORD.

The principal grape varieties here are Cabernet, Gamay, Gris Meunier, Pinot Noir and Chardonnay. The last two are known locally as Auvernat Noir and Auvernat Blanc.

The Clos St-Fiacre is a small *domaine* in the village of Mareau-aux-Prés, where the Montigny family farm about 20 hectares of vines producing red wines from Gris Meunier and Auvernat Noir, red and rosé from Cabernet, and white from Auvernat Blanc. Vin de Pays with the regional appellation of Jardin de la France is also produced from Gamay and Sauvignon Blanc.

There is a *cave co-opérative* near the village and another in the town of Olivet, almost a suburb of Orléans.

From the village of Cléry-St-André a small road leads eastwards through the hamlets of Le Trepoix and Les Groisons to St-Hilaire-St-Mesmin, closely following the left bank of the Loire with constantly pleasing views of the river and some good picnic spots on the water's edge.

The vineyards of the Orléannais lie on the edge of the region called the Sologne, a mysterious landscape of heathland, forest and silent pools which has been a preserve of hunters for centuries. The countryside of the Sologne looks its best in the early autumn, when the heather is in bloom.

The pretty village of Jouey-le-Potier, 10 kilometres or so to the south of Mareau-aux-Prés, is typical of the region, with a collection of old half-timbered houses and a number of ancient pottery kilns to be seen in the surrounding countryside. The old quarter of the market town of La Ferté-St-Aubin, a short distance to the south-east, has some delightful old houses grouped around a château built in the style of Louis XIII.

LOIRE-ET-CHER
Cheverny

CHEVERNY LIES ON the western edge of the Sologne region and possesses one of the most striking châteaux of the Loire. Built in the classical style with brilliant white stone, it was completed in 1634 by Hurault de Cheverny and has remained in the same family ever since. The town gives its name to one of the region's VDQS wines, which are produced from 23 communes on the left bank of the Loire between Muides in the north and Sambin in the south.

The principal grape varieties are the Gamay, Cot, Pinot Noir, Sauvignon Blanc, Menu Pineau – known locally as Arbois – Pineau d'Aunis, a variety which is used mainly for making rosé, and Romorantin, used extensively for white wines. This variety is so named because it was introduced into the region when François I bought 80,000 vines from Beaune in Burgundy and planted them around the town of Romorantin-Lanthenay.

There is a *cave co-opérative* in the neighbouring village of Mont-près-Chambord on the edge of the forest of Chambord. A red wine is produced here from Gamay, varietal whites from both Sauvignon Blanc and Romarantin, and a rosé from Pineau d'Aunis.

Of the many independent producers in the area, I visited Patrice Hahusseau in the village of Muides on the banks of the Loire. Here he produces a Cheverny Blanc from Sauvignon, red and rosé wines from Pineau d'Aunis, as well as varietal reds from Cabernet, Pinot Noir and Gamay.

The vineyards of Cheverny envelop a number of other impressive châteaux. Chambord lies in the heart of the forest surrounded by parkland and is, perhaps, the most spectacular of all the Loire châteaux; it is certainly the largest, with no fewer than 440 rooms. Seen at the end of a grand tree-lined avenue, its roofline appears like a forest of turrets, pinnacles and towers and, among numerous other beautiful features, contains a magnificent spiral staircase over 30 metres high.

A short distance to the north-east of Cheverny is the Château de Villesavin, built at the beginning of the sixteenth century by the Lord of Villandry, Jean le Breton, who was in charge of the construction of Chambord. The interior can be visited, and there is a collection of old carriages, as well as a large sixteenth-century *pigeonnier*.

A few kilometres south-west of Cheverny is the attractive little Château de Troussay, where the outbuildings contain a collection of old utensils, implements and agricultural tools from the Sologne region. A little further to the south-west is the picturesque village of Fougères-sur-Bièvre, which has a feudal castle dating from the fifteenth century.

About 20 kilometres south-east of Fougères is the fifteenth-century Château de Moulin, near the Sologne village of Lassay-sur-Croisne. Built of red brick, the château is surrounded by a moat which is fed from the River Croisne. The interior contains some fine furniture, a beautiful painted ceiling and tapestries from the fifteenth and sixteenth centuries.

Coteaux du Vendômois

Fifty kilometres or so to the north-west of Cheverny the charming old town of Vendôme sits astride the little River Loir. An ancient stone bridge and a fortified gateway lead into the town, and the ruins of a feudal castle stand impressively on a steep rounded hill behind. There are numerous old houses with turrets, gables and towers, and in the town centre, now pedestrianized, is the sixteenth-century tower of Saint-Martin. The abbey church, La Trinité, founded in the eleventh century, has a magnificent Gothic façade and a beautiful bell tower.

The Coteaux du Vendômois is a VDQS appellation which covers the communes of Houssay, Lavardin, Lunay, Mazange, Montoire-sur-le-Loir, Naveil, Thoré-la-Rochette, Villiersfaux and Villiers-sur-Loir. The permitted grape varieties are Chenin and Chardonnay for white wines, Pineau d'Aunis for rosé, and Pineau d'Aunis, Cabernet Franc, Pinot Noir, Gamay and Cot for red.

The village of Villiers-sur-Loir, just a few kilometres north-west of Vendôme, is the location of the region's one and only co-operative, where they also produce a Vin de Pays du Jardin de la France from Chardonnay.

The stretch of river between Vendôme and Montoire-sur-le-Loir is very peaceful and unspoilt and can be followed quite closely by road on both banks. The village of Les Roches-l'Evêque has a number of troglodyte houses carved into the tufa rock, and Montoire-sur-le-Loir, an old town, has a ruined château, several fine old houses and a bridge with pleasing views of the river.

A few kilometres away, on the left bank of the Loir, is Lavardin, a village with a ruined feudal château set on a hill above. It was the stronghold of the counts of Vendôme in the Middle Ages, but was dismantled by Henri IV during the Wars of Religion.

Downstream from Montoire, on the right bank of the river, is the curious troglodyte village of Trôo. It is set on a steep rounded hill and has a warren of dwellings that have been carved into the rock. Many can be reached only by a zig-zag footpath and series of steps. The homes are much more than simple caves, with gardens, patios and luxurious interiors. At the highest point of the village is a burial mound, from which there are superb views of the Loir valley.

ABOVE: A VIGNERNON'S HOUSE NEAR BOURGUEIL.
OPPOSITE TOP: VINEYARDS NEAR MAREAU-AUX-PRES.
OPPOSITE BELOW: A FARMHOUSE NEAR CHINON.

Nearby is an ancient well and an eleventh-century church which was a place of pilgrimage during the Middle Ages.

Mesland

The vineyards of the Touraine begin in earnest around the town of Amboise, about 40 kilometres downstream from Blois. Just before this, however, is one of the least known AOC wines of the Loire region, Mesland. The name is taken from a village which lies on the right bank of the river amid peaceful countryside where cattle and crops are raised.

The vineyard was first planted here by the Romans, but grew in the eleventh century when part of the forest was cleared by the monks of Marmoutier Abbey, near Tours, who had moved into their newly-built priory in Mesland. The appellation of AOC Coteaux de Touraine was granted to the area in 1939, but it was not until after the end of the war in 1945 that a group of *vignerons* began to shape the autonomy of the region's vineyard, with the denomination Touraine Mesland being finally recognized in 1955. Even today the production is relatively small, with only 8,000 hectolitres of red wine, 1,000 of rosé and 1,500 of white sold annually from a vineyard of about 300 hectares.

The white Mesland wine is made chiefly from Pineau de la Loire (Chenin), but a small proportion of Chardonnay or Sauvignon is allowed. A varietal Sauvignon is produced as Touraine Blanc, and the rosé, usually vinified as a *vin gris*, is from Gamay. A Crémant, made using the champagne technique, is also produced. The red wine is a blend of Gamay, Cabernet Franc and Malbec (Cot). The vineyards are planted in small parcels of land around the villages of Mesland, Chousy-sur-Cisse, Molineuf, Chambon-sur-Cisse and, in particular, Onzain.

SARTHE
Coteaux du Loir & Jasnières

IN THE FAR north-western corner of Indre-et-Loire are 22 communes entitled to the appellation of Coteaux du Loir, which also extends just over the border into the département of Sarthe, and within this region is the appellation of Jasnières, for white wine only, which applies only to the vineyards around the villages of Lhomme and Ruillé-sur-Loir on the slopes bordering the right bank of the Loir to the east of La Chartre-sur-le-Loir. Red Coteaux du Loir is produced from pure Pineau d'Aunis, while the rosé is made from Gamay. Both white Coteaux du Loir and Jasnières are made from 100 per cent Chenin.

The attractive little town of La Chartre-sur-le-Loir makes a good base from which to explore the vineyards, and several of the producers are based here. The Hôtel de France has an excellent restaurant and is a popular place for drivers and their colleagues to stay during the Le Mans race.

The principal vineyards, which are planted in small pockets, extend along the Loir valley, beginning in the east around Ponce-sur-le-Loir and extending to Vaas in the west. At Ponce there is a sixteenth-century château with a magnificent Renaissance staircase and gardens containing a maze and one of the most beautiful dovecotes in France. The village also houses an arts-and-crafts centre with pottery, glass blowing, weaving and enamel workshops. At the village of Couture, nearby, the Manoir de La Possonnière was the birthplace of the poet, Pierre Ronsard. The largest concentration of vineyards are on the hillsides above the villages of Ruillé and Lhomme on the right bank of the river. Nearby, north of Chahaignes, the Château de Bénéhart has a restored medieval winepress. The vineyards also extend in isolated plots to the south, around the villages of Chenu and St-Christophe-sur-le-Nais where the hillsides are planted with orchards and vast fields of maize.

A few kilometres to the west of La Chartre, Vouvray-sur-le-Loir has a *caveau* tunnelled into the rock where the local wines can be tasted and bought. Beyond Château-du-Loir, near Vaas, is a watermill, Le Rotrou, with guided tours to demonstrate traditional flour making. To the north is the deep, dark forest of Berce, and among 200-year-old oaks at Chenne Boppe you can see the stumps of massive, centuries-old trees – all that remains following a fierce storm. Nearby the springs of Fontaine de la Coudre and Sources de la Hermitière bubble up from the earth. Near the latter, hidden in the trees, is a delightful *auberge* where you can enjoy specialities like *petit sauté sarthois au jasnières*, in which pieces of chicken are cooked with snails, cream and white wine.

INDRE-ET-LOIRE

THE WINES

THE APPELLATIONS TO which Indre-et-Loire is entitled are: Bourgueil – St-Nicholas-de-Bourgueil – Chinon – Touraine – Azay-le-Rideau – Vouvray – Montlouis – Amboise – Vin de Pays du Jardin de la France – Coteaux du Loir.

The wines of this *département* are especially varied: red, white and rosé wines are all made here, from a wide range of grape varieties. Excellent red wines, such as those from St-Nicolas-de-Bourgueil and Bourgueil, are made from the Breton grape, a variety of Cabernet Franc. Gamay and Pinot Noir are also used to produce both red and rosé wines. Chenin Blanc, or Pineau de la Loire, is the classic white grape of Touraine, used to produce Vouvray and Montlouis; white wines are also made from Sauvignon Blanc and Chardonnay. Both *méthode champenoise* and *pétillant* wines are also made in the region.

THE VINEYARDS

The Route des Vins is well signposted in Touraine; however, it seems to have been designed by an over-zealous wine enthusiast since the signs indicate every single village of any interest – and it's not uncommon to be pointed in two or three directions at once. I have suggested a rather more selective – and more rational – route, from which you can be distracted at will.

A good place to start is Selles-sur-Cher, about 48 kilometres from the Blois exit of the A 10 autoroute. This village was built around a steep-sided curve in the River Cher. Nearby are the ruins of a thirteenth-century fortress and the Château de Selles, which is set in a small park on the riverside. From here the route starts along the D 17 through the small villages of Meusnes and Couffi, then heads off through Châteauvieux and Seigy, towards St-Aignan. All along this route you will see Route des Vins signs leading away from the river, up into the vine-covered hillsides and the peaceful countryside of the *vignerons*. This is the time to follow the local signs: you won't see most of the vineyards from the roads that run close to the riverbank, and driving along these quiet lanes you will come across farms and houses where you can sample the wines.

St-Aignan, with its narrow cobbled streets, medieval houses, Romanesque church and imposing Renaissance château, is a very appealing town. Just across the river are the small wine villages of Noyers-sur-Cher and St-Romain-sur-Cher. The Route des Vins continues along the riverside on the D 17 through Mareuil-

ABOVE TOP AND OPPOSITE: THE CHATEAU OF CHENONCEAUX.
ABOVE: THE CHATEAU STEPS IN THE VILLAGE OF ST AIGNAN.

sur-Cher and Pouillé. Just across the river from Pouillé are the wine villages of Thésée and Monthou-sur-Cher.

On the north side of Monthou is the château of Le Gué-Péan, built in the late fifteenth century by the Italian, Nicolas Alaman, who was *valet de chambre* to both Louis XII and François I; his blue and white building displays a quirky individuality, notably in its towers – one pointed and one bell-shaped. The château is open to visitors and also offers *chambre d'hôte* accommodation and a riding stable.

Follow the route to Angé, St-Julien-de-Chédon and Faverolles-sur-Cher; there are many diversions along the tiny vignerons' roads among the vines, and it is worth going a few kilometres out of your way to see the ruined Abbaye d'Aiguevive set among remote fields and woods, just south of Moutrichard, and Chisseaux, to the west of it, where you can try Fraise d'Or, the local strawberry liqueur. Just across the river from there, a small detour takes in the wine villages of St-Georges-sur-Cher, La Chaise and Durdon.

Now take the D 40 to Chenonceaux. This is the site of one of the most popular and grandiose châteaux in the whole of the Loire region. Henri II gave the unfinished Château de Chenonceaux to his lover Diane de Poitiers; on the king's death, his widow, Catherine de Medici, reclaimed it. Nearly two centuries later, Jean-Jacques Rousseau spent several years there as the owner's secretary. It is a magnificent Renaissance building of epic proportions, with an extraordinary three-storey classical arched bridge spanning the Cher. The château contains some fine paintings, including works by Rubens, del Sarto, Correggio and Murillo.

The Route des Vins continues towards Tours along the N 76 on the south bank of the Cher, passing through the towns of Bléré and Veretz. From here the D 85 heads north for a few kilometres, across the narrow strip of countryside which separates the converging Loire and Cher rivers, to Montlouis-sur-Loire. The town is known for its subtle, dry white wine, meant for early drinking.

The drive on the D 751 to Amboise is a worthwhile diversion: Leonardo da Vinci spent the last few years of his life here at the invitation of François I, and is reputedly buried in the chapel of the château.

Follow the N 152 along the north bank of the river towards Tours and you come to Vouvray, known for its white wine, which is made both dry and sweet, as well as still, *pétillant* and sparkling. This small region has its own wine circuit which leads into a succession of small valleys and villages, first along the River Brenne to Vernou-sur-Brenne, Chançay-la-Vallée and Reugny, then to La Vallée-de-Cousse and the villages of Vaugondy and Jallanges. Just to the west of Vouvray are the villages of Parçay-Meslay, where there is a medieval fortified farm, and Rochecorbon, famous for its plums. Then there is Vallée Coquette, where the *cave co-opérative* of Vouvray is situated, and where you can eat grilled goat's cheese dusted with herbs, among other local specialities, in a troglodyte cave at a restaurant called Saint Martin.

The Route des Vins continues west, along the south bank of the Loire, through the village of Savonnières to Villandry, which has a château surrounded by a superb formal garden in the Italian style. The route continues along the D 7 through Lignières-de-Touraine and Rivarennes to Ussé. Here an enchanting chateau with towers and gables is built high above the banks of the River Indre. It looks particularly beautiful from the bridge opposite, with its terraces descending steeply to the riverside; Charles Perrault is supposed to have been inspired by it when he wrote *Sleeping Beauty*. A little to the south is the town of Azay-le-Rideau. The château here was Balzac's favourite ('a diamond cut in facets').

Chinon marks the western limit of the wine route and it is a delight, set beside the broad, lazy waters of the River Vienne. The village is renowned for its excellent red and rosé wines. It is built on a hill, the top of which is ringed by the remains of ramparts and fortifications. In Vieux Chinon, the old town that dates from the fifteenth century, the streets are lined with lovely old timbered and gabled houses.

From Chinon take the D 749, which crosses the Loire at Port-Boulet. Nearby is a small château, Les Reaux, which offers *chambre d'hôte* accommodation. A little further north are the villages of Bourgueil and St-Nicolas-de-Bourgueil. At the latter there is a Cave Touristique where you can taste the wines and visit the museum. To complete the wine circuit, drive along the riverside road, the N 152, towards Tours. This takes you past the attractive towns of Langeais, Cinq-Mars and Luynes, each of which has a château. The first was built by Louis XI and has not been altered since; the second was owned by a favourite of Louis XIII but was largely destroyed on the orders of his neighbour, the king's chief minister, Cardinal Richelieu at the third château, Luynes. At Cinq-Mars there is also an oddly shaped square tower, with four of its five pinnacles remaining.

INDRE
Valençay

THE HILLTOP VILLAGE of Valençay is a quintessential French country market town, with old houses lining its narrow streets and an attractive square bristling with excellent *boulangeries*, *patisseries*, and *charcuteries*. There is a sixteenth-century château on the very edge of the hill from where there are fine views over the valley of the River Nahon. The building is set in the midst of a lovely park populated by deer, peacocks and other exotic birds. At the beginning of the nineteenth century the château was acquired by Prince Talleyrand, a bishop under Louis XVI and a leading figure in French politics. He often used the château for lavish entertainment; Napoleon, who made him a prince, was among the many famous guests.

There is a lively country market on Thursdays where you find the distinctive pyramid-shaped cow's-milk cheese to which the village gives its name. A festival of wine and cheese is held in Valençay on the Sunday following Ascension (Ascension day is 40 days after Easter).

THE WINES

The wines of Valençay have a VDQS appellation which covers 40 communes around the villages of La Vernelle, Lye, Villentrois, Faverolles, Veuil, Luçay-le-Mâle, Poulaines, Parpeçay, Menetou-sur-Nahon, Varennes-sur-Fouzon, Chabris, Selles-sur-Cher and Fontguenand. The countryside is one of open rolling farm-land, with the vineyards, totalling about 750 hectares, scattered throughout in smallish plots, the largest concentration being to the south of Meusnes.

The permitted grape varieties are Gamay, Cot and Pinot Noir for reds; Gamay, Cot, Cabernet and Pineau d'Aunis for rosés; and Sauvignon Blanc, Chardonnay and Menu Pineau – also known as Arbois – for whites.

The region's *cave co-opérative* is situated on the D 956 near the village of Fontguenand and is open every day except Sundays. There are also a number of independent producers. The small village of Meusnes, which has a very attractive eleventh-century church, is the centre for ten of them, and a wine fair is held here each year at Pentecost (the seventh Sunday after Easter).

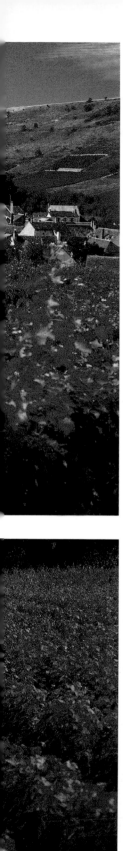

ABOVE: THE FOREST OF BERCE NEAR LA CHARTRE-SUR-LE-LOIR.
OPPOSITE TOP: THE WINE VILLAGE OF CHAVIGNOL NEAR SANCERRE.
OPPOSITE BELOW: PRUNING IN THE VINEYARDS OF VOUVRAY.

THE VINEYARDS

The D 15 leads south-west of Valençay through the pretty valley of the Nahon to Vicq-sur-Nahon, where there is an elegant eighteenth-century château, La Moustière, and the Château de Coubloust, which has a curious separate tower. Ten kilometres to the west of Valençay is the village of Lucay-le-Mâle, where there is a fifteenth-century château, the fine old manor house of La Foulquetière and an eleventh-century church. Nearby is the lake of Foulquetière and the River Modon, known for its trout fishing.

You can make a round trip through the vineyards along quiet country lanes by following the CD 22A and the D 128 west of Valençay to the village of Villentrois on the edge of the Forêt de Gatine. There are 50 kilometres of caves here, used for mushroom cultivation, a fifteenth-century château and a Roman chapel. From here the D 33 continues north to Lye, in the valley of the Modon, with the sixteenth-century Château de Saray and the Cave de Vaux, from which the stones for the cathedral of Bourges were quarried.

The route leads east from Lye to Fontguenand, which has a manor house with a tower, La Drevaudière, and then continues north through the hamlets of Le Musa and Porcherioux to La Vernelle, in the valley of the Fouzon, where you can visit the *fromagerie* of M. Jacquin. On 22 January the fête of St Vincent is held at La Vernelle, incorporating a competition of Vins de Pays. From here the route heads south, back towards Valençay, through the hamlets of Launay, Lucioux, l'Epinat and Les Jumeaux.

CHER
THE WINES

THE ROLLING HILLS overlooking the upper reaches of the Loire are planted with the Sauvignon Blanc Grape. From it are produced two of France's greatest wines: Pouilly-Fumé and Sancerre. The two towns around which the wines are produced are separated by the river and lie in different regions. Why Sancerre and Pouilly-Fumé are so different is a matter of endless debate. There are certainly differences in the soil; Sancerre's is composed of clay and limestone, and the best of its wine is produced where there is most limestone. Which is the better of the two wines is also hotly disputed.

The appellations to which the *département* is entitled are: AOC Sancerre – Menetou-Salon – Quincy – Reuilly – VDQS Châteaumeillant – Vin de Pays.

The wines of this region are predominantly white and are made from Sauvignon Blanc, but in Sancerre and other outlying villages some red and rosé is also made from Pinot Noir, Pinot Gris and Meunier grapes. In addition to the wines of Sancerre, interesting wines of all three colours are produced around the villages of Menetou-Salon, Quincy and Reuilly, which are situated further to the west, away from the Loire. Reuilly is known for its white wine made from the Sauvignon grape and also for a rosé made from Pinot Gris. Quincy has its appellation for white wine, also made from Sauvignon Blanc, while Menetou-Salon, like Sancerre, makes all three types from the same varieties.

THE VINEYARDS

Sancerre is one of the prettiest of all the wine villages, with its network of steep, winding, narrow streets lined with crumbling stone houses. There are some wonderful restaurants and enticing food shops as well as numerous places where you can sample and buy the wines. It has a dramatic setting on a hill which is itself surrounded by other hills; the effect is impressively like an amphitheatre.

It also has an interesting history. In the ninth century a colony of Saxons, banished by Charlemagne, settled in the area, and a fort was erected to keep them in order. It was occupied by Huguenots during the religious wars of the sixteenth century; they lost it after a siege lasting 220 days, and it was finally destroyed in 1621, leaving only the twelfth-century Tour des Fiefs. Later, in 1745, a group of Bonnie Prince Charlie's Scottish followers settled at Sancerre and one of their descendants became a marshal under Napoleon.

From Sancerre the wine route – not a true circuit – goes off in several directions. Just north of Sancerre is the beautifully situated village of Chavignol, which produces some of the best Sancerre wine and a famous goat's-milk cheese, Crottin de Chavignol. The vineyards rise up steeply all around the cluster of houses and the village church, and there are many places where you can try the local wines. The communes of Sury-en-Vaux and Ste-Gemme are north of Chavignol. Here the countryside is much more open, with rolling hills covered in meadows and a variety of crops as well as the vineyards. Two villages, Crézancy and Menetou-Râtel, mark the limit of the Sancerre vineyards to the west. Close by is the sixteenth-century Château de Boucard.

In the foothills a few kilometres east of Sancerre are two adjoining villages on the Canal Latéral, which runs parallel to the Loire. St-Satur is a canal port and boasts a Gothic church which was based on the designs for Bourges Cathedral but was never completed. It was built by Augustinian monks, who were also responsible for introducing grapes to the area in the twelfth century. St-Thibault, between the Loire and the canal, was a thriving port at one time; the river is wide and shallow at this point, with large sandy beaches. Ménétréol, also on the Canal Latéral, is shaded by tall, slender trees and there is a château nearby in the village of Thauvenay.

The stone houses of Bué, a few kilometres south of Sancerre (take the D 955 and turn off at the sign), with their brown-tiled roofs, nestle in a steep-sided valley. Bué is an important wine centre, selling the excellent wines from the surrounding vineyards. There is a popular small restaurant here, Le Caveau des Vignerons, which is owned and run by a co-operative of *vignerons*, and serves very good, simple country food. It is particularly busy at Sunday lunchtimes when its long wooden tables are full of noisy local families. There are fewer vineyards to the south-west, but it is worth visiting the communes of Veaugues and Montigny just off the D 955, and then taking a detour to the vineyards of Menetou-Salon, 10 kilometres away. The appellation covers vineyards which extend to around 500 hectares. Although a modest town, set in a delightful wooded region, it possesses a magnificent château. It was once the property of Jacques Coeur, who acquired it in 1450, but it was largely destroyed during the Revolution and was rebuilt, on a grand scale, in the nineteenth century.

About forty kilometres to the south-west of Menetou-Salon are the small wine towns of Quincy and Reuilly, the former lying in the valley of the Cher, the latter in the valley of the Arnon. Both towns have a rather tired and undistinguished air and offer little of interest apart from their wines, of which the combined output is less than 7,000 hectolitres.

Châteaumeillant

About a hundred kilometres south of Menetou-Salon is Vesdun, a rather nondescript village which has gained fame by its claim to be the geographical centre of

France. Although there has been some dispute in this matter, there is now a monument recording the claim, which has become a tourist attraction.

The village is one of the communities which own the right to the small VDQS appellation of Châteaumeillant, a town some 20 kilometres to the west. In practice there is only 1 hectare of vines to be found in the vicinity of Vesdun, most of them being nearer to Châteaumeillant, around the villages of Feusines, Urciers, Champillet, Néret, St-Maur, Reigny and Beaumerle.

There is a *cave co-opérative* on the outskirts of Châteaumeillant which has been in existence now for over 30 years. It is responsible for the majority of production, although there are a few individual producers. Red wine from Gamay is made there, together with a *vin gris* from a blend of Gamay and Pinot Noir, while some white is produced and sold as Vin de Pays du Jardin de la France.

There are about 50 members of the co-operative, farming a total of about 50 hectares. The produce of the 15 hectares belonging to the Domaine des Garennes is vinified and bottled separately.

The classic wine of Châteaumeillant is considered to be the *vin gris*, a very pale rosé made by pressing the juice from black-skinned grapes before it has time to take on much colour. Patrick Lanoix, of the Cellier du Chêne Combeau in the hamlet of Beaumerle, makes a particularly good *vin gris* from Gamay alone with a vineyard of about 6 hectares.

Near Culan, 12 kilometres south-east of Châteaumeillant, is a feudal fortress set above the gorges of the Arnon. On the Route Jacques-Coeur, it was built in the thirteenth century and reconstructed in the fifteenth. It has impressive walls and tall round towers, and the interior contains fine fifteenth-century furnishings and Flemish tapestries.

THE CUISINE

Good food abounds in this region, and freshwater fish from the Loire, Cher and Indre and their tributaries appear on most menus. *Friture de la Loire* is a dish of tiny fish dusted with flour and quickly sautéed in butter or oil. Salmon from the Loire is highly regarded; it is often served with *beurre blanc*, the light creamy sauce of the Anjou region. *Sandre* (zander), which is like a large perch, is another delicious freshwater fish of the region, and *alose* (shad) is also caught in the river; it is usually served *à l'oseille*, with a sorrel sauce. *Anguilles* (eels) are a regular feature served as a *matelote*, stewed in wine with onions and mushrooms.

The meadows and hillsides of this region are not only covered with vines, they are also dotted with herds of rusty brown goats that produce the milk for an enormous range of cheeses. Crottin de Chavignol, from the countryside around Sancerre, is one of the most famous. It starts life as a small, flat cylinder of soft creamy curd, quite mild in taste, about 10 to 12 centimetres in diameter; as it ages it shrinks and forms a crust, becoming firmer and stronger in flavour. In addition to being served as part of the cheeseboard, the cheeses are often sprinkled with herbs and toasted under the grill: served on a croûton with a garnish of green salad they are a delicious variation on the cheese course.

Rillettes are a famous local speciality, soft creamy pâté made from slowly cooked pork which is finely shredded and blended with the fat produced. They are found on every menu and in every *charcuterie* in the region, but those from the Sarthe, Le Mans in particular, are considered to be the best. *Rillons* are small pieces of pork, cooked to a golden brown and usually served as part of a *salade composé*. *Grattons* are nuggets of pork skin cooked until they are crisp.

ALSACE-LORRAINE

HE REGION OF Alsace-Lorraine lies in the extreme north-east corner of France, bordering the countries of Belgium, Luxembourg, Germany and Switzerland. It encompasses the *départements* of Meuse, Moselle, Meurthe-et-Moselle, Bas-Rhin, Haut-Rhin and Vosges – the only one which has no vineyards. The landscape is both dramatic and varied: the rugged Vosges mountains with their wooded slopes extend for almost 160 kilometres north to south, running parallel to the River Rhine. The Ardennes rise on the northern borders of the region, which also includes the great forest of Argonne and the valleys of the Meuse and Moselle. Within this domain are crystal-clear lakes, woodland walks, fairy-tale villages and, of course, superb vineyards.

MEUSE
Côtes de la Meuse

SOUTH-EAST OF VERDUN, between the valley of the Moselle and the course of the River Meuse to the west lies the Parc Régional de Lorraine. The Rupt de Mad carves an attractive valley which bisects the region, at the centre of which is the Lac de Madine, one of the numerous lakes and pools scattered throughout an area known as the Woëvre.

The plain of the Woëvre is separated from the River Meuse by Les Côtes, a range of hills with densely wooded crests. On the slopes are large areas of

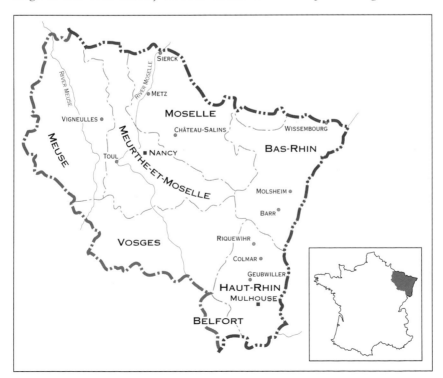

orchards, producing the region's speciality crop, the mirabelle. Between the orchards are small plots of vines which produce a wine that is locally renowned, but otherwise almost unheard of, Vin de Pays de la Meuse.

The production area is very small, with a total of just 35 hectares spread between six producers in the villages of Combres-sous-les-Côtes, St-Maurice-sous-les-Côtes, Billy-sous-les-Côtes and Creuë.

Véronique and Jean-Marc Léonard farm 5 hectares of vines at the Domaine de Muzy, near the village of Combres-sous-les-Côtes. The Auxerrois variety is the predominant crop, from which they make a varietal white wine. They also make a locally-acclaimed Chardonnay as well as a Vin Gris from Pinot Noir or Gamay – or sometimes a blend of the two. These vines are also used to produce small quantities of varietal red wines.

In the centre of this region lies the village of Vigneulles-les-Hattonchâtel, where a shop called La Ferme Gourmande sells many of the wines from local producers together with a variety of regional products, including Mirabelle de Lorraine, jars of preserved mirabelles, *quetsch foie gras*, *confits* and *charcuterie*.

The old village of Hattonchâtel is set on a hill above Vigneulles, with commanding views over the surrounding countryside. It has a church with a sixteenth-century carved stone altarpiece and a château which was destroyed in 1634 and reconstructed in medieval style by an American owner in 1927.

Nearby, beside a forest road, is a memorial to Alain-Fournier, the author of *Le Grand Meaulnes*, who was killed in action here during the First World War. This region was the site of many battles, and there is an impressive American memorial in the style of a Greek temple constructed on the Butte de Montsec, a wooded hill overlooking the Lac de Madine.

At Hannonville-sous-les-Côtes, a small museum of rural crafts and traditions has been established in a pair of village houses, including displays showing the region's culture of vines, linen and hemp.

To the west of Les Côtes, beyond the valley of the Meuse, is the Forêt d'Argonne, a beautiful, peaceful region of densely wooded hills. It was once an autonomous county ruled by the bishops of Chalons, Reims and Verdun, and in its centre, set on a ridge, was a Benedictine abbey around which the small village of Beaulieu-en-Argonne developed.

All that remains today is a charming street of old houses decked with flowers and creepers. One of them contains a thirteenth-century winepress constructed of massive wooden beams which was used by the monks to press 300 kilos of grapes at a time. There is an attractive group of traditional Argonne houses and farms to be seen in the neighbouring village of Brizeaux.

MEURTHE-ET-MOSELLE
Côtes de Toul

THE RIDGE OF hills which forms Les Côtes de la Meuse continues south beyond the town of Toul which is set beside the River Ingressin, linking the Moselle and the Meuse. Between the villages of Trondes and Barissey-la-Côte are the vineyards of the Côtes de Toul, which were given VDQS status in 1951.

Vines have been grown here for more than two thousand years. At the end of the nineteenth century there were 17,000 hectares of vines in the *département* of Meurthe-et-Moselle, 2,000 of which were planted on the Côtes de Toul. Today there are only about 100 hectares, with a mere 15 producers making a living from wine production alone.

While Pinot Noir is used here for red wine, and Auxerrois for white, the region's most renowned wine, Vin Gris, is made from Gamay. Vin Gris is produced by pressing the grapes and fermenting the separated juice without skin contact, in exactly the same way in which white wine is made. The colour can vary from being almost indistinguishable from a white wine to a deep rosé. Claude Vosgien, in the village of Bulligny, told me that it depends upon the amount of summer sunshine, the less there is, the paler the wine.

My visit in the middle of April was a couple of months before M. Vosgien's new, very pale Vin Gris was due to be bottled, but he gave me the opportunity to sample it. I commented on the faintest degree of sparkle, and he said it was known as *frétillant*, which translates as wriggling or quivering, and is the mark of a good, young Gris de Toul.

There is a signposted Route du Vin et de la Mirabelle which leads through the principal wine villages, from Barisey-la-Côte in the south via Bulligny, Mont-le-Vignoble and Charmes-la-Côte to Bruley and Lucey in the north, with plenty of opportunities to taste and buy the wines along the way.

The neighbouring and rival villages of Bruley and Lucey, just north of Toul, harbour the greatest concentration of producers, including Marcel and Michel Laroppe, Pierre Prévôt and Dominique Goujot at Bruley, and Lièvre frères and Michel Goujot at Lucey.

There is an excellent opportunity to taste and buy many of these wines, as well as other regional specialities, at the Promotion Centre of the products of the Côtes de Toul in the village of Bruley, where there is also a *caveau* and a small museum of viticultural equipment. It is open every day except Monday (2–7 p.m.) from March until December.

MOSELLE
Vin de Moselle

THE CHAMPAGNE VINEYARDS which encircle the Montagne de Reims are generally considered to be the most northerly in France. A more legitimate claim, however, can be made by the group of *vignerons* based in the small town of Contz-les-Bains, on the left bank of the River Moselle, just a few kilometres from the Luxembourg border. Here the vines are planted on the steep slopes beside the river and along the south-facing hillside of the valley of the little River Altbach which flows into the Moselle at Contz.

About a dozen producers farm a total of 10 hectares producing Vin de Moselle, which received its VDQS appellation in 1984. The total vineyard area around Contz is more extensive than this, but some of it is owned by Luxembourg *vignerons* and is only in France as a result of border changes. The grapes from these vines are taken over the border to the co-operative at Remerschen, a few kilometres away, and some of the smaller Contz wine-growers also have their wine vinified here.

The principal grape varieties grown in the Moselle vineyards are Pinot Noir, Pinot Gris, Pinot Blanc, Auxerrois and Müller-Thurgau. Vin de Moselle is the only delimited French wine using the latter variety, which is more commonly associated with German wines, and until 1871 these vineyards were within the German border. However, the Müller-Thurgau vines now found around Contz are largely the result of recent plantings by the French growers.

Joseph Simon, in Contz, is one of these *vignerons*, making an excellent example of a varietal Müller-Thurgau from his single hectare of vines planted on

ABOVE TOP: A FARMER HARVESTING MAIZE NEAR COLMAR.
ABOVE: AN AUTUMN MEADOW NEAR THE VILLAGE OF HATTONCHATEL.
OPPOSITE: THE FORTIFIED CHURCH OF HUNAWIHR.

the sharply-angled slope which faces his village house. M. Simon also produces an Auxerrois and a Pinot Blanc, which had just been bottled at the time of my visit in mid-April.

M. Simon had just finished planting a plot of Pinot Noir which will be used to produce both a red wine and a Vin Gris. He told me that the largest of the Contz vineyards was one of just 3 hectares which belonged to his neighbour M. Mansion at the other end of the steep, narrow Rue du Pressoir.

A few kilometres to the west of Contz-les-Bains is Rodemack, which has been given the rather optimistic title of the Carcassonne of Lorraine. Named after an ancient Celtic tribe, the Rhoetes, in medieval times the village was the centre of a powerful feudal domain within the county of Luxembourg. It has many old buildings, the ruins of a castle and a fortified gateway, the Port de Sierck, which was reconstructed after partial demolition during the Second World War to allow American tanks to pass through.

A short distance downstream from Contz, on the right bank of the Moselle, Sierck-les-Bains presents an attractive view of a riverside promenade with an imposing castle set on a hill above.

Vin de Moselle is also produced in the Moselle valley to the south of Metz. The vineyards here were of considerable importance during the Middle Ages, when their income helped to finance the construction of Metz cathedral.

Later, in the nineteenth century, the grapes from the vineyards of Metz were used in the production of champagne, and the tradition lingers, with many of the Lorraine wine-producers still making sparkling wines by the *méthode champenoise*. The vines now occupy only about 20 hectares in all, but there is enthusiasm among the local wine-growers to continue their regeneration.

One of the leading instigators of the renaissance is the CDEF, an experimental agricultural station near the village of Laquenexy. In addition to 16 hectares of fruit trees planted around the village they also have a plot of 3 hectares of vines on the slopes above Scy-Chazelles, near Metz, on the left bank of the river. In the Middle Ages this was considered the most prestigious vineyard of the region, and its terrain the most favoured.

The CDEF produces both fruit and wine on a commercial scale, and the latter has already received considerable recognition, with the 92 Müller-Thurgau receiving a gold medal at the Concours Général in Paris. The range of wines is extraordinary, although quantities of each are small. The current tariff lists varietal wines made from Müller-Thurgau, Auxerrois, Pinot Noir, Pinot Blanc, Pinot Gris, Riesling, Gewürztraminer, Gamay, Muscat, Chardonnay, Sauvignon Blanc, Poulsard and Cabernet. In addition, a white wine is made from a blend of Pinot Blanc and Auxerrois, and a red from Pinot Noir and Gamay.

A few kilometres upstream is the village of Vaux, around a rather faded eighteenth-century château. Here Jean-Marie Diligent and his daughter Marie farm 3½ hectares of vines on the hillside overlooking the valley. M. Diligent grows a small amount of Chardonnay, Pinot Gris and Pinot Blanc but his main varieties are Auxerrois, Müller-Thurgau and Pinot Noir. The château and its *caveau* are only open to visitors on Saturdays (2–6 p.m.), but on other days the wines can be bought in the village's *épicerie* in the Rue des Mirabelles.

Gris de Vic

The third pocket of vines of the Vin de Moselle can be found to the south-east around the villages of Vic-sur-Seille and Marsal. Gris de Vic is a wine with a long history, and Raymond André of Vic was one of the few main producers, with 4 hectares of vines on the hillsides above the hamlet of Vic-Salon. Before his retirement, M. André made only Vin Gris from a blend of Pinot Noir, Auxerrois, Pinot Gris and Gamay, but he sold his vineyard to Jean-Marie Diligent a few years ago. The wine is still called Gris de Vic, and the label, rather touchingly, acknowledges its creator: 'Vignes de M. Raymond André'.

Clause Gauthier, at the hamlet of Manhoué, further along the valley of the Seille to the north-west, makes Gris de Vic together with red and rosé wines from Pinot Noir and white wines from Müller-Thurgau and Auxerrois. MM. Walter and Marchal at Marsal also make white Vin de Moselle from Müller-Thurgau and Auxerrois as well as a rosé from Pinot Noir.

Marsal is a curious village a few kilometres to the east of Vic, dominated by a massive fortified gateway and the remains of ramparts. These were built by Vauban to protect the deposits of salt which had made the region wealthy during the Middle Ages. A museum, La Maison du Sel, explains the 4,000-year history of salt extraction and how it is achieved today.

BAS-RHIN & HAUT-RHIN
The wines

THE WINES OF Alsace are predominantly white and, unlike the wines of other regions, are identified primarily by grape type. The main varieties are Sylvaner, Muscat Riesling, Pinot Gris, Gewürztraminer, Pinot Blanc and Pinot Noir, from which red and rosé wines are made. In addition, there is a wine called Edelzwicker, which is a blend of various grape types, including the Chasselas; Edelzwicker is the basic, everyday wine of the region, often served in restaurants in the traditional blue-and-white earthenware jug.

Cleebourg

Marlenheim, on the busy N 4, a few miles west of Strasbourg, is where the official Alsace Route des Vins starts. But there is also a small pocket of vineyards further to the north near Wissembourg, almost on the German border.

Unlike the main Alsace wine-growing region, the wines here are produced exclusively by a single co-operative based near Cleebourg, a few kilometres south-west of Wissembourg in the heart of the Northern Vosges regional park. This village nestles in a hollow, surrounded by steep vine-clad hills, and during the summer its ancient timbered houses are ablaze with flowers, planted in hundreds of window boxes and in tubs and barrels placed in every available corner.

The vineyards are planted around the communes of Cleebourg, Oberhoffen, Rott and Steinselz, and 190 individual growers, farming 60 hectares, bring their grapes to the co-operative for vinification. This was established in 1946 and was the first regrouping of a co-operative to take place after the Second World War.

In addition to the varietal wine names common to Alsace, the region gives its own names (lieux dits) to the very best wines produced from a specific vineyard. This highly sought-after distinction is only bestowed, however, when the quality reaches the required level in a specific year. Keimberg is Pinot Blanc Auxerrois produced from a 3-hectare plot near Cleebourg, Hannesacker from a similar sized vineyard of Riesling near Rott. Brandhof is produced from 2.5 hectares of Tokay Pinot Gris at Steinselz, Karchweg from the same variety in the village of Oberhoffen. Huettgasse is a rosé wine made from a small plot of Pinot Noir at Steinselz, and Riefenberg from a 7-hectare vineyard of Gewürztraminer

AUTUMNAL VINEYARDS NEAR THE VILLAGE OF EGUISHEIM.

near Cleebourg. The co-operative also produces wines from Sylvaner and Muscat as well as making Crémant and Edelzwicker.

Wissembourg has numerous timbered buildings grouped around a meandering river which runs through the town centre, giving rise to the inevitable title of Petite Venise (Little Venice). Nearby are the picturesque villages of Hatten, Betschdorf, Soultz-sour-Forêts, Woerth and – the region's gem – Hunspach.

Alsace – Route des Vins

The main wine-growing area lies to the south of Marlenheim, a small town about 20 kilometres west of Strasbourg, and this is where the official Route des Vins begins. Marlenheim is noted for its rosé wine, called Vorlauf, made from the Pinot Noir grape, and for the important wine festival it holds every September; and there are a number of attractive half-timbered houses near the Hôtel de Ville.

To begin the route, head south from Marlenheim on the D 422. Here, on the rolling hills, there are vineyards side by side with fields of food crops and grazing animals. The best time to visit this rich agricultural region is in late autumn, when the harvest is taking place and the turning leaves create vivid bursts of colour, while the upper slopes of the Vosges glisten with the first dustings of snow.

Although tiny tractors have taken the place of horses, the other traditional harvesting methods survive. The grapes are still collected in wooden tubs and re-loaded on to ancient wooden carts. The vineyards hum with excitement and it seems that the entire population is recruited to help. The narrow, cobbled village streets are jammed with tractors towing cart-loads of grapes; drying tubs are stacked everywhere and the air is heady with the smell of fermenting juice.

The Route des Vins meanders along a quiet country road that twists and turns its way through several small villages to the west of the main road. The university town of Molsheim is situated below the vine-clad Molsheimer Berg on the River Bruche. There is an unusual sixteenth-century Renaissance building, the 'Metzig', which was erected by the butchers' guild and now houses the museum. Obernai, a market town, has a sixteenth-century corn market and an Hôtel de Ville, and you can look towards the forests of Vosges from its medieval ramparts.

A little to the west are the slumbering old village of Boersch and the small town of Ottrott, known for its red and rosé wines. Barr, an important wine centre, is the next large town on the route and nestles below a steep hill lined with vines. It would make a good base from which to explore the northern part of Alsace, especially in March when there is a wine fair centred around its seventeenth-century château.

Nearby is Mont Ste-Odile, a hilltop convent established by Alsace's patron saint, who is buried in the small twelfth-century chapel; it is a spectacular viewpoint and a place of pilgrimage. Two other attractive villages within a short distance are Mittelbergheim and Andlau, the latter tucked into a niche in a steep-sided green valley. A little further south you come to Itterswiller, a welcoming little village perched on the edge of the vineyards, its single, narrow street lined with houses that always seem to be decked with flowers. The Hôtel Arnold, with its adjoining *winstub* (a cross between a *bierkeller* and a wine bar) is a memorable place to stay with its views over the vineyards to the wooded Vosges beyond.

The next main town on the route is Dambach-la-Ville, the home of a number of important growers; there are medieval ramparts, three fortified gates and a sixteenth-century town hall to see here as well. Continuing south, the road leads you through the small villages of Orschwiller, St-Hippolyte and Bergheim towards Ribeauvillé. Here the Vosges become more rugged and dramatic and the vineyards creep up the lower slopes. You can take a minor detour from Orschwiller up to the castle of Haut-Koenigsbourg; a small road winds up through beautiful woods to the summit of the mountain, from where you can see over the vineyards to the distant Rhine – on a clear day you can even see the Black Forest.

Ribeauvillé is known for its Gewürztraminer and Riesling – and its music: on its annual feast day, the first Sunday in September, the fountain in the main square flows with wine, and there is a street festival of strolling musicians. Set in a narrow valley in the foothills of the Vosges, it is ringed with vineyards. The cobbled streets are lined with beautiful old timbered houses and you'll find many places to taste and buy the wines of local growers, as well as *charcuteries*, *pâtisseries* and *épiceries* selling the culinary specialities of the region. Nearby is the little village of Hunawihr, with its fortified church overlooking the vineyards.

Riquewihr, next on the route, is the pride and joy of Alsace – and undoubtedly one of the loveliest wine villages in France, if at times a little crowded, especially at the height of summer when busloads of tourists descend on it. It has everything a perfectly preserved, historical village should have: ramparts, fortified gates, fifteenth-century houses with sculptured doorways, ornate balconies, wrought-iron signs, cobbled courtyards and winding narrow streets, all a blaze of floral colour. But it's not all show; there are many important growers based here, including Hugel and Dopff. It is well worth walking up through the vineyards beyond the village ramparts to look out over to the distant Vosges.

From Riquewihr the wine route continues through the small villages of Mittelwihr, Sigolsheim and Kientzheim to Kaysersberg, at the entrance to the Weiss valley. This is where Albert Schweitzer was born in 1875. The town is dominated by a ruined castle, the streets are lined with medieval and sixteenth-century houses and there is a fifteenth-century fortified bridge incorporating a chapel. The next village is Turckheim, where a platform has been built high up, as in many other Alsatian villages – usually around a church steeple or tower – in the hope that a pair of storks will build their nest on it; the stork is the local symbol for good luck.

Colmar is the centre of the Alsace wine trade and hosts an important wine fair in mid-August. It is a lovely town set on the River Lauch, with many important old buildings, including the Maison Pfister (a fine example of a carved wooden façade), l'Ancienne Douane (the old customs house) and a medieval guard house. The museum of Unterlinden, in a thirteenth-century Dominican monastery, houses an extensive collection of medieval religious art; best of all is Mathias Grünewald's Issenheim altarpiece, a superb example of German Renaissance art. In the modern galleries downstairs there are works by Picasso and Braque. The museum also contains a section on the local wine history: it is a colourful past centred around the *poêles*, private drinking clubs whose exclusive membership demanded exclusive – and excellent – wines. There is a lively weekly market in the old central square, where the local farmers sell their produce, and there are many *caveaux* where the regional wines can be found. Colmar has a number of excellent restaurants, *winstubs*, and hotels too; it is a good base from which to explore the surrounding vineyards and villages,

Continuing south, the Route des Vins leads you to Eguisheim, a village which has changed little since the sixteenth century. Its cobbled circular street, which runs around the inside of the rampart walls, is lined with old houses and

ABOVE: THE VILLAGE OF RIQUEWIHR SEEN FROM THE VINEYARD.
OPPOSITE TOP AND BELOW: STREET SCENES IN THE VILLAGE OF EGUISHEIM.

ABOVE TOP: A CHAMPAGNE WINE PRESS FULLY LOADED AND READY FOR PRESSING.
ABOVE: THE PROCESS OF REMUAGE IN THE CHAMPAGNE CELLARS OF VEUVE CLIQUOT IN REIMS.
OPPOSITE: CHAMPAGNE VINEYARDS NEAR VENDRESSE IN THE MASSIF DE ST THIERRY.

CHAMPAGNE VINEYARDS OVERLOOKING THE CANAL DU MARNE
NEAR TOURS-SUR-MARNE.

Ambonnay, a flower-decked village with an ancient winepress, a stone fountain and the fine old church of St-Réol. At Condé-sur-Marne, beside the Canal du Marne, is a particularly striking timbered market hall which is still used regularly for a lively country market. Nearby, the village of Bouzy is famed for its red Coteaux Champenois.

At Tours-sur-Marne is the champagne house of Laurent Perrier and beyond the route leads to the village of Louvois, with a park designed by La Notre, and then through Tauxières-Mutry and Fontaine-sur-Ay to Avenay-Val d'Or. From here some of the finest views of the Champagne vineyards and the Marne plain can be enjoyed from the small road which leads up to the village of Mutigny and then down again to Ay, an important town and Grand Cru commune where the champagne houses of Deutz & Gelderman, Ayala and Bollinger are based.

The route ends at Epernay, where a stunning sequence of magnificent classical mansions lining the Avenue de Champagne reflect the world-wide importance of the town. Below the avenue, over one hundred kilometres of tunnels and caverns house many millions of bottles of champagne from world-famous champagne houses such as the prestigious Möet et Chandon, Mercier, Perrier Jauet and Pol Roger.

Côtes des Blancs & Coteaux du Sézannais

The Route des Vins for this part of the Champagne vineyards begins in Epernay and passes the villages of Pierry and Moussy on the way to the summit of Mont Félix, where an isolated church among the vines is all that's left of a hilltop village. From here a scenic road through the vineyards leads through the villages of Monthelon and Mancy to Cuis, where there is a fine Romanesque church below an escarpment offering sweeping views across the plain.

The route now follows the D 10 and D 9 to a sequence of Grand Cru villages; Cramant, marked by a huge champagne bottle on the roadside, then Avize and Oger – which a sign proclaims as 'Un des Plus Beaux Villages de France'. One of the finest views of the Côtes des Blancs can be obtained from the road which leads up from it towards Grauves. Beyond is Le Mesnil-sur-Oger and Vertus, where there is a particularly lovely twelfth-century church built above an ancient well.

The route has descended now and crosses the plain with the vineyard slopes on one side and the distinctive chequerboard landscape of fields stretching away to a far horizon on the other. A few kilometres to the south of Bergères-les-Vertus there is a magnificent view from the road which leads up to Mont Aimée. Three hundred thousand troops were massed here in 1815 by Czar Alexander, and the ruins of the castle of Queen Blanche of Navarre acknowledge the dominating position of the site. Today it makes a perfect spot for a summer picnic.

The vineyards of the Côtes des Blancs have now been left behind, and the route continues through flat farmland to Coligny, Vert-la-Gravelle and Toulon-la-Montagne, where there is a sixteenth-century church, containing the tombs of the lords of Etoges, and a twelfth-century castle surrounded by a moat.

From here the route follows the D 343 through a sequence of quiet villages before vineyards reappear at Allemant and Broyes, set on the edge of a ridge. There are fine views across the plain from the steeply-angled vineyards which are planted along the hill slope. Afterwards, the route descends into the medieval town of Sézanne, with its cobbled streets, numerous old houses and an alley which traces the outline of its former ramparts.

A signposted wine route continues to the south of the town, where the majority of the vineyards are planted, along quiet country lanes through a sequence of peaceful little wine-villages; Vindey, Saudoy, Barbonne-Fayel, La Celle-sous-Chantemerle, Chantemerle, Bethon, Montegost and, just over the border into the Aube, Villenauxe-la-Grande, known for its china and ceramics.

In contrast to the more prestigious regions of the Côtes des Blancs and Montagne de Reims, the vines do not dominate the landscape here and are dotted among fields of grain and sunflowers which mingle with meadows and forests. The larges concentration of vineyards is to be found around Bethon, where the highly-regarded co-operative of Le Brun de Neuville is based, farming a total of 140 hectares.

Vallée de la Marne

The Route des Vins for the Vallée de la Marne begins in Epernay and leads initially northwards through Magenta and Dizy to Champillon, where there is a magnificent view back over the vineyards to Epernay, the River Marne and the Côtes des Blancs.

From here the route continues along the N 51 to St Imoges and then leads south-west along the D 71 to Hautvillers, from where there are more stunning views of the Marne valley. Here is the Benedictine Abbey, now owned by Moet & Chandon, where Dom Pérignon honed his skills. Hautvillers has many fine old houses decorated with ornate wrought-iron signs, and there are numerous opportunities to taste and buy champagne direct from the makers. There is a picnic area within the Abbey gardens.

Leaving Hautvillers, the route continues along the D 1 to the Grand Cru village of Cumières, on the banks of the Marne, which is also famous for its red Coteaux Champenois. Beyond, at Damery, there is a magnificent avenue of plane trees, and the route continues to Venteuil, from where a loop detours further up into the vine slopes to Fleury-la-Rivière, Belval-sous-Châtillon and la Neuville-aux-Larris. It then circles back to the banks of the Marne at Reuil and onwards to Châtillon-sur-Marne, which is dominated by a monolithic statue of Pope Urban II, who lived in the region and initiated the First Crusade. You can climb an interior staircase into the figure's arm, where there is a *table d'orientation* identifying the numerous villages which can be seen from this viewpoint.

The route continues along the right bank of the Marne to Verneuil and Vincelles and then crosses into the *département* of Aisne, where the vineyards continue as far as Crouttes-sur-Marne. At the centre of this region is Château-Thierry, where medieval remains include two fortified gateways and a thirteenth-century castle.

In this region the Marne becomes a more meandering, steeply banked river, and the vineyards, often planted on terraces, are not at all typical of the Champagne region. Most of the vineyards in the Aisne are on the right bank of the river, and the route leads to several villages with a long history of wine-making, like Essomes, which produced the wine for the court of King François I, and Bonneil, which had a reputation for Vin Gris at the end of the last millennium. At Charly-sur-Marne there is a statue to Emile Morlot, who was the village mayor at the end of the nineteenth century and was largely responsible for having the Aisne vineyards accepted into the Champagne appellation.

At Crouttes-sur-Marne the route crosses to the left bank and returns towards Epernay through the villages of Grand-Porteron, Nogent l'Artaud, and Chézy-sur-

ABOVE: AUTUMNAL VINEYARDS OVERLOOKING THE VILLAGE OF OGER.
OPPOSITE TOP: BARGES ON THE CANAL OF THE AISNE, NEAR BERRY-AU-BAC
OPPOSITE BELOW: VINEYARDS OF THE COTES DES BLANCS
SEEN FROM MONT AIME.

Marne to Nogental, Etampes-sur-Marne, Chierry, Blesmes and Crézancy at the beginning of the Surmelin valley. There were extensive vineyards here until the onset of phylloxera, when they all but disappeared, but they are now being steadily replanted.

At Condé-en-Brie you can see the castle of the Prince de Condé as well as a particularly lovely covered market hall. The route continues up the Surmelin valley as far as Baulne-en-Brie, where there is a fine view of the valley from the summit of the vineyards. From here it returns along the opposite side of the valley to the Marne and the villages of Moulins, Reuilly, Corthiezy and Dormans, where there is an impressive castle dating back from the time of Louis XIII and a vast park which contains a monument to the First World War battle of the Marne, with sweeping panoramic views over the valley.

From Dormans the route leads back to Epernay through Chavenay, Leuvrigny-Festigny, and Chene-la-Reine. From here the D 36 and the D 222 take you through Oeuilly, Montvoisin and Villesant, overlooking the winding Marne. Beyond, at Vaucienne, the route leaves the valley to cross the eastern edge of the Brie plateau and descends to Epernay through the wine-villages of Vinay, Moussay and Pierry.

Massif de St-Thierry

This is perhaps the least known region of the Champagne vineyards, but in the eleventh century the vines here were owned by the abbey of St-Thierry and were of considerable importance. Today they are of quite modest extent, occupying only 830 hectares. Farmed by 132 *vignerons*, they are largely scattered in small parcels among fields of sunflowers, wheat, barley, pasture land and woods in a landscape of gentle hills and small river valleys. The region has been known in the past for the production of the black-skinned varieties of Pinot Noir and Pinot Meunier, but more recent plantings have included Chardonnay.

The wine-producing area is centred around a group of small villages which lie to the north-east of Reims, on both the left and right banks of the River Vesle. The most important of these villages include Brimont, Cauroy-les-Hermonville, Cormicy, Hermonville, Merfy, Montigny-sur-Vesle, Pouillon, St-Thierry, Thil, Brouillet, Savigny-sur-Ardes, Serzy-et-Prin, Jonchery-sur-Vesle, Prouilly, Trigny and Pevy. There is also one single producer at the hamlet of Craonelle in the *département* of Aisne, a little to the north of this region. Independent wine producers can be found in all the villages mentioned, and there are *caves co-opératives* in Cormicy, Prigny, Pouillon and Trigny.

A very enjoyable tour of the vineyards leads along a sequence of country lanes through quiet unspoilt countryside to each of these villages. At Montigny-sur-Vesle there is an ancient fountain and wash-house and nearby, at Pevy, the church is listed as an ancient monument because of its fourteenth-century chancel, twelfth-century portal and sixteenth-century altarpiece. At Cheney there is a wash-house dating from the time of Henri IV, as well as a fine view of Reims and its cathedral in the distance.

At Montigny-sur-Vesle is a beautiful little church, built in the twelfth century on the site of the ancient temple dedicated to Jupiter, and a farm built at the time of Henri IV. The village of Merfy offers another fine view of Reims, and at St-Thierry is an eighteenth-century château built on the site of a sixth-century abbey. Two Kings of France, Saint Louis in 1248 and Louis XI in 1461, rested here after their coronation at Reims cathedral.

The hilltop village of Brimont has a château built in 1761 and a fort from the late nineteenth century. The village church was destroyed in the First World War but was rebuilt in 1925. Hermonville has a very pretty eleventh-century church and the medieval Château de Marzilly.

Joan of Arc passed through Cormicy in 1429, and you can see a church dating from the twelfth century. Nearby, at Berry au Bac, is a fascinating canal port where the great barges moor up at the junction of the Aisne and Ardennes canals. There is a grassy bank which makes a good place to have a picnic while you watch these huge craft come through the lock.

AUBE
THE WINES

THE VINEYARDS OF the Aube are mainly in the hills surrounding the valleys of the Aube, Seine and Ource, between the towns of Bar-sur-Seine and Bar-sur-Aube, lying about 40 kilometres east of Troyes and about 100 kilometres south of the Marne vineyards. The Aube vineyards are in fact part of Champagne, entitled to the same appellations, made from the same grape varieties and in the same way. However, the region tends to be the poor relation, and the majority of the most famous and respected Champagne houses are based mainly around Reims in the more northerly vineyards of the Marne.

It is generally accepted that the wines produced in the Aube are of a lesser quality than those of its more illustrious neighbour to the north. At the end of the nineteenth century the vineyards of the Aube were badly affected by phylloxera, and the depleted vineyards became separated from those of the northern Champagne and excluded from the appellation. A succession of bad harvests and problems experienced in selling and transporting the Aube wines led many thousands of *vignerons* and their supporters to descend upon the city of Troyes in the spring of 1911 to protest at their exclusion. As a result the government redefined the limits of the appellation and gave them back their earlier status. To some extent this reunion has not been entirely successful, because the wines from the Reims region have retained their reputation for superiority and are much more widely exported. However, there is much of interest here for the wine lover, including some excellent champagne as well as interesting Coteaux Champenois wines. Rosé de Riceys, of which Louis XIV was extremely fond, has its own appellation; it is a delightful deep pink, full-bodied rosé which is quite unusual and rarely found outside the region.

THE VINEYARDS

The Route des Vins in the Aube is quite well signposted and easy to follow. It is a complete circuit and so can be joined at any convenient place. But a good starting point is Bar-sur-Seine, whose narrow streets are lined with medieval houses with timbered façades. Two buildings to look out for are the sixteenth-century church of St Etienne and the Château des Comtes de Bar, above the town, with its unusual clock-tower. From here and from the footpath that leads to it there are fine views of the countryside and the town below.

Leave the town on the main road, the N 71, going towards Châtillon-sur-Seine (where the archaeological museum displays important Grecian artefacts found locally). After a kilometre or so you will come to a small road on the left that leads to Merrey-sur-Arce, a wine village that has some old houses typical of the region. Continuing on the D 167, you come to Celles-sur-Ource, where you can sample and buy wine. The countryside here is quite open with gentle hills; the vineyards are confined mainly to the tops and slopes of the slight hills.

After crossing the N 71, take a quiet country road, the D 452, to the village of Polisy situated at the confluence of the Seine and the Laignes. It is a sombre place made up of some austere old stone houses, a gloomy sixteenth-century château and a church containing an interesting *Virgin and Child* and some fine murals. The wine route continues to the hamlet of Balnot-sur-Laignes, which is known for its red and rosé Coteaux Champenois wines, set at the head of a valley. Here the Route des Vins climbs along the side of the valley into the wood of Riceys. A left turn on to the D 142 takes you to the top of a steep hill; from here you can see Les Riceys, a village where the wines are extensively cultivated.

Les Riceys is in fact three villages in one. The first you encounter is Ricey-Bas, which has an elegant Renaissance church beside the River Laignes. Nearby is a château, the oldest parts of which date back to the eleventh century. A little further along the road, virtually merged, are Ricey-Haut and Ricey-Haut-Rive, both with distinctive churches. There are several places where you can taste and buy the local Rosé des Riceys and champagne.

Return to Ricey-Bas, and continue on the wine route along the D 70, crossing the N 71, to the village of Cye-sur-Seine, which has a twelfth-century church and the remains of a fourteenth-century château. From here, you can make a small detour to Neuville-sur-Seine, which has a *cave co-opérative* and is dominated by a statue of Notre Dame des Vignes set on the top of the hill above the village. This is the perfect place to lie in the grass with a baguette, a piece of Chaource and a bottle of Rosé des Riceys, and allow the world to pass you by.

Follow the Route des Vins through a peaceful little valley along the D 103 to Loches-sur-Ource, then cross its Roman bridge and turn on to the D 67 to Essoyes, through which the River Ource meanders. The great impressionist painter, Pierre-Auguste Renoir, his wife and two famous sons – actor Pierre and film-maker Jean – are buried in the churchyard. The house they lived in between 1897 and 1916 is on the edge of the town, marked with a plaque.

There are fine views over the vineyards as the Route des Vins continues along the D 70 to the village of Fontette; there is a *cave co-opérative* here. Just before the next village, St-Usage, there is a detour to the high point of the downs giving some breathtaking panoramas over the plateau of Blu. Then on to Champignol-lez-Mondeville, a small village set in a wide valley and surrounded by cornfields, meadows, vineyards and fields of sunflowers. The route now continues along the D 101A to Arconville and then to Baroville, where there is another *cave co-opérative*. Continuing along the D 396 you come to Bayel, where you can visit the famous crystal glass works, la Cristallerie de Champagne.

The route follows the D 47 to Lignol-le-Château, at the crossroads with the N 19. There are two twelfth-century buildings here – a church and a château. You can make a detour to the village of Colombey-les-Deux-Eglises, where Charles de Gaulle lived; he is buried in the local cemetery. The next village is Rouvres-les-Vignes, then Colombé-le-Sec, home to an important *cave co-opérative*. Nearby are the ancient cellars of the Abbaye de Clairvaux; these date back to the twelfth century and can be visited.

Go through the small village of Colombé-la-Fosse to Arrentières, where there are remains of a fourteenth-century castle; it was demolished on the orders of Louis XIII. From here the route continues to the bustling market town of Bar-sur-Aube. This ancient town has a number of medieval buildings with timbered façades, an Hôtel de Ville dating from the seventeenth century, and the twelfth-century church of St Pierre, whose striking interior includes a wooden gallery. There is a wine-tasting chalet on the outskirts of the town beside the N 19 in the direction of Chaumont.

The route back towards Bar-sur-Seine starts off along the D 4 towards Proverville. Shortly after leaving the town you take a small road to the left to the chapel of Sainte-Germaine, set high on the hill above the town and offering splendid views of the Aube valley. A delightfully scenic road completes the circuit back to Bar-sur-Seine, passing through wine villages such as Meurville, with its twelfth-century church, Chacenay, which has a fifteenth-century château, and Ville-sur-Arce, where there is the cave co-operative of the Coteaux de l'Arce.

Montgueux

There is one small outpost of the Aube vineyards which remains from the pre-phylloxera period. The village of Montgueux lies about ten kilometres due west of the city of Troyes and is set on a steep-sided round hill overlooking the valley of the Seine. The south-facing slopes below the village are extensively cultivated with vines and have the appearance of a mini Montagne de Reims. Only champagne is made here, and the appellation was granted at the same time as those of the region around Bar-sur-Seine and Bar-sur-Aube. There are about 30 wine-growers in the village and just 12 who produce and sell commercially.

HAUTE-MARNE
Coteaux de Coiffy

IN THE FAR south-eastern corner of Haute-Marne is one of the least-known vineyards in France, near the spa town of Bourbonne-les-Bains. A few kilometres to the south-west is the small hilltop village of Coiffy-le-Haut. In countryside which is a considerable distance from any familiar wine-growing regions it comes as something of a surprise to discover neatly-planted rows of vines decorating the slopes around the village.

The area has a long wine-growing history. In the 1800s there were 300 hectares of vines here, and there have been small family plots of vines since the phylloxera destruction, but the Coteaux de Coiffy appellation, or the Vin de Pays de la Haute-Marne, is a quite recent development.

A vineyard of just 8 hectares was planted in 1983 by a group of four farmers who also raise cattle, maize and wheat, but this has been increased over the years to a total of 20 hectares. The production is mainly white wine from both Auxerrois and Chardonnay, with a smaller quantity of Pinot Noir and Gamay. There is a small *caveau* in the village of Coiffy-le-Haut which is open at weekends, and one of the *vignerons* lives in the last house on the village's single street opposite the church and is happy, when at home, to welcome buyers.

Around Coiffy you will find yourself in typically French rural backwaters which time seems to have passed by. A drive through the valleys of the Mance, the Petite Amance and the villages of Varennes-sur-Amance, Champigny-sous-Varennes, Laferté-sur-Amance and Vernois-sur-Mance provides an enjoyable hour or so of exploration.

Châtillon-sur-Saône also deserves exploration: a partially derelict hill village of considerable antiquity, it has the remains of ramparts and towers, as well as numerous old houses, and is currently being restored.

THE CUISINE

This region of France does not, perhaps, have the most distinctive cuisine in the country. The best-known regional specialities are those featuring champagne-based sauces: dishes like *poulet au champagne* and *écrivisses au champagne* (crayfish). *Potée champenoise* is a cross between a soup and a stew made from pork, sausage, ham and chicken with a mixture of vegetables and is traditionally served at harvest time to the hungry grape pickers. A sorbet made with Marc de Champagne is often served as a palate freshener between courses.

The town of Ste-Menehould is famed for its pig's trotters. These are cooked for up to a day and a half in stock with white wine, cloves and herbs, so that even the bones are reduced to a soft gelatinous texture. They are then made into a sausage-like preparation which is glazed with butter, coated in breadcrumbs and then grilled.

The hams and pâtés of Ardennes are renowned, for example *pâté de sanglier* made from the wild boar which roam the Ardennes forests. *Boudin blanc* is another local speciality, made from the best fillet of pork with nothing added but onions, milk, salt and spices; some say the best comes from the town of Rethel.

Andouillettes are found all over France, but those from Troyes are especially sought after. A sausage made from the intestines of pigs, *andouillette* is a popular lunchtime dish often served with puréed potato, *choucroute* and mustard.

Some of the great cheeses of north-eastern France originate from the neighbouring *département* of Aisne. One is the classic Brie de Meaux, a great wheel of creamy velvet-skinned cheese made from unpasteurized milk and bearing no resemblance to the bland, factory-made product found in supermarkets. Another distinctive cheese is Maroilles. Made from cow's milk, it has a rust-brown crust, a rich smell and a powerful flavour.

The Aube produces the luscious Chaource, which has been made since the fourteenth century, its neighbour Mussy, a cheese of similar appearance but with a firmer texture and slightly stronger flavour, and Caprice des Dieux, a cow's-milk cheese with added cream. From the Haute Marne come the strongly flavoured washed-rind cheese of Langres and the cone-shaped Chaumont.

FRANCHE-COMTÉ

THE REGION OF Franche-Comté occupies the countryside between Burgundy and Switzerland, and its landscape reflects the transition from French heartland to the Alps, becoming increasingly rugged and mountainous as you go from east to west. The region consists of three *départements*, Jura, Haute-Saône and Doubs. The latter is without an appellation, while Haute-Saône possesses only small areas of vineyards making Vins de Pays; it is the Jura alone in this region which produces wines in any quantity, but these have a unique character and quality.

JURA

THE WINES

THE WINES OF the Jura have long been regarded with respect. Pliny mentioned them, and they were greatly appreciated by the Romans. They have also graced the tables of many discerning people from the dukes of Burgundy to Rabelais and Brillat-Savarin, the French writer and gastronome.

Among the grape varieties grown here are Poulsard (or Ploussard), from which rosé wines are made, Trousseau for red, Savagnin (from which the renowned *vin jaune* is made) and Chardonnay for fine white wines that can be kept for many years. The Poulsard and Trousseau grapes are often blended during harvesting, as are the Chardonnay and Savagnin, to produce wines with a considerable variety of colour, from very pale gold through yellow, amber and light pink to rich ruby.

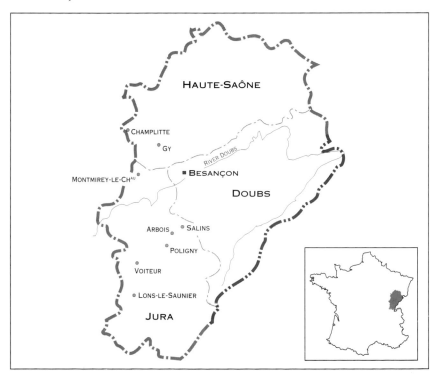

ABOVE TOP: VINEYARDS NEAR ARBOIS.
ABOVE: VINEYARDS NEAR CHATEAU CHALON.
OPPOSITE: A WATERFALL BELOW THE CIRQUE DE BAUME NEAR LONS-LE-SAUNIER.

The soil on which the vines are grown is mainly limestone, often combined with clay, the subsoil being a compacted marl. In the Arbois area the land is particularly favourable to the Savagnin and Poulsard grapes, traditional varieties which are unique to this region. Vine cultivation is hard work in the Jura: many of the vines are planted on terraces cut into the steep hillsides, and when the soil is washed down, as often happens during heavy rainfalls, it must be carried back to the vineyards.

For such a relatively small area, the Jura produces an amazing variety of wine. The regional speciality, *vin jaune*, or 'yellow wine', is made by an unusual method, shared by the Spanish Jerez wines. The Savagnin grapes are harvested late, often not until November, and are pressed in the same way as for a conventional white wine, but the juice is then put in barrels and kept for up to ten years (six is the legal minimum). During this period a veil of yeasts develops on its surface, the wine begins to oxidize, creating the characteristic deep yellow colour, and at the same time a subtle and unusual bouquet and flavour develop, often compared to hazelnuts. The exact nature of this transition is not fully understood, nor can it be totally controlled. The natural loss of wine from evaporation in the cask (ullage) is not made up, as with normal wines during ageing, and this makes good *vin jaune* a rather expensive and relatively rare commodity. It is usually drunk chilled as an aperitif or at room temperature with the local Comté cheese.

Another unusual wine for which the Jura is famous is *vin de paille*, or straw wine, so called because the grapes are dried on a bed of straw for three months before pressing. This makes them sweeter and produces a highly alcoholic dessert wine which compares favourably with a Sauternes; it can be kept for fifty years or more. Sparkling wines are also produced in the Jura, and Henri Maire extols the virtues of his *vin fou*, or mad wine, on hoardings throughout France.

Of the other wines, the rosés are of particular interest and are as highly rated as the well-known Rhône wine, Tavel, for their body and strength. Most rosé wines are left only briefly in contact with the skins of the black grapes to give them colour. But the Poulsard grapes of the Jura have less pigmentation than other varieties, which means that the juice and skins can be left to ferment together for many days, as they would for a red wine, without losing the delicacy of colour expected of rosé. This gives the Jura rosés well-defined body and flavour and means that they can be kept.

THE VINEYARDS

The Route des Vins leading through the Jura has been signposted relatively recently and provides an easy-to-follow tour through the most important vineyards and the most attractive villages and countryside. Although most of the vineyards are contained within a narrow strip of land, rarely more than about 15 kilometres wide, alongside the N 83 between Arbois in the north and St-Amour in the south, it is possible to tour the vineyards all day and hardly be aware that the main road is so near.

Driving south on the N 83 from Besançon, you will get your first glimpse of the Jura vineyards a few kilometres north of Arbois, where the rolling hills that signal the approach of the Jura plateau also define the eastern border of the plain of Bresse.

Just north of Arbois and to the east of the N 83, in the valley of the River Furieuse, lies the thermal spa of Salins-les-Bains. This is a good starting-point for a tour through the wine-growing area of the Jura. To reach the town, leave the N

83 a little way north of Arbois and, if time allows, stop on the way at Port-Lesney, to the west of the main road on the banks of the River Loue. This offers a peaceful retreat for anglers and campers, and there are walks along the river and through the surrounding woods.

The signposted Route des Vins begins at the village of Les Arsures, just north of Arbois, and offers not only its fine wine but also the seclusion of its quiet lanes and vine-clad hills. I passed a memorable hour here in a meadow just a few hundred metres from the main road, watching a pair of kestrels riding the thermals above my head, with a simple picnic of bread, Morbier cheese and a good bottle of Arbois red wine, while remaining blissfully unaware of traffic.

From here the route winds through country lanes to Montigny-les-Arsures before descending into Arbois; there are many wine-growers' establishments around the Place de la Liberté selling their products, and the town's Fruitière Vinicole (the name for the wine co-operatives of the region) is here too. Just along the main street is the imposing Les Deux Tonneaux, owned by Henri Maire, a grower whose wines are known throughout France. Nearby, in a small street behind the Hôtel de Ville, is a museum of wine.

The Fête de Biou, one of the most spectacular harvest festivals in France, is held in the streets of Arbois on the first Sunday in September; the high point of the festival is when about 100 kilogrammes of grapes are carried in procession through the town to the church.

Arbois was the boyhood home of Louis Pasteur; the house he lived in on the bank of the River Cuisance is still there. He did much of his experimental research into fermentation and wine-making at a small vineyard in Les Rosières, just north of Arbois.

Continue south from Arbois on the D 246, climbing into the foothills of the Jura towards the little village of Pupillin, which is said to make the best red wine of the region. Here you really know that you are in mountain country, although it is only a few hundred metres above Arbois. Even at the height of summer, there are massive piles of wood stacked against every house in readiness for the cold, dark evenings ahead. And, as if in defiance of the rigours of mountain life, every house will be ablaze with bright geraniums and petunias adorning all available corners and ledges, soaking up every ounce of the summer's warmth and colour as an antidote to the oncoming winter. It was up here in the mountains that an elderly *vigneron* explained to me that the Jura vines are among the purest strains in France; only grapes of noble lineage are grown, and, if necessary, he added, vineyards are compulsorily uprooted in order to maintain this tradition.

From Pupillin the D 246 rejoins the N 83 via the wine village of Buvilly. Follow this a short distance until you get to the fortified village of Poligny, which is an important wine centre; many growers have establishments in its narrow streets, and the Fruitière Vinicole (called the Caveau des Jacobins) is situated in an old church.

Among the many buildings of architectural interest here are the seventeenth-century Ursuline convent and the Hôtel Dieu with its vaulted halls and kitchens and old pharmacy; there is also a superb collection of Burgundian documents in the church of St-Hippolyte. A few kilometres from Poligny, towards Champagnole, is the beautiful and dramatic wooded gorge at Vaux, from which there are fine views over the surrounding countryside.

A little way further south from Poligny along the N 83 turn left on to the quiet D 57 towards St-Lothain, and you will come to a succession of pretty vil-

ABOVE: THE CHATEAU OF LE PIN NEAR THE WINE VILLAGE OF ETOILE.
OPPOSITE TOP: THE VILLAGE OF BAUME-LES-MESSIEURS.
OPPOSITE BELOW: THE PERCHED VILLAGE OF CHATEAU CHALON.

lages, including Passenans, Frontenay, Menetru-le-Vignoble and Domblans. You will be able to taste the local wines as you go. This area is known as the Revermont, literally 'the back of the mountain', and some of the more dramatic scenery – wide rolling landscapes with distant views of mountains, sudden surging hills and abrupt escarpments – can be seen at Château-Chalon, a village famed for its *vin jaune*, perched on a 460-metre peak overlooking countryside patterned with vineyards. Further south the imposing escarpment of the Cirque de Baume towers above the twelfth-century Romanesque abbey of Baume-les-Messieurs. From here you can follow a small road through the wine villages of Voiteur, Lavigny and Pannessières into Lons-le-Saunier.

A few kilometres west of Lavigny lies the village of l'Etoile, where a particularly notable white wine with a remarkable bouquet is made; its appellation also covers *vin jaune* and *vin de paille*. St-Germain-les-Arlay and nearby Château d'Arlay also produce fine white wines.

Lons-le-Saunier, the chief town of the region, has been a spa since Roman times; it has a beautiful park which contains the thermal baths and a casino. It is an excellent alternative to Poligny or Arbois as a base from which to explore the Jura vineyards.

If you follow the D 471 east out of Lons-le-Saunier you will reach a spot with a spectacular view over the Cirque de Baume and the distant village of Baume-les-Messieurs. Here the rift drops sheer for hundreds of metres into the valley, but a tiny, steep lane leads down into the valley, where there is an impressive waterfall at the foot of the cliff. From here you can return to Voiteur, Domblans and the RN 83 and back into Lons-le-Saunier, where the Route des Vins leads further south to the limit of the Jura vineyards at St-Amour, a small resort beside the River Besançon that has a lively holiday atmosphere during the summer.

HAUTE-SAÔNE
Coteaux de Champlitte

EVEN IN THE small Vin de Pays regions the presence of vinous interest is usually marked by the sight of vineyards, but the Coteaux de Champlitte could qualify as France's most secret vineyards, since they are tucked away on a remote hillside and can be approached only along a small country track.

Champlitte lies south-west of Coiffy, on the D 67, about half-way to Dijon and 20 kilometres north of Gray. It has a number of old houses, a church with a fifteenth-century Gothic tower and a château dating from the sixteenth century, which is now the town hall and houses a museum of local history and folklore. The town holds the fête of St Vincent, the patron saint of *vignerons*, on 22 January, a tradition which has been maintained since its instigation in 1632.

The main production of the Coteaux de Champlitte, or Vin de Pays de Franche-Comté, is by a group of 12 *vignerons* who farm the 40 hectares of vines planted largely on a single well-exposed, east-facing hillside to the west of the town. The winery and *caveau* can be found in the town centre, where they are well signposted.

Before phylloxera, the Coteaux de Champlitte was an important vineyard with over 600 hectares, but the present venture only began in 1975. Mostly Chardonnay and Pinot Noir are grown with a small quantity of Auxerrois, Gamay and Pinot Gris, and the wines have attracted numerous medals since the first harvest in 1979.

The valley of the River Salon to the east of Champlitte makes a peaceful and attractive detour, and the village of Leffond, to the north-west, an ancient wash-house and stone bridge create a particularly appealing corner.

About 30 kilometres south-west of Champlitte is Bèze, set at the source of its namesake river, which is a tributary of the Saône. Once a dependency of an abbey founded in the seventh century, it has retained two towers from the building, and a lovely thirteenth-century house overlooks the square. A famous son of the village was Félix Kir, who was the curate there in the early part of the century and subsequently a mayor of Dijon. He is best remembered now as the inventor of the popular aperitif of Cassis-spiked Aligoté to which he gave his name.

Roche-et-Raucourt

Vin de Pays de Franche-Comté is also made by just one producer in the village of Roche-et-Raucourt, 15 kilometres or so east of Champlitte in the valley of the little River Vannon. Here the Garnéry family farm 8 hectares of vines producing red and rosé wines from Gamay, Pinot Noir and Pinot Gris, together with a white wine from Chardonnay.

Although small family plots have existed in this region for many years, the present vineyard produced its first harvest in 1987. Wheat and maize also form an important part of the farm's production but cattle are no longer raised, I was told by Madame Garnéry senior, who observed that the younger generation like to have their holidays.

Gy & Charcenne

The ancient village of Gy lies about 30 kilometres to the south of Roche-et-Raucourt, and further pockets of vines producing Vin de Pays de Franche-Comté are to be found here, and in neighbouring Charcenne, under the care of Henri Guillaume. He also runs a large nursery specializing in vine cultivation, and told me that he has supplied plant stock to many of the English vineyards.

There were around 10 hectares in production at the time of my visit, with new plantings in progress. Chardonnay accounts for about half of the vines, with a balance of Pinot Noir and Gamay, together with a small planting of Pinot Gris.

Once the property of the bishops of Besançon, the village of Gy has old houses, a fine eighteenth-century church, an ancient fountain and a château with an unusual angular tower.

Offlanges

About 30 kilometres south-west of Gy, the hill village of Offlanges looks out over the Forêt de la Serre. The prestigious vineyards of the Côte d'Or are about 60 kilometres to the west, and at one time the hillsides around Offlanges were almost as densely cultivated, with over 500 hectares of vines before the advent of phylloxera.

A few plots of vines for family consumption have always remained, but in 1973 two local farmers, M. Lormet and M. Guell, began small commercial vineyards which have grown to 8 hectares of Gamay and Chardonnay.

It is interesting to note that the favoured grape varieties here, like others of the Vin de Franche-Comté, are from Burgundy instead of those grown in the vineyards of the Jura, a short distance to the south.

This small community is one of many throughout France that are busy reviving a wine-making tradition lost for several generations.

THE CUISINE

The trout, perch, pike (*brochet*) and carp from the region's fast-flowing rivers are excellent, and its forests and hills produce plenty of game, including hare, pigeon, woodcock (*bécasse*) and pheasant, which are used to make some intriguing pâtés and terrines. You can find the local smoked hams, *saucissons* and *andouillettes* in every *charcuterie*. Jesus de Morteau, considered to be one of the finest French sausages, has quite a unique taste.

One typical Jura dish is *coq au vin jaune*, a delicious concoction of chicken in a rich but light sauce made with cream and *vin jaune* and thickened with egg yolks; in spring it is served with morels, dark brown wild fungi of subtle texture and flavour.

The brown and white cows that graze on the hillsides and meadows provide milk for the region's cheeses. These include the famous Comté, much of which is produced in co-operatives – many of the individual herds are quite small and Comté is a very large cheese! At one small co-operative in a hill-town above Salins-les-Bains the proprietor showed me the vast copper vats holding over 1,000 litres of milk which, she explained, is made into two cheeses weighing about 45 kilos each. Another mountain cheese of note is Morbier: smaller than Comté, it is distinguished by a thin blue vein running through its centre and a distinctive nutty flavour and firm texture.

BOURGOGNE

T HE REGION OF Burgundy is perhaps the one most closely associated with the French tradition of good food and wine. In the
Middle Ages it was an independent kingdom, stretching from
the Low Countries in the north to Switzerland in the east. Today it
encompasses four *départements*, Yonne, Côte-d'Or, Nièvre and Saône-
et-Loire, each with its own well-defined character and distinctive landscape. There are important vineyards in each *département* and each has
its own renowned appellations.

YONNE

THE WINES

T HE SMALL COUNTRY town of Chablis is 12 kilometres to the east of the A 6
– *Autoroute du Soleil* – near Auxerre. Here and in a few surrounding villages one
of the greatest white wines of all is produced. There is nowhere else in the world
where the Chardonnay grape, from which Chablis is made, thrives the way it
does here on these sunny limestone hills.

Although Yonne is known mainly for Chablis, it possesses a variety of
appellations: Chablis – Sauvignon de St-Bris – Côtes d'Auxerre – Irancy –
Coulanges la Vineuse – Chitry – Epineuil – Tonnerre – Côte St-Jacques – Vézeley.

While the reputation and importance of Chablis are immense, the vineyard
area where it is produced covers only about 1,500 hectares – and the Grand Crus
vineyards about 100 hectares. However, there are more vineyards in the valley of
the Yonne, where other types of Burgundy are produced.

Chablis is one of the world's best-known wines and has virtually become a generic term for white wine. It is made exclusively from the Chardonnay grape – which is used for all the great white wines of Burgundy. Chablis is crisp and dry, making it the ideal accompaniment to seafood and shellfish; it also has a clear, crystalline quality with a greenish tinge and looks as refreshing and pleasing as it tastes.

There are four classifications of Chablis: Grand Cru, Premier Cru, Chablis and Petit Chablis. Seven Grands Crus – Blanchot, Bougros, Les Clos, Grenouilles, Les Preuses, Valmur and Vaudésir – come from the three communes of Chablis, Poinchy and Fyé; the vineyards are on the slopes of the prominent hill to the north-east of the town between the D 150 and the D 216. The wines must reach a volume of alcohol of at least 11 per cent and should be kept for at least two years; they continue to improve for up to ten years.

The Premiers Crus – there are 27 of these – come from the next most favourably sited vineyards; they have a similar capacity for ageing and must contain at least 10.5 per cent alcohol. Chablis is produced from 19 different communes, the best of the remaining vineyards, while Petit Chablis is from the least favourable terrain and is best drunk quite young.

The production of Chablis is fraught with difficulties, since it is an area prone to spring frosts. Considerable effort is made to combat them. Whenever frost is forecast, oil-fired stoves are placed among the vines to keep the temperature above freezing point. Another measure involves spraying water from a system of pipes ranged along the vines. The water comes from an artificial lake created specially for this purpose; the principle depends upon the fine spray of water freezing as it coats the vines, forming a protective barrier of ice.

In addition to Chablis the region is entitled to the appellation Bourgogne, and red, white and rosé wines are also made from the Gamay, Pinot Noir and Aligoté grapes. Passe-Tout-Grains is a red wine made from a blend of Gamay and Pinot Noir. In the village of St-Bris-le-Vineux a white VDQS wine from the Sauvignon grape, Sauvignon de St-Bris, is made, as well as Crémant de Bourgogne, a sparkling wine, which is made using the *méthode champenoise*. Smaller quantities of other grape varieties are also grown in the Yonne: Sacy for Crémant de Bourgogne, Melon de Bourgogne for Bourgogne Blanc Grand Ordinaire, Auxerrois for some Vins de Pays, Pinot Gris for La Côte St-Jacques, and César for some Irancy red.

THE VINEYARDS
Chablis

The Route des Vins in Chablis, and the Yonne generally, is not signposted. The route I have suggested follows the most interesting and important villages. The town of Chablis is an ideal starting-point for the tour. There are countless places where you can sample and buy the wines of the region and, during the summer, the Syndicat d'Initiative mounts a small exhibition of tools, implements, pictures and displays which explain the history and development of wine-making in the region. A lively market takes place on Sunday mornings, and there is a wine fair on the last Sunday in November. The town itself is small but has considerable charm and character. There are a number of interesting medieval buildings, including the church of Saint-Pierre and the collegiate church of Saint-Martin, both dating from the twelfth century. There is also an excellent *cave co-opérative* here which is open throughout the week, including Sundays.

To start the tour, leave the town on the D 965 heading towards Auxerre. The first wine village is Milly, high up on the hilly slopes to the west; a small road leads up into the village and its surrounding vineyards. A little further along the main road is the Grand Cru commune of Poinchy, designated as a *Village Fleuri* (flower village): in the spring and summer every available container – old wine casks, stone troughs, baskets – is crammed with a vivid display of flowers. Here the route leaves the main road and continues along the D 131 to the village of La Chapelle-Vaupelteigne and Villy along the banks of the River Serein. Then it is on to Maligny, where there is an ancient château.

From here the route climbs up out of the valley towards Fontenay-près-Chablis and then to Fyé, a Grand Cru village in a small valley with the vineyards planted on the steep slopes above it at a dizzy angle; here you are in the midst of the finest of the Chablis vineyards. Returning briefly to the D 965 and heading towards Tonnerre you come to the wine village of Fleys. Just after this, take the small road to the right which leads to Béru, a cluster of ancient grey stone houses. The next village is Viviers, a crumbling hamlet in a small valley. The wine road now climbs to the top of the hill towards Poilly-sur-Serein and, as you drive along, there are wonderful views of the vast, open landscape through which the River Serein weaves its gentle course, the rolling hills patterned with vineyards and fields of grain.

The road follows the Serein back towards Chablis through the hamlet of Chemilly-sur-Serein and the attractive little village of Chichée. On the outskirts of Chablis take the D 2 through a small wooded valley to Préhy and then Courgis; these two villages with their vineyards spread around the hill slopes mark the western limit of the Chablis vineyards.

From here you can head back towards Chablis through quiet, almost remote countryside and the hamlet of Montallery before rejoining the main road, the D 965, at the busy wine village of Beine. This is close to the artificial lake which feeds the vineyard sprinkling system. A little road leads up out of the village over the vine-covered hill to Lignorelles and then onwards through Villy and Poinchy to Chablis.

Côtes d'Auxerre

The A 6 autoroute is, effectively, the western limit of the Chablis vineyards. However, a tour through the Auxerrois vineyards can be made, beginning in Chitry, a small town dominated by a fortified church which has a huge round tower. This region is where the ordinary Burgundy wines are produced. St-Bris-le-Vineux, though, makes an unusual dry white VDQS wine from the Sauvignon Blanc grape, which is also used for the great white wines of Sancerre and Pouilly-sur-Loire, a little further to the south-west. The Route des Vins here has beautiful and extensive views of the rolling landscape.

Next you come to Irancy, situated in an idyllic spot, almost surrounded by steeply sloping hillsides planted with vineyards and cherry orchards; of the rosé and red wines produced here, Palette, a wine made from a plot of land overlooking the River Yonne, is especially sought after.

From Irancy the route continues to the twin towns of Vincelottes and Vincelles, separated by both the River Yonne and the Canal du Nivernais, running side by side. There is a towpath from which you can watch the boats and barges making their unhurried progress along the waterways. Downriver a short distance are the Caves de Bailly, where excellent Crémant de Bourgogne is

THE PILGRIM VILLAGE OF VEZELEY SEEN FROM ITS VINEYARDS.

produced; beyond are the wine villages of Champs-sur-Yonne and Vaux. To the south, the road continues alongside the canal to the old town of Cravant. A few kilometres west of the Yonne is Coulanges-la-Vineuse, with a mellow old church set in the middle of vine-clad hills. A little further to the south in peaceful unspoilt countryside are the small wine villages of Mige and Charentay.

Vézeley

At the southernmost point of the *département* of Yonne, on the edge of the great forest of Morvan, is the historic hilltop village of Vézeley overlooking the valley of the Cure. Set on a terrace at the northern tip of the ridge is the basilica of Sainte-Madelaine, the largest convent church in France. It was founded by Girard de Roussillon, a Count of Burgundy, and consecrated in 878 by Pope John VIII. In the tenth century the supposed relics of Mary Magdalene were placed in its care, and it became a major place of pilgrimage as well as a resting place on the route to Santiago de Compostela.

The vineyards of Vézeley, which were destroyed at the end of the nineteenth century by phylloxera, were replanted in 1970 on the hills surrounding the village. With the appellation Vins de Bourgogne, they now extend over 100 hectares in the communes of Vézelay, Asquins, St-Père-sous-Vézelay and Tharoiseau. There is a *cave co-opérative* based at St-Père which represents 13 *vignerons*, as well as four independent producers. A white wine is produced here from Melon de Bourgogne as well as a Chardonnay, labelled Henry de Vézeley, a red Pinot Noir and Passe-Tout-Grains.

Joigny – Côte St-Jacques

At the time of the Revolution there were over a hundred wine-growers in the vicinity of Joigny, a town about 25 kilometres to the north-west of Auxerre on the banks of the River Yonne. Today there are just two making commercial quantities from a total plot of 10 hectares of vines planted on the Côte St-Jacques, a steep hill which rises above the river valley on the north-western edge of the town. To see the vineyard, and a splendid sweeping view of Joigny and the Yonne, follow the D 20 for a short distance towards Dixmont. In addition to a red wine made from Pinot Noir, a delicate rosé is made from Pinot Gris.

Epineuil & Tonnerre

The wines of Tonnerre, a small town on the Armançon to the east of Auxerre, were reputed in the Middle Ages to be among the best of the Yonne and were held in great favour by both Henri IV and Louis XIV. In 1827, before phylloxera, they extended over 5,300 hectares, producing wine of a quality compared to Pommard and Meursault.

The vineyards were replanted in 1970, with a total of 160 hectares, around Epineuil, Tonnerre and Molosmes. There are 20 individual producers making red and rosé wines from Pinot Noir with the Epineuil appellation and white from Chardonnay with the Tonnerre appellation.

CÔTE-D'OR

THE WINES

THE APPELLATIONS TO which the *département* of Côte-d'Or is entitled are: Hautes Côtes de Nuits – Côtes de Nuits – Marsannay – Fixin – Gevrey-Chambertin – Morey St-Denis – Chambolle-Musigny – Vougeot – Vosne-

Romanée – Nuits-St-Georges – Côtes de Beaune – Hautes Côtes de Beaune – Ladoix – Pernand-Vergelesses – Aloxe-Corton – Chorey-lès-Beaune – Savigny-lès-Beaune – Pommard – Volnay – Volnay-Santenots – Monthelie – Auxey-Duresses – St-Romain – Meursault – Blagny – Puligny-Montrachet – St-Aubin – Chassagne – Montrachet – Santenay.

These famous names all lie within quite a small area. The Côte d'Or is a ridge of hills that runs almost parallel to the *Autoroute du Soleil*, and the vineyards that stipple its slopes start just south of Dijon and continue in an almost unbroken band to the village of Santenay, some 48 kilometres to the south. There is, however, one small outpost of vines within the *département* of Côte-d'Or around the town of Châtillon-sur-Seine to the east.

The soil of the Côte d'Or is a reddish clay containing fragments of chalk, with a subsoil rich in minerals. In addition, the disposition of the hills creates an ideal microclimate for the Pinot Noir and Chardonnay grapes, from which the greatest of the Côte-d'Or wines are made. This does not mean, however, that wine-making here is a trouble-free occupation. When the first buds appear in April they often have to be protected from hard frosts, while heavy rain in the summer months can easily create the conditions for rot.

But the diverse climate and soil in the Côte-d'Or mean that there is an extraordinarily rich variety of wine, in terms of character and quality. Often a distance of only a few hundred metres can make the difference between a good wine and a really great one: for this reason, vineyards in the region are called *climats*, since each has its own unique combination of soil, sun, wind and rain. As a general rule the best wines are made from the grapes grown on the middle of the slope.

As well as the fine – and expensive – wines from the famous vineyards and villages of the Côte-d'Or there are wines under the appellations Côtes de Nuits and Côtes de Beaune, from communes in these general areas; Côtes de Beaune-Villages and Côtes du Nuits-Villages, from specific communes; and Hautes Côtes de Beaune and Hautes Côtes de Nuits, from the vineyards higher up the hill beyond the more famous slopes.

THE VINEYARDS

The Côte-d'Or is divided, geographically and by wine types, into two quite separate areas – the Côtes de Nuits in the northern half and the Côtes de Beaune in the south – although the vines are virtually continuous. The northern half runs south from Chenôve, a suburb of Dijon. The distance from Chenôve to Corgoloin, where the Côtes de Beaune route starts, is little more than 24 kilometres. The countryside on the short northern tour is best explored on foot along the tiny lanes that meander up into the vineyards from the villages.

Côtes de Nuits

The Côtes de Nuits Route des Vins starts just outside Dijon, at Chenove, on the N 74. It is well signposted, rather proudly, as the Route des Grands Crus. From Chenôve the route follows the D 122, a small road that winds its way up on to the gentle slopes of the Côtes de Nuits towards the village of Marsannay-la-Côte, noted for its rosé; it has its own appellation, Bourgogne Rosé de Marsannay. The next village is Fixin, the first of eight major communes of the Côtes de Nuits; in the park just above the village is a bronze statue of Napoleon, sculpted in 1846 by François Rude, whose most famous work is the decorative panels of the Arc de Triomphe in Paris.

ABOVE: THE WALLED VINEYARD OF LE MONTRACHET IN THE SNOW.
OPPOSITE TOP: THE OLD VILLAGE OF CHABLIS SEEN FROM
THE BANKS OF THE RIVER SEREIN.
OPPOSITE BELOW: THE CHATEAU OF COUCHES IN THE CHALONNAIS.

From Santenay you can follow the signs to small villages such as Dezize-lès-Maranges, and then to the top of the Montagne des Trois Croix, where there are stunning views of the Côte-d'Or and the Chalonnais. The route continues from here through the villages of Sampigny-lès-Maranges and Changé, then on towards Nolay on the D 973. Nolay has many fine old buildings, including an oak-beamed market hall. Nearby is a spectacular gorge, le Cirque du Bout du Monde (World's End), where sheer cliffs surround a meadow through which a stream wends its way. At the base of the cliff is a waterfall.

The village of La Rochepot is close by; its spired and turreted château was badly damaged during the Revolution and was restored last century. From here the Route des Hautes Côtes winds up towards the highest point in the wine-growing area. You go through Orches, stunningly located beside dramatic rock formations; it is also known for its delicate rosé wine. Near the village of Nantoux follow a narrow road on a detour up the side of a valley, through precariously sited vineyards, over the steep hill and down into the village of Bouze-lès-Beaune.

Further north, over the autoroute towards the small hamlet of Bouilland, the route goes through what is now the Hautes Côtes de Nuits and continues up steep-sided, wooded valleys towards Marey-lès-Fussey, where the Maison des Hautes Côtes is situated. This is a centre that promotes the local wines; you can taste and buy them, and sample the regional culinary specialities in the Maison's restaurant. In these wild and often rugged surroundings, soft fruit, particularly blackcurrants, are grown along with the grapes. Much of the fruit for Cassis, the blackcurrant liqueur for which the region is also famous, is grown here; Kir is traditionally made with a glass of chilled Bourgogne Aligoté and a dash of Cassis. There are many lanes you can take to return to Beaune or the villages along the Route des Grands Crus.

Châtillonais

The town of Châtillon-sur-Seine lies about 80 kilometres north-west of Dijon, at the north-eastern tip of the *département* of Côte-d'Or, bordering that of Aube. It is situated on a curious loop in the river Seine and, because of its strategic position, was an important stronghold of the Duchy of Burgundy. The town was extensively damaged during an aerial bombardment in 1940 but there is still much of interest to be seen: the ruins of the château of the Dukes of Burgundy, the tenth-century church of Saint-Vorles, the Cistercian church of Saint Nicholas and an archaeological museum containing the treasure of Vix.

The countryside surrounding Châtillon is one of forests, lakes, meandering rivers and meadows where quiet country lanes link a series of peaceful villages. Once an important vineyard, the Châtillonais is beginning to revive its wine-growing tradition and there are increasing areas of vines to be seen among the fields of sunflowers, maize and wheat. The wines are entitled to the Bourgogne appellation, and Crémant de Bourgogne is an important part of the production. The principal communes are Molesmes, with its ancient abbey, Griselles, Larrey, Marcenay, beside a peaceful wooded lake, and Massingy.

SAÔNE-ET-LOIRE
Côte Chalonnaise

THE CHALONNAIS IS, effectively, an extension of the Côtes de Beaune; in fact, part of the Hautes Côtes de Beaune falls within the *département* of Saône-et-Loire. It is a small area in terms of vineyard acreage – smaller even than Chablis – and the vines are less intensively cultivated. The vineyards of the Chalonnais extend south from just beyond Chagny to St-Boil, on the D 981, a distance of about 30 kilometres, and they are seldom more than a few kilometres wide.

THE WINES

The wines of the Côte Chalonnaise are, perhaps, less well known than those of the rest of Burgundy, particularly outside France. However, the grape varieties are the same and the soil has much in common with the more illustrious neighbouring vineyards and, while they do not have the same reputation for character and quality, Chalonnais wines have become more popular, perhaps because the high cost of the better-known wines from Burgundy make these seem good value. The appellations to which the vineyards of the Chalonnais are entitled are: Hautes Côtes de Beaune – Maranges – Bourgogne Côte Chalonnaise – Bouzeron Aligoté – Rully – Mercurey – Givry – Montagny.

As in the rest of Burgundy, the best white wines are made from the Chardonnay grape, and the best reds from Pinot Noir. However, the Aligoté thrives well on this terrain and the region's Bourgogne Aligoté is highly regarded, in particular that from the commune of Bouzeron. Sparkling wines are also made here by the *méthode champenoise*; in addition there is the Bourgogne Passe-Tout-Grains, a red wine made from a mixture of Pinot Noir and Gamay grapes.

THE VINEYARDS

The northern gateway to the Chalonnais Route des Vins is the town of Chagny; one of the best restaurants in the region, in the Hôtel Lameloise, is here. You take the D 981 to the first of the four main wine communes, Rully. As you approach the village you will see little evidence of vines, since most of the vineyards are on the hillside behind the village to the west; access is via a narrow road that leads past an imposing château.

Although this was a red wine area originally, today the *vignerons* rely mainly on the Chardonnay grape, from which they make a fine white wine that is steadily increasing in both quantity and reputation. Crémant de Bourgogne, is also made here.

A short detour from Rully will take you back towards Chagny along a narrow country road through unspoilt, almost deserted countryside to Bouzeron, a sleepy little village of ancient stone houses and crumbling farm buildings. It is known for its white wine made from the Aligoté grape: Bourgogne Aligoté. Then go west on to the D 109, which will take you south through a green valley and the small wine village of Aluze, perched precariously on a hill surrounded by vineyards.

From here the Route des Vins continues towards the second of the major wine centres, Mercurey, a one-street town ranged along the D 978. But don't be deceived – Mercurey is, in fact, the largest producer of all the Chalonnais communes. Red wines predominate, made from the same Pinot Noir grape as the red Burgundies of the Côte-d'Or, while a small quantity of white wine from the Chardonnay grape is also produced. There is a tasting cellar where you can sample a variety of these local wines. Before returning to the D 981, it is worth making a small detour to St-Martin-sous-Montaigu, another village of stone houses surrounded by vine-patterned hills.

As you approach Givry, another important wine town, you'll see signs proclaiming that its wines were Henri IV's favourite tipple. An old town with a bustling atmosphere, Givry makes a good base for exploring the region. As in

Mercurey, most of the wine made here is red, with only a small amount of white being produced.

Montagny is the most southerly commune of the Chalonnais appellations. A peculiarity of the Montagny wines is that the term Premier Cru here simply denotes a higher degree of alcohol rather than a superior or specific vineyard, as would normally be the case. This is a white wine area and the vineyards are scattered over the surrounding hillsides, some of which are over 400 metres high. The quiet, narrow lanes that wind through the vineyards offer a succession of rural landscapes and will lead you to some delightful little villages, including Jully-lès-Buxy, a picturesque cluster of weathered, golden-stone farmhouses, and St-Vallerin. Buxy, which is larger and busier, has a *cave*, the Caveau de la Tour Rouge, where you can taste and buy the local wines. Regional specialities are served in its restaurant, attractively situated in an old tower within the remains of the ramparts. On the outskirts of Buxy, towards the autoroute, there is a large, modern and highly regarded *cave co-opérative*.

Couchois

To the west of Mercurey, on the road towards Autun, is Couches, where you can see the impressive remains of a fifteenth-century castle and a thirteenth-century church. Once an important iron-mining community, Couches is now the centre of a small wine-growing area within the Côte Chalonnaise.

Here, among steep rounded hills, the vineyards are even more widely scattered than in the main Chalonnais region but a drive through the principal wine villages of St-Maurice-lès-Couches, St-Sernin-du-Plain and Dracy-lès-Couches, the last with its sixteenth-century château, will provide an enjoyable hour or two and the opportunity to taste and buy some very good wines at reasonable prices.

The Mâconnais

Wines have been grown in Mâcon since Roman times, but it wasn't until an inspired publicity stunt by a local grower in the seventeenth century that they gained wider recognition: Claude Brosse loaded two casks of his wine on to a cart and travelled for 33 days until he got to the court at Versailles. Louis XIV was very impressed by him – and by his wine, declaring it to be of a better quality than the Loire wines he had been drinking. In recent years the wines of the Mâconnais have become more and more popular and therefore production has increased accordingly.

Although Mâcon itself is the centre of the region's wine trade, the vineyards are situated further to the west, along a line of low hills rising from the valley of the Saône. As you travel south, it is around Mâcon that your thoughts start turning towards the Mediterranean. The climate is more southerly, the land lush but rugged, and the houses have flatter, red-tiled roofs and open-galleried façades. Indeed, the grapes ripen a week or so earlier here than in the more northerly Burgundian vineyards, and the harvest, too, is sooner.

THE WINES

Although red, white and rosé wines are all made here, the dominant type is white, made from Chardonnay and Aligoté, as in the rest of Burgundy. The red and rosé wines are made from Gamay and Pinot Noir.

The basic appellations of the wines are Mâcon, Mâcon Supérieur and Mâcon-Villages. The difference between the first two is simply that Mâcon Supérieur has a higher minimum level of alcohol. Mâcon-Villages is made from 43 specific communes within the region, and the quantity of wine allowed to be produced from each hectare of vines is limited, resulting in a better quality wine. In addition there are the named Crus from the small region in the south of the Mâconnais: Pouilly-Fuissé, Pouilly-Vinzelles, Pouilly-Loché and St-Vérand.

THE VINEYARDS

Although the most important wine-growing area is situated immediately to the west of Mâcon, the Route des Vins starts further north, just south of the Chalonnais region beyond Buxy. Drive south on the D 981, a quiet road leading to the heart of the Mâconnais through undulating countryside. The first towns reached are St-Boil and Sercy; from the road at Sercy a spectacular château is visible. A short detour to St-Gengoux will reveal an attractive medieval town with a twelfth-century château, cobbled streets and many old houses. It also has a good *cave co-opérative* where many wines from the Mâconnais and the Chalonnais regions can be tasted.

After this, the vineyards become less frequent, but the road is a continuing pleasure with vistas of rolling, wooded landscape. Stop at Cormatin to see the fifteenth-century solid gold *Vierge de Pitié* in the church. You can also visit the magnificent Renaissance château set in its great park. From here, take the D 14 west towards Ozenay where another turreted château can be seen from the roadside. The vineyards begin in earnest again around the village of Plottes, near Ozenay, on the D 56.

The road continues through a succession of small wine-growing villages, including Chardonnay, where there is an excellent *cave co-opérative*, Viré, Lugny and Azé. This is gently contoured, open countryside, criss-crossed by quiet lanes. The meadows and fields are planted with grain and vegetables while the orderly rows of well-tended vines in the vineyards pattern the slopes.

Many of the villages have wine co-operatives where visitors are welcome and buy the local wines. I visited that of Viré in late September as convoys of tractors queued up to deposit their cut loads of greenish-yellow Chardonnay grapes. I asked how the harvest was this year, and received the true Gallic response – with downturned mouth and shoulders shrugged – 'Moyen, M'sieu, moyen' (so-so).

Although the vineyards here are less well known than those of the villages further south, much of the good, honest wine (red, white and rosé) sold under the Mâcon-Villages and Mâcon Supérieur appellations is produced from around these sleepy slopes. Further south is the curiously named town of La Roche-Vineuse. If you have the time, you should go for a walk up the steep, winding lane via the church to the hilltop, from where there is a superb view of the surrounding countryside.

The real heart of the Mâconnais is a small area just south of the N 79. The villages of Pouilly, Fuissé, Solutré, Vergisson, Davayé, Vinzelles, Loché, St-Vérand and Chasselas are clustered almost on top of each other, linked by a number of narrow winding roads. They are all quite small and quiet but are full of character. In addition to the many individual *vignerons* inviting you to visit their *caves*, there are a number of renowned *caves co-opératives*.

The Route des Vins is well marked but this is hardly necessary, since even an aimless drive in this region will take you to most of the important wine villages. The scenic splendour here is matched by the excellence of wines: Pouilly-Fuissé is considered by many to be one of the greatest white wines of France, certainly

ABOVE TOP: THE ROCK OF SOLUTRE IN THE MACONNAIS.
ABOVE: A VINEYARD IN THE CHATILLONAIS NEAR THE VILLAGE OF LARREY.
OPPOSITE: A MACONNAIS VINEYARD NEAR THE VILLAGE OF FUISSE.

of the Mâconnais. The vines which produce this great wine are planted over a landscape of dramatic character and proportion, dominated by two rocky outcrops, Vergisson and Solutré, which rise cathedral-like above the vineyards.

The rock of Solutré, a natural fortress, was the gathering place for the Gauls during their final battle for autonomy in 511; a huge bonfire of discarded vines is lit on the summit every Midsummer's Day to mark the event. A vast deposit of prehistoric bones – one layer made up entirely of broken horsebones – was found at the base of the rock in 1866: this site is so important that one period of the Palaeolithic area is now known as Solutrian (18,000–15,000 BC). Many of the archaeological finds are at the Musée des Ursulines in Mâcon.

The busy river port of Mâcon is some way from the vineyards, but it would certainly be a pity to bypass it. In the old part of town there is a wine centre, as well as the Maison du Mâconnais, a restaurant serving regional food.

NIÈVRE
THE WINES

THE NIÈVRE CONTAINS the smallest area of vineyards within Burgundy but possesses one of the most highly-regarded appellations, Pouilly-Fumé, along with Pouilly-sur-Loire, the VDQS wines of Coteaux Giennois and the Vins de Pays of Nièvre and Coteaux Charitois. The wines differ considerably from the rest of Burgundy since the main grape variety for white wine is the Sauvignon Blanc but both Gamay and Pinot Noir are grown for red and rosé wines. Some Chardonnay is grown for Vins de Pays and Chasselas for Pouilly-sur-Loire.

THE VINEYARDS

The Route des Vins centres around Pouilly-sur-Loire, on the western edge of the Burgundy region, only about a dozen kilometres from Sancerre. This tranquil, one-street town on the eastern bank of the Loire is a good place to stop overnight; there are several hotels, a campsite by the river, restaurants and numerous places to taste the local wines.

Pouilly-sur-Loire

The small wine circuit takes you into the gentle countryside which is flatter and has less immediate appeal than that of the Sancerre region on the western bank of the river, but it has a rural charm all of its own. A few kilometres to the northwest is the village of Les Loges, its old stone houses lining a steep street that rises away from the river; there are a number of *vignerons* here who welcome visitors. The route continues through the communes of Les Girarmes and Bois-Gibault, then returns to the river at Tracy, with its impressive fourteenth-century château.

The route continues away from the river through a number of hamlets such as Bois Fleury, St-Laurent, Soumand and St-Martin-sur-Nohain. The largest community, and the most important Pouilly-Fumé wine village, is St-Andelain, set on a hill; its slender-spired church is visible from miles around. Close by is the largest and best-known estate of Pouilly-Fumé, Château de Nozet. Returning towards Pouilly you arrive at the hamlet of Les Berthiers, where there are a number of signs inviting visitors to taste and buy wine.

Coteaux du Giennois

The Coteaux de Giennois is a VDQS appellation which applies to a small winegrowing region of about 100 hectares in the Loire valley between Cosne-sur-Loire

and Gien, about 40 kilometres downstream. Although there are small plantations of vines on both sides of the river along this reach, the largest concentration is to be found on the right bank to the east of Cosne-sur-Loire, around the
villages of Cours, St-Loup, St-Père and Pougny.

This countryside is one of sweeping, rounded hills and broad vistas, and the
vineyards occupy small plots within fields of wheat, maize and pasture land. I
visited Jean Jarreau in Villemoison, a pretty hamlet near St-Père, where he farms
about 8 hectares of vines producing red, white and rosé wines. He said ruefully
that the VDQS appellation means that he is obliged to charge prices well below
those of his more famous neighbours in Sancerre and Pouilly, although his wines
are very similar, both in terms of grape varieties and the terrain on which the
vines are planted. There is some talk that the Coteaux du Giennois may be elevated to AOC status in the not-far-distant future.

The symbol used on many of the wine labels for the Coteaux du Giennois is
derived from an emblem in the ancient Commanderie of the Knights Templars,
which can be found on the outskirts of Villemoison.

The *cave co-opérative* at Pouilly-sur-Loire produces a red Coteaux du Giennois
from Pinot Noir in addition to AOC Pouilly-Fumé and Sancerre.

Coteaux Charitois

One of the least known, and newest, Vin de Pays is to be found in the countryside to the east of La Charité-sur-Loire, about 14 kilometres upstream from
Pouilly-sur-Loire. The Vin de Pays des Coteaux Charitois was granted its appellation in 1986. At the time of writing there are only about 25 hectares of vines, but
new plantings will double this within a few years.

The vineyards are situated around the villages of Raveau, Nanny, Chasnay,
Murlin and La Celle-sur-Niève, on the edge of the Forêt des Bertranges, and also
in the hamlet of Tronsanges on the right bank of the Loire a few kilometres south
of La Charité. Varietal red and white wines are made from Pinot Noir, Gamay,
Sauvignon Blanc and Chardonnay. The largest vineyard is the Société des Hauts
de Seyr at Chasnay, with 15 hectares, which began production of Chardonnay in
1993 and Pinot Noir in 1994.

Coteaux de Tannay

The village of Tannay lies on a range of low hills bordering the left bank of the
River Yonne about 15 kilometres south-east of Clamecy. A community has
existed here since the ninth century and was granted the right to be fortified by
Louis IX in the fifteenth century. Today it is a peaceful little village, where not
much remains of its fortifications but you can see the thirteenth-century church
of St Léger, the fifteenth-century Maison des Chamoines in the Rue de Bèze, the
Château de Pignol, built in the seventeenth century and, a short distance to the
south, the beautiful fifteenth-century Château de Lys.

Wine has been produced in the village since the twelfth century, when it had
a reputation for fine whites. In the fifteenth century François I allowed the wine
to be sold in order to reconstruct the ramparts, and Louis XIII served it at his
table at the beginning of the sixteenth century. Phylloxera destroyed the vines in
1868, but the vineyard is now being revived and there is a local *confrérie vineuse*,
Les Chanoines de Tannay.

One producer in Tannay is currently making Chardonnay together with red
and rosé Pinot Noir from a vineyard of 6 hectares. A new planting of Melon de

ABOVE TOP: THE GILDED MOSAIC ROOF OF THE HOSPICE DE BEAUNE.
ABOVE: THE ANCIENT COVERED MARKET HALL OF NOLAY.
OPPOSITE: THE CHATEAU OF RULLY IN THE CHALONNAIS.

Bourgogne has been made recently by another *vigneron*. The wines are entitled to the appellation Vin de Pays de la Nièvre, which extends to a number of other villages: Talon, Vignol, Asnois, Pouques-Lormes and La Maison-Dieu.

THE CUISINE

Heartiness is the essence of Burgundian cuisine, where wholesome ingredients are combined with strong flavours and rich sauces to create dishes which many feel reflect the true tradition of the French culinary art. Wine figures extensively in many dishes; *coq au vin* and *boeuf à la bourgignonne* have become standard menu items the world over. In a similar vein, *oeufs en meurette* are eggs poached in red wine and flavoured with shallots. Burgundy is also famous for its *escargots* stuffed with garlic, parsley and butter; *jambon persillé*, where chunks of ham are set into a wine-rich jelly marbled with finely chopped parsley; the superb Charolais beef served with a red wine sauce: and wild rabbit cooked in a sauce made with white wine, egg yolks and Dijon mustard. *Gougères* are light golden buns of *choux* pastry studded with Gruyère cheese, while the *charcuterie* of the region includes such delights as hams from the Morvan, an air-dried *saucisson* called *rosette*, made from pork and various spices, and the renowned *andouillettes* of Chablis.

Among the excellent cheeses found in the region are Epoisses, which is soft and creamy with a dusty reddish coating, and St-Florentin, similar in appearance but with a stronger flavour; both are made from cow's milk. A creamy, mild cow's-milk cheese you will find in the region is Brillat-Savarin, a smallish disc with a golden crust named after the nineteenth-century gastronome. There is also Cîteaux, a larger cheese with a firmer texture, and Soumaintrain, both made from cow's milk. Cendre d'Aisy is a cow's-milk cheese steeped in Marc for several weeks and then dusted with wood ash, while Claquebitou is a creamy goat's-milk cheese flavoured with garlic.

AUVERGNE

T HE AUVERGNE IS the region of the Massif Central, the great mass of mountainous and volcanic terrain which rises up from the central plateau. It consists of four *départements*, Haute-Loire, Cantal, Puy-de-Dôme and Allier. Only the last two have vineyards producing appellation wines and these are, only designated as VDQS.

ALLIER
St-Pourçain-sur-Sioule

THE RIVER ALLIER flows from its source in the Cevennes to join the Loire at Nevers. Like its bigger sister, the Allier is also a wine river. On the western side of its broad valley between Moulins and Vichy, at the point where it is joined by the River Sioule, are the vineyards of the VDQS appelation, St-Pourçain.

Vines have been grown here since before the Roman occupation. It is recorded that the Phoenicians founded a colony at Chantelle and planted the first vines on the slopes overlooking the Bouble, a tributary of the Sioule. The Romans arrived in around 50BC, and at first continued to work the vineyards, but during the first century AD the Emperor Domitian banned the cultivation of vines and for more than two centuries wine-making ceased in the region.

During the Middle Ages the vines flourished again with the encouragement of the abbeys and were extended on to the slopes around the villages of Saulcet, Contigny and Montfand. At this time the wines of St-Pourçain were considered worthy of comparison with those of Bordeaux, Burgundy and Champagne. They were transported throughout France by river and canal, and reached the tables

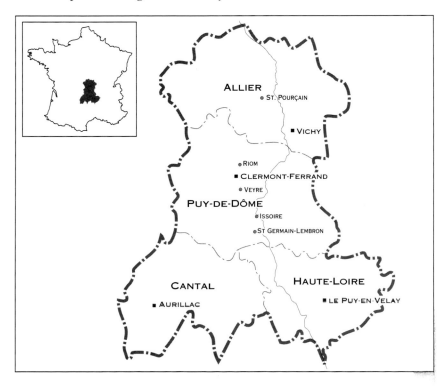

A WINTER LANDSCAPE IN THE COUNTRYSIDE TO THE WEST OF ISSOIRE.

of the highest in the land. Pope Clément VI, Charles VI and Henry IV are all recorded as being great admirers of the wines.

Towards the end of the eighteenth century the vineyards of St-Pourçain covered more than 8,000 hectares, but today there are only about 800. Two-thirds of the total production is from the *cave co-opérative* at St-Pourçain, but there are over twenty individual producers. Most are members of the Caves Particulières association, whose distinctive brown-and-white signs at the road-side draw in potential buyers.

THE WINES

The vineyards are planted on the low hills bordering the Allier, Bouble and Sioule rivers, occupying a strip of land 5 kilometres wide and 30 kilometres long. The region was originally known for its white wines, and the region's distinctive grape variety was the Sacy, known locally as the Tresallier. It was once widely planted in the Yonne and even began to rival Chardonnay in the Chablis region. It is still used in some of the sparkling Crémant de Bourgogne made in that area.

Today, however, both Chardonnay and Sauvignon Blanc are used for white wines, although a proportion of Sacy is required under the appellation regula-tions and its inclusion is considered to be essential for a characteristic St-Pourçain white wine. Both red and rosé wines made from Gamay and Pinot Noir have become increasingly important in the region and now account for three-quarters of the total production.

THE VINEYARDS

St-Pourçain is set by the river, and holds a lively country market each Saturday in the church square. The museum of wine is open from March until December, a wine festival is held each August, and a wine fair on St Vincent's day at the end of January.

The countryside is a pleasure to explore, with quiet lanes threading through a succession of slight hills and shallow valleys, vineyards mingling with fields of grain and meadows dotted with creamy white Charolais cattle. Here and there, small châteaux can be seen in villages and hidden behind trees along the way.

A round trip of the southern part of the wine region can be made by follow-ing the road from St-Pourçain to the village of Saulcet, where there is a twelfth-century church. At Bransat, a little further west, there is an old stone bridge over the Gadenet. The route continues south-west to Chantelle, where one can see the remains of the fifteenth-century château of the Dukes of Bourbon, together with old timber-framed houses and a twelfth-century Romanesque church. A fine view of the village can be seen from the gorges of the little River Bouble nearby.

From here you can make a short detour south to the delightful walled village of Charroux, set on a hill overlooking the valley of the Sioule. During the Middle Ages it was one of the 19 manors of the Barony of Bourbon, and its ramparts and fortified gateways provide a hint of its former importance. Today it is a sleepy and secretive place, with many old houses along its narrow cobbled streets together with a wash-house, ancient wells and castle ruins. From Chantelle the wine route continues back to St-Pourçain via the villages of Fourilles and Chareil, where there is an attractive château.

The northern section of the wine-growing region can be explored by follow-ing the road from Saulcet to Verneuil-en-Bourbonnais, a very pretty medieval village with a gateway and walls remaining from a feudal castle. There are many old timber-framed houses and a twelfth-century Romanesque church. On the outskirts of the village a very attractive old *pigeonnier* stands in a field.

From Verneuil the route continues northwards to Meilland, the château of Aix and a twelfth-century church, and on to Bresnay and Besson, where another twelfth-century church has been designated as a national monument.

There are also three châteaux in the vicinity of the village: the fourteenth-century Vieux-Bost, hidden behind trees a short distance to the west; the fifteenth-century Château de Ristz, on the north-western edge of the village; and the very attractive Château de Fourchaud, south of the village on the D 292. The last has an impressive rectangular keep dating from the fourteenth century and is considered to be the finest example of a fortified house in the Bourbonnais.

PUY-DE-DÔME
Côtes d'Auvergne

THE PRESENCE OF vineyards in the Auvergne were mentioned by Sidonious Appollinaris, Bishop of Clermont in the fifth century, who likened them to those of Sicily. Records show that as early as the twelfth century the wines of Clermont were being transported by boat along the Allier and that they were being sold in the markets of Paris and consumed by the French nobility during the centuries which followed.

In the seventeenth century the wines of the Auvergne were considered to be among the best in the land, with the *crus* of Chanturgue, Nérat, La Barre, Pompignac and Bourassol being singled out for special praise. At this time the dominant grape variety of the region was Burgundy's Pinot Noir, but in the eighteenth century these vines were replaced by Gamay, a variety which gave a greater yield and was better suited to the terrain.

In those days it was known as the wine of the *bougnats*, or coal merchants, as it was transported on roughly-built barges which were also loaded with coal, their departure timed to reach Paris before the end of the autumn flood. On arrival, both the wine and the coal were sold, together with the timber from the barge, which was broken up, and the bargee would then walk back to the Auvergne. This routine would be repeated each year until he had enough money to marry and settle down in Paris as a trader, selling the wares of his fellow *bougnats* still in the Auvergne.

The phylloxera blight reached the Auvergne considerably later than most other regions of France, providing an initial advantage, but when it did its effect was devastating. Before it arrived in the late nineteenth century, the Auvergne vineyards had increased in the course of the century from about 18,000 to 60,000 hectares.

The destruction of phylloxera was followed by a plague-like attack of mildew in 1910. The vineyards' demise was accelerated during the next decade by the effects of the First World War and the gradual withdrawal of the labour force from agriculture as manufacturing industries like Michelin became established in Clermont-Ferrand. By 1920 the vineyards had shrunk to less than 15,000 hectares.

In 1936 the few remaining *vignerons* began to re-develop the vineyards on the most favoured slopes, and the renewal of the Vins d'Auvergne was under way. Now the plantations of vines are widely spaced between crops of maize, wheat and pasture land and it is possible to drive along the N 9 from Riom to

ABOVE: AN OLD WINE CELLAR IN THE VILLAGE OF BOUDES.
OPPOSITE TOP: AN OLD HOUSE IN THE VILLAGE OF
VERNEUIL-EN-BOURBONNAIS.
OPPOSITE BELOW: AN ANCIENT COTTAGE NEAR THE
AUVERGNE WINE VILLAGE OF BOUDES.

St-Germain-Lembron, through the heart of the wine-growing region, seeing only the occasional small plot of vines.

THE WINES

There are more than 2,000 hectares in total, with the most important vineyards grouped in three main areas: around the town of Riom, to the south of Clermont-Ferrand, and in the countryside to the west of St-Germain-Lembron. Just 500 hectares of these vines are delimited for the VDQS appellation of Côtes d'Auvergne which was granted in 1977, and elevation to AOC status is anticipated in the near future.

Gamay has remained the dominant grape variety, with about 95 per cent, but plantings of Pinot Noir, Chardonnay and Sauvignon Blanc are regularly increasing. The wines are predominantly red, with about 40 per cent made as rosé or *vin gris*.

There are still five defined *crus*: Madargues, around the town of St-Bonnet-près-Riom; Châteaugay, near the village of that name about 10 kilometres to the south; Chanturgues, on the outskirts of Clermont-Ferrand; Corent, on the slopes around the hill village of that name; and around Boudes, a medieval village to the west of St-Germain-Lembron.

The *cave co-opérative* at Veyre-Monton is responsible for about 45 per cent of the total production, and the Côtes d'Auvergne organization lists 23 individual producers who account for most of the rest.

THE VINEYARDS

M. Bernard Boulin-Constant is one of just three producers in the area making the wine of Madargues. He has about 8 hectares of vines, three of which are Pinot Noir, on the slopes around the village of St-Bonnet-près-Riom, together with a newly-planted plot on the northern outskirts of Riom itself. His most favoured slopes are a few kilometres from the village, where the distant Monts d'Auvergne create an impressive backdrop. There is a small plantation here of vines which were planted during the century's first decade, from which he makes a wine with the label 'Cuvée des Grandes Heures'.

The medieval hill village of Châteaugay lies about 10 kilometres south-west of Riom, overlooking the plain of Limagne. The wines made here had a considerable reputation during the Middle Ages and were, records attest, greatly appreciated by both Charles VI and Henry IV.

There are a number of *vignerons* making the *cru* of Châteaugay, of whom Pierre Lapouge and Michel and Raymond Rougeyron are the most important producers. The château, which dominates the small village, was built in the fourteenth century by Pierre de Giac, who was a member of the court of Charles VII. From the castle keep there is a splendid view of the plain of Limagne, the mountains of Forez and Livradois and the range of volcanic peaks which form the Chaîne des Puys.

Chanturgue is the smallest of the five *crus*, being produced from vines grown on the volcanic soil of the northern slopes of the 1,700 foot Puy de Chanturgue, now part of the suburbs of Clermont-Ferrand. Pierre Lapouge makes three-quarters of the average annual total of 200 hectolitres.

The village of Corent is set on a hill just east of Veyre-Monton. Terraces of vines occupy the steep slopes all around the village, which is an attractive cluster of old stone cottages and farms linked by a single narrow street. The *cru* of Corent is known especially for its rosé, and there are half a dozen or so producers in and around the village offering wines to taste and buy.

On the right bank of the Allier, a little to the north-east of Corent, is the Château de Busseol. Built by the counts of the Auvergne in 1170, it is one of the oldest castles in the region.

A short distance south-west of Le Crest is St-Saturnin, sheltering in the valley of the River Monne with a number of fine old houses and small manors. The village was formerly the residence of the barons of La Tour d'Auvergne, ancestors of the Medicis. On the edge of the village there is an impressive fourteenth-century feudal castle with triple walls, machicolations, crenellated towers and ramparts. It is considered by historians to be an outstanding example of medieval military architecture.

Nearby is the curious fortified village of La Sauvetat. Almost completely encircled by ramparts and threaded by a maze of narrow lanes, the village is now partially derelict.

The countryside in this area is particularly appealing, with narrow country lanes winding through the rounded hills to small wine villages like Parent and Buron. Nearby is the medieval village of Montpeyroux, entered by a fortified gateway. At the eastern end of the village a thirteenth-century castle looks out over the valley of the Allier. For those seeking a quiet, comfortable hotel with excellent cuisine, only a stone's throw from the N 9, the atmospheric Auberge de Tralume is ideal.

The little village of St-Floret lies only a dozen kilometres or so to the south-west of Montpeyroux in the peaceful valley of the Couze de Pavin. The village dates from the thirteenth century, when land here was given to an aide of the Dauphin of the Auvergne. He took the name of St-Floret and built a castle on the site. On a hill opposite the village is a fourteenth-century chapel, containing medieval wall paintings, and a churchyard with tombs carved into the rock.

About 20 kilometres to the east of St-Floret, on the far side of the Allier valley, the ancient village of Usson is built on a rock which juts out abruptly from the plain. At the summit is a chapel with a monumental statue of the Virgin which was erected in the nineteenth century. Nearby are the remains of a feudal castle which, for 19 years, was the prison of Henry IV's wife, Marguerite de Valois, punished for an infidelity with a member of her husband's court.

The village of Boudes is set in the valley of the same name a short distance to the west of St Germain-Lembron. The old centre of the village, which dates from the eleventh century, has retained a strong medieval atmosphere, with its narrow streets and alleys, a small square and an ancient church surrounded by old stone houses containing wine cellars.

One of these cellars contains the winery of André Charmensat, a leading producer of the *cru* of Boudes. He has about 8 hectares of vines, a quarter of which are young Pinot Noir, while some of his Gamay vines are more than 80 years old.

There are seven producers based in Boudes, farming a total of about 40 hectares of vines planted on the steep hillsides surrounding the village. Claude and Annie Sauvat have a vineyard of similar size to that of André Charmensat, mainly of Gamay but with half a hectare of Pinot Noir and a more recently planted hectare of Chardonnay.

A few kilometres to the north of Boudes is the Château de Villeneuve, set on a ridge overlooking a peaceful valley. Built in the fourteenth century with a round

ABOVE TOP: VINEYARDS NEAR ST POURCAIN-SUR-SIOULE.
ABOVE: MADARGUES VINEYARDS NEAR THE VILLAGE OF ST BONNET-PRES-RIOM.
OPPOSITE: A WATERFALL NEAR THE VILLAGE OF BESSE-EN-CHANDESSE.

tower in each corner, it contains a number of fifteenth-century frescoes, together with furniture and paintings of the period. To the south of Boudes, the Vallée des Saintes extends deep into the hills, providing a blissfully peaceful retreat for walkers and picnickers.

There is one small outpost of the Côtes d'Auvergne near Billom, a town some 20 kilometres south-east of Clermont-Ferrand. Many of the small vineyards planted on the hillsides around the town are primarily for family consumption, but I found one commercial producer, Les Caves de l'Abbaye, in Chauriat.

The community originally developed around a tenth-century priory. By the nineteenth century the village was surrounded by vineyards and had a thriving population of over 2,000. Many of the houses in the old quarter have wine cellars below. Les Caves de l'Abbaye are, appropriately enough, installed in an old church and, along with Côtes d'Auvergne, the speciality of Maison Dhôme has for several generations been the production of sparkling wine made by the *méthode champenoise*.

A short distance to the south-east is the pretty hill village of Montmorin and, a little further to the east, the remains of the Château de Mauzun, a powerful fortress built on an outcrop of rock by the bishops of Clermont. From there there are sweeping views of the countryside, west to the Volcans and the Monts Dore and east to the Monts du Forez.

THE CUISINE

While the *charcuterie* of the Auvergne is superb, it is the wonderful cheeses for which this corner of France is especially renowned. The rich, creamy-yellow St-Nectaire with its orange rind is one of the great classic cheeses, said to be the favourite of Louis XI; and many consider the firm, strongly-flavoured cheeses of Cantal, and especially Salers, to be superior even to Cheddar! Other great cheeses of the region include Fourme d'Ambert, a tangy, pressed blue-veined cheese made from cow's milk, Chevrotin de Bourbonnais, a conical goat's-milk cheese from Allier, and Gaperon, a soft, creamy conical cheese made from cow's buttermilk and flavoured with garlic and pepper.

Cheese also features in the dish called *aligot*, a rich combination of Cantal cheese curd and creamed potato. A similarly comforting dish is *pounti*, made by baking a mixture of chopped pork, ham, bacon, eggs, cream and a variety of green vegetables, while *potée auvergnat* is a soup-like stew of meat and vegetables. The green lentils of Le Puy are much more than a vegetarian's alternative – small and round, like minute peas – and when simmered in stock until tender, glazed with garlicky butter and sprinkled with parsley, they make a wonderful addition to any meal.

AQUITAINE

THE REGION OF Aquitaine occupies the south-west corner of France and encompasses five *départements*, Gironde, Dordogne, Lot-et-Garonne, Landes and Pyrénées-Atlantiques. The land-scape varies enormously from the vast pine forest of the Landes to the Pyrenean massif, from the endless, tide-swept beaches of the Atlantic coast to the fertile river valleys of the Dordogne and Garonne.

GIRONDE
THE WINES

THE APPELLATIONS D'ORIGINE Contrôlées to which the Gironde is entitled are: Bordeaux – Bordeaux Superieure – Bordeaux Clairet – Bordeaux Rose – Bordeaux Sec – Médoc – Haut-Médoc – Margaux – Moulis – Listrac-Médoc – St-Julien – Pauillac – St-Estephe – Graves – Graves Superieres – Pessac-Léognan – Cérons – Sauternes – Barsac – Entre-Deux-Mers – Entre-Deux-Mers Haut-Bernage – Bordeaux Haut-Benauge – Premier Côtes de Bordeaux – Cadillac – Graves de Vayres – Côtes de Bordeaux St-Macaire – Ste-Foy Bordeaux – Loupiac – Ste-Croix-du-Mont – Côtes de Castillon – Bordeaux Côtes de Francs – Côtes de Bourg – Blaye – Côtes de Blaye – Premières Côtes de Blaye – St-Emilion – St Emilion Grand Cru – Lussac-St-Emilion – Montagne-St-Emilion – Parscac-St-Emilion – Puisseguin-St-Emilion – St-Georges-St-Emilion – Pomerol – Lalande de Pomerol – Néac – Fronsac – Canon-Fronsac – Côtes Canon-Fronsac.

The great wines for which this region is renowned are largely red, but it also produces rosés and very fine white wines. The main grape types use for the red

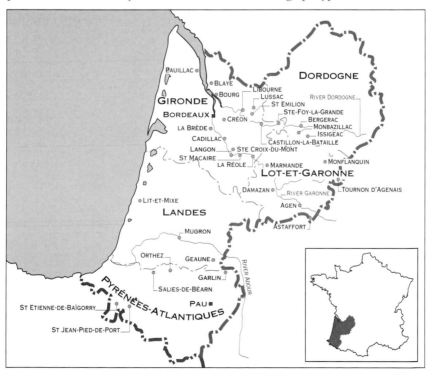

129

ABOVE TOP: VINEYARDS OF THE COTES DE BLAYE NEAR THE VILLAGE OF CARS.
ABOVE: THE CHATEAU OF MONBAZILLAC NEAR BERGERAC.
OPPOSITE: THE CHATEAU OF THEOBON AND THE VINEYARDS OF THE CÔTES DE DURAS.

and rosé wines are Cabernet Sauvignon, Cabernet Franc, Merlot, Petit Verdot and Cot (Malbec), while Sauvignon Blanc, Semillon and Muscadelle are used for whites. Clairette is a light red wine which is deeper in colour and more full-bodied than a rosé.

THE VINEYARDS

The vineyards of the Gironde can be divided into three broad sections: the Northern Bordelais, which covers those planted on the right bank of the Dordogne and the Gironde, reaching from the Côtes de Blaye in the west to the Côtes de Castillon in the east; the Southern Bordelais, which includes the Graves region, Sauternes and Entre-Deux-Mers; and the Médoc, where the vineyards are planted on the left bank of the Gironde estuary to the west of Bordeaux.

The Northern Bordelais

Undoubtedly some of the finest wines of this region are to be found in the small area immediately around Libourne, St-Emilion and the surrounding villages of Puisseguin, Montagne, Lussac, St-Georges and Parsac, all of which are hyphenated with the name St-Emilion; as well as Fronsac, Canon-Fronsac, Pomerol and Lalande-de-Pomerol.

The route given here is not a signposted Route des Vins, and not a circuit as such, but it takes you through the most important villages and vineyards and can easily be extended to the regions of Graves and Entre-Deux-Mers. If you are travelling from the north along the A 10 autoroute (l'Aquitaine), the best place to start the tour is at Blaye (off the motorway at exit 28, along the D 254 and then the N 137). The town is situated beside the broad estuary of the Gironde, north of Bordeaux. It is the centre of the Côtes de Blaye, a region not known for any very great wines but one that produces a large volume of honest red wine as well as some white and rosé.

Blaye is an interesting fortified town, surrounded by moats with an imposing citadel, a fortification built by the famous seventeenth-century military engineer, Sébastien de Vauban; within its walls is a large open park from where there are sweeping views over the river to the island fort of l'Île Pâté (also built by Vauban), and towards the distant south bank and the vineyards of the Médoc. The Hôtel de la Citadelle, which is situated within the ramparts, provides ideal accommodation and there is a Pavillon du Vin in the centre of the town where wines can be sampled and bought.

From Blaye there is a very enjoyable scenic drive through the vineyards with fine views over the Gironde by following the N 137 from Blaye to the village of Cars and then turning right on to the D 135 to St-Ciers-de-Canesse and right again for Thau, where a narrow road, the D 669, runs close beside the river bank. Here the vineyards sweep right down to the water's edge. Continue on this road towards Bourg, where the vineyards of the Côtes de Bourg begin. Just outside the town is the Château de Tayac, once the home of the Black Prince; it stands among the vineyards overlooking the river.

Bourg is built on the banks of the Dordogne. Its Château de la Citadelle, first built in the thirteenth century and rebuilt in the eighteenth, was once the summer residence of the archbishops of Bordeaux; you can visit the building and wander through its magnificent park planted with magnolias and pistachio trees. The terrace beside the old church commands fine views over the river.

The small village of Lansac is a few kilometres north-east of Bourg; during the Middle Ages, the eleventh-century monastery of La Croix-Davide here was a stopping-place for pilgrims travelling to Santiago de Compostela. A little further to the east, near the village of Prignac, are the grottoes of Pair-non-Pair, while just outside the village there is the *cave co-opérative* of Tauriac, where you can taste and buy the local wines.

The route continues through St-André-de-Cubzac and then along the D 670 towards Libourne. The vineyards of Fronsac are cultivated on the hillsides to the north of the village and you can follow a narrow signposted wine route through the vineyards and villages such as St Aignan and Saillans. Just to the west of Fronsac is the magnificent thirteenth-century Château de la Rivière, set high on the hillside above vast areas of vines; you can visit the château and sample its wines in *caves* carved into the rock.

Libourne, a thirteenth-century *bastide* and once a busy river port, is a bustling town with old quarters and quaysides. This is the trading centre for the wines of Fronsac, St-Emilion and Pomerol. The vineyards of Pomerol, which occupy a small area just to the east of Libourne, produce some of the great French wines; you can see the town's tall church spire rising high above the vineyards for miles around.

Among the many important wine châteaux in this area, that of Petrus is one of the most highly acclaimed, making a superb wine from the Merlot variety. It is a relatively modest and low-key building, quite unlike the magnificent, ostentatious examples found in the Médoc. Just across the river from Libourne are the vineyards of Graves de Vayres, and there are two châteaux in this region which are worth visiting too: Château des Vayres, with a peaceful riverside park, and Château le Grand Puch, surrounded by ancient farm buildings and vineyards. A small detour leads to St-Pardon – a hamlet beside the Dordogne – where people gather to watch the periodic tidal bores which sweep up the river with waves which are sometimes large enough to attract surfers.

The Route des Vins now leads up to St-Emilion, an ancient wine village where the Roman poet Ausonius was supposed to have lived. Its narrow, winding cobbled streets are lined with lovely pale medieval houses built of the local limestone, with rust-coloured slate roofs. There are ruins of Dominican and Franciscan convents, and the fourteenth-century cloisters of the collegiate church, which are superbly proportioned. St-Emilion has a wine museum and many ancient tasting cellars, as well as shops and restaurants. You could stay in the Hostellerie de Plaisance, a splendid hotel sited on a terrace overlooking the rooftops of the village.

From here numerous quiet roads lead through the vineyards to small villages such as Montagne, which has a handsome Romanesque church, Lussac, Puisseguin, where there is a Maison du Vin, and Parsac, all of which have their own appellations. There are three châteaux you can visit on the way. The first, Château des Tours, is near Montagne; it dates from the fourteenth century, has a Renaissance façade and is set in an elegant park surrounded by vast areas of vineyards. The next is near the village of St-Georges. Lastly, just to the north-east of Puisseguin, high up on a wooded hillside, is the fourteenth-century feudal château of Monbadon, looking down over the vineyards that carpet the fertile valley below.

A little further to the east are the Côtes de Francs, around the villages of Tayac, Francs and St-Cibard. From here the route leads south through the vineyards to the villages of St-Genès-de-Castillon and Belvès to Castillon-la-Bataille,

ABOVE: HARVESTING THE GRAPES AT CHATEAU LASCOMBES IN THE MEDOC.
OPPOSITE TOP: THE COURTYARD OF CHATEAU CARBONNIEUX
IN THE GRAVES REGION.
OPPOSITE BELOW: THE VILLAGE OF POUDENAS NEAR
MEZIN IN THE AGENAIS.

an historic town which is the centre of the Côtes de Castillon and marks the eastern limit of the vineyards of the northern Libournais. The vines continue, however, almost without a break to the beginning of the Côtes de Bergerac.

To the south are the vineyards of the Guyenne and St-Foy, both with the appellation of Bordeaux. Sauveterre-de-Guyenne is an attractive *bastide* built in the late thirteenth century with fortified gateways and a large central square surrounded by arcades. On the outskirts of the town is a *cave co-opérative* where you can taste and buy the local wines.

The Southern Bordelais

The name Graves means gravel – and this is what the vines grow on, over a bed of clay. In fact, this type of soil is characteristic of most of the region, but it is only the wines of Graves that take their appellation directly from the earth in which they thrive. In many ways Graves is an extension of the Médoc, but whereas the Médoc is influenced by the geological formations of the broad Gironde estuary, the vineyards of Graves are cultivated on the terraces of the River Garonne.

Red, rosé and white wines are produced in the Graves region, using blends of the same varieties permitted for all the Bordeaux appellations. As well as dry white wines, some of France's best sweet dessert wines – Sauternes and Barsac – are made in this region. The unique feature of these wines is that they are made from Semillon, Sauvignon and Muscadelle grapes which have developed *pourriture noble*, or 'noble rot'. This is a fungus called *Botrytis cinerea* which grows on the grapes, encouraged by the micro-climate peculiar to the region – high daytime summer temperatures combined with damp, misty mornings and evenings. The combination of *Botrytis* and over-ripe grapes increases their sugar content, while the volume of juice decreases and becomes very concentrated. When the juice is fermented it produces a sweet wine which attains a level of alcohol of between 14 and 15 per cent. Because all the grapes do not reach the optimum degree of over-ripeness at the same time, the harvesting has to be carried out over a period of many weeks, as the grapes reach this critical stage – thus the same vine may be gleaned many times, virtually a bunch at a time, which makes the best of these wines very expensive.

The ring-road around Bordeaux makes a good starting-point for this Route des Vins (which is partly signposted). Bordeaux is a sprawling city which, over the years, has encroached on some of the traditional vineyard areas; indeed, many of them are now within its outer suburbs, including one of the most prestigious, Château Haut-Brion. It is in Pessac, which can be reached by leaving the ring-road at exit 14 and driving for a short distance towards the city centre. Samuel Pepys recorded the wonderful qualities of this superb French wine 'Ho Bryan' in his diary. In 1855, when the official classifications were established, Haut-Brion was the only wine outside the Médoc to be accorded a Premier Grand Cru Classé.

Close by, and originally part of the same estate, is the Château la Mission Haut-Brion, where the dates of the best vintages of the last century are inscribed in gold on the roof of the adjoining chapel. Also in the vicinity are Château Latour Haut-Brion and Château Laville Haut-Brion. Drive a few kilometres to the south of Bordeaux, on the D 111, to the village of Cadaujac, the site of Château Bouscaut and Château Carbonnieux. The latter, known for its white wine, was owned by the Benedictine monks of the abbey of Ste-Croix-du-Mont who, it is claimed, exported their wine to Turkey as 'mineral water of Carbonnieux' in order to satisfy that country's religious laws and its sultan, who was very fond of their product.

A number of important vineyards and châteaux are found close to the town of Léognan. A sign on the D 111 indicates the Route des Graves, which guides you around the region. Of particular note are Château Haut-Bailly and Château La-tour Martillac. In this part of the Graves the vines are not cultivated intensively and there are large areas of woods, pine forests and meadows. A short drive from Léognan will bring you to the village of La Brède, where you can visit Château de la Brède, the family home of the eighteenth-century political satirist Montesquieu; it is just outside the village in a wooded setting and is open only at weekends and holidays. The small village of St-Selve, a few kilometres away, holds a lively, colourful wine fair in the streets and the church square during the first weekend of June.

Continue south on the N 113 for a short distance to the Sauternais, where the sweet dessert wine is produced. This wine has been famous since the twelfth century, and Richard Lionheart is said to have had a weakness for it. The Sauternais has its own wine circuit which is clearly signposted from the N 113 just south of Barsac or from the village of Preignac, a little further south. These are two of the five communes of the region, the others being Fargues, Sauternes and Bommes. The route winds its way through a series of quiet country lanes to each of these small villages in turn. The countryside here is captivating with its meadows and farmland, its vineyards and its gently rolling hills swathed in woods and pine forests. Preignac and Barsac are both busy villages situated beside the main road, and close to Preignac is the elegant Château de Malle, set in beautiful formal gardens, where visitors are welcome.

Sauternes is a sleepy little village nestling in a hollow, surrounded by vine-clad hills. At the Maison du Vin in the square you can use the information service as well as taste and buy wines. With the rather extraordinary exception of the famous Château d'Yquem, the many châteaux in this region are clearly signposted along the way. Although this is to deter visitors and overcrowding, you will be welcome if you do take the trouble to find it. This is not too difficult, since it occupies a prominent position on a hilltop near Sauternes. The château is built on the site of a fortress and dates back to the twelfth century, although it was heavily restored in both the sixteenth and eighteenth centuries. Thomas Jefferson visited it in 1787, and today it is the venue for the Bordeaux May Music Festival.

The estate has over 160 hectares of vines, of which 120 are entitled to the appellation. Every year 2 or 3 hectares are uprooted and replanted, and it is then a further six years before they are productive. The equipment used in the château's wine cellars is surprisingly modest – just three presses, a crusher and a wooden émietteur. This would be enough to handle only about 4 hectares of normal vines, but because of the unique way in which Sauternes is made, the cellar needs only to deal with one day's selective harvesting at a time.

Although not on the Route des Vins circuit, the twelfth-century Château de Roquetaillade is worth a short detour; it is set on a hill in a park and looks just the way a medieval castle should, with battlements and towers.

The limit of the Graves region is just south of Langon, a busy market town situated beside the Garonne. Here there is a Maison du Vin de Graves (there is also one at Podensac) and the well-known hotel-restaurant of Claude Darroze, making it an ideal base from which to explore the area. You can cross the river to the ancient walled village of St-Macaire, known for its sweet white dessert wines.

Head back northwards on the D 10, which stays quite close to the river and passes through a succession of wine villages.

A kilometre or so to the east, high up on the hill that borders the Garonne, are Verdelais and Ste-Croix-du-Mont. At Verdelais, at the end of a shady promenade, is the church where Henri de Toulouse-Lautrec is buried. Ste-Croix-du-Mont has the appellation Grand Vin Liquoreux de Bordeaux. Right on the edge of this village, on the hill beside the church, is a terrace with wonderful views over the Garonne valley and the Sauternais; there is a Maison du Vin in the château nearby. This is particularly appealing countryside, with tiny lanes and steep, rounded hills.

A little further north, the small village of Loupiac also has its own appellation for dessert wines, as does its neighbour Cadillac and the village of Cérons, across the river. Hereabouts during the fishing season you often see signs advertising *alose* for sale. Cadillac is a large fortified village with its fourteenth-century ramparts still intact. The somewhat severe Château des Ducs d'Eperon sits high above the village, and houses the Maison du Vin. Every Saturday, the village centre is closed to traffic and a lively market selling local produce is held. A few kilometres to the north-east of Cadillac is the region of Haut-Benauge, named after the château which is set impressively on a hill. Some of the best Entre-Deux-Mers is produced in the countryside around the villages of St-Pierre-de-Bat, Escoussans and Soulignac.

From here, drive to Rions, a few kilometres to the north. Surrounded by medieval ramparts, it has a fortified gate, an old church and narrow streets lined with crumbling stone houses. Just beyond the town is the ruined Château de Langorian; here a small road winds up past the château to the hamlet of Haut-Langoiran, from where there are wonderful views down over the vine-clad hill to the River Garonne and the countryside of Graves. The village of Langorian is set right beside the wide, rusty Garonne – it has a riverside promenade and is a stopping-place for the barges which ply up and down to Bordeaux.

Now you can either cross back over the river and return towards Bordeaux along the N 113, or you could extend your tour to include some of the Premières Côtes de Bordeaux and Entre-Deux-Mers vineyards. This region, which lies between the Garonne and Dordogne rivers, has a signposted circuit through the countryside. Of particular interest is the majestic ruined Romanesque abbey of La Sauve Majeure, an important stop for medieval pilgrims following the Way of St James to Santiago de Compostela. Nearby Créon, situated in a hilly region known as Petite Suisse, has an arcaded square dating from the thirteenth century. It is the capital of Entre-Deux-Mers and holds an agricultural market on Wednesdays.

The Médoc

The Médoc is situated on a peninsula about 100 kilometres long, extending from just north of the city of Bordeaux to the Pointe de Grave, immediately opposite the seaside resort of Royan. It is bordered by the wide estuary of the Gironde to the east and by the vast pine forest of the Landes to the west. The vineyards run for almost the entire length of the peninsula on a low-lying, gravelly hill range, in a band about 10 to 15 kilometres wide. It is divided into two areas: the Médoc to the north, as far down as St-Seurin-de-Cadourne, where the lesser wines are produced, and the Haut-Médoc, stretching from St-Seurin to Blanquefort. It is in the Haut-Médoc that the finest wines and the most famous names are to be found – St-Estèphe, Pauillac, St-Julien, Margaux and Cantenac.

The wines produced here are predominantly red. The finest are made mainly from the Cabernet Sauvignon and Merlot varieties but the Cabernet Franc, Petit Verdot and Malbec are also grown. The classification method of the Médoc wines originated in 1855, when the Cru Classé was instigated by Napoleon III for the Exposition Universelle de Paris; the system is essentially the same today. The classification ranges from Premier Grand Cru Classé through Cru Bourgeois, Cru Artisan and Cru Paysan to the basic Appellation Contrôlée Médoc.

The way the vines are grown and the wine produced is strictly controlled, even to the method of pruning, and the best wines must come from vines that are at least ten years old. Many vines remain productive for up to eighty years, by which time they will have driven their roots down through the meagre soil to a depth of 3 metres or more. Although the quality of the wine improves as the vine ages, fewer grapes are produced, a factor which contributes to the dramatic difference in cost between a fine wine and a good one. As in all the best wine-producing regions, both the climate and the soil are such that the vine has to struggle to survive; ironically, it is usually these very conditions which create the best and most subtle wines.

THE VINEYARDS

The Route des Vins in the Médoc is a single road which runs through the narrow-ish region, with smaller roads leading off to individual châteaux – indeed it is really much more a tour of the châteaux. In wine country a château can mean almost anything from a magnificent building to a modest farmhouse or even a bungalow; here they tend very much towards the magnificent.

There is an element of formality to observe when visiting some of these châteaux: many prefer visitors to make appointments. These can be made through the various Maisons du Vin in the region. There is one in Bordeaux, near the Grand Théâtre, and others in Pauillac, St-Estèphe and Margaux; they provide a wealth of other useful travel information.

The signs indicating Circuit du Médoc refer to three general tourist circuits which will take you to the beaches, lagoons and forests as well as to the vineyards; if you have the time and the inclination this can be an ideal way of exploring the region. But the route suggested here concentrates on the villages, vineyards and châteaux associated with wine.

The tour starts at Bordeaux. Leave the ring road around the city at exit 7 and head for Blanquefort on a road which runs through the heart of the vineyards. Near here is Taillan, the first of the many impressive châteaux encountered the Médoc. It dates from the early eighteenth century, is set in stately grounds and has an ancient double-vaulted *cave*. As well as making wine, the proprietor raises thoroughbred horses. The Château de la Dame Blanche where, according to legend, the ghost of a beautiful Moorish princess, Blanca, can be seen riding her winged horse around the castle, is here too: both the château and the town of Blanquefort are named after her.

From this point the route continues along the D 2 to Cantenac. The prestigious wine châteaux are concentrated around this very flat region where there is only a slight suggestion of rise and fall in the landscape: the highest hills you can see are on the other side of the wide, muddy Gironde in the Côtes de Blaye. Woods and meadows dominate the landscape at this point. You can visit Château Prieuré-Lichine, the domain of the famous wine writer Alexis Lichine; he has a collection of fire-backs from all over the world decorating the courtyard.

Just beyond Cantenac is Issan. There are two châteaux in this tiny village: the sixteenth-century moated Château d'Issan in a peaceful wooded setting along a small lane to the east of the village, and the immaculate Château Palmer, set beside the main road. The next village is Margaux: its château, with its Empire-style façade framed by an avenue of plane trees, is one of the most famous in France – and deservedly so. Although the château is privately owned, its *chais* can be visited; the wine made here is renowned as one of the Premiers Crus of the Médoc.

The route continues northwards via Soussans, detours to Moulis, which has a twelfth-century Romanesque church, and Listrac, then back to the D 2 at Arcins, and Lamarque. Few of the villages are noteworthy, often consisting of a few rows of rather austere, single-storey terraced cottages – but they are invariably brightened up by a blaze of flowers. In contrast to the low elevation of the houses and some châteaux, the church steeples are remarkably high. The church in Lamarque, for instance, has two enormous towers; there is an imposing château-fort here too, built in the eleventh century to resist the Viking invasion. A short distance further along the route a sign indicates a small road to the east leading to Fort Médoc, in a quiet place close to the river. It was built by Vauban during the reign of Louis XIV as part of a three-pronged defence line (with l'Île Pâté and the Blaye citadel).

A few kilometres further on, you get to the vineyards of Château Beychevelle, overlooking the river. The name of this grand château is said to be derived from the command 'Baissez les Voiles' (lower the sails) – to salute the Duc d'Epernon, an admiral who lived here in the seventeenth century; the château's emblem is a ship with lowered sails. A small road beside the château goes down the riverbank, an ideal place to sit and watch the boats go by, or to watch the fishermen work their huge nets which they suspend from a gib at the end of a little pier. Many of the beautiful Médoc châteaux can be seen from the wine route. Often they are clearly signposted and you reach them along quiet lanes deep in the countryside; none is more than a few kilometres from the D 2.

You can't miss the village of St-Julien. It has a large notice somewhat immodestly commanding passers-by to salute its celebrated vineyards; the point is reinforced by a monolithic wine bottle beside the road. Just to the north are two châteaux which you should not miss: Pichon-Longueville, an elaborately elegant building, and, along a small road to the west, Château Latour, one of the Premiers Crus of the Médoc.

Next you reach Pauillac, situated beside the now very broad estuary. It is the largest centre on the Route des Vins and has the atmosphere of a seaside town (which it very nearly is), with its wide tree-lined promenade, a busy harbour and pavement cafés. In addition to Château Latour, two other Premier Crus lie within the commune of Pauillac: Château Lafite-Rothschild and Château Mouton-Rothschild. They are quite close together to the west of the D 2 north of Pauillac. The ostentatious Château Cos-d'Estournel, which is right beside the road, demands attention with its ornate, oriental-style turrets and façade. This domain is within the most northerly of the great Haut-Médoc communes, St-Estèphe.

The route continues beyond St-Estèphe, at times running alongside the Gironde, to St-Seurin-de-Cadourne and St-Yzans-de-Médoc, where Château Loudenne dominates the hills to the west of the road. The small village of St-Christoly-Médoc marks the northern limit of the route. Although there are some vineyards further north these are mainly for the production of the more anonymous, basic Médoc wines. From here you can return towards Bordeaux by taking the D 103 E 5 to Lesparre-Médoc and then the fast main road, the N 215, back through St Laurent-Médoc and Castelnau-de-Médoc.

DORDOGNE

THE WINES

THE WINES OF Bergerac, red, white and rosé, are sold under the following appellations: Bergerac (red, white and rosé); Côtes de Bergerac (red and white); Bergerac and Côtes de Saussagnac (white); Monbazillac (white); Montravel, Côtes de Montravel and Haut-Montravel (white); Pecharmant (red), and Rosette (white). The grape types used are principally the Cabernet Franc, Cabernet Sauvignon, Merlot, Cot (or Malbec), Semillon, Muscadelle, Chenin and Sauvignon Blanc.

Monbazillac is one of the best-known wines of the region. It is sweet and white, and can be drunk chilled as an aperitif, as an accompaniment to *foie gras* or as a dessert wine. As with the great sweet wines of neighbouring Sauternes and Barsac, Monbazillac is made from grapes affected by the *Botrytis* fungus.

THE VINEYARDS

The Bergerac Route des Vins is a complete, if meandering, circuit and is well signposted. It is also particularly well planned and easy to follow if you begin in the town of Bergerac which has a fascinating old quarter, with narrow cobbled streets, medieval houses and courtyards, and a Maison du Vin. Tobacco is an important product of the region too – indeed, you can follow a Route des Tabacs as well as the Route des Vins.

If you leave by the bridge near the old quarter and cross over to the south bank of the Dordogne, you will pick up the signposts, starting on the D 933, the main road to Marmande. Very soon the route turns left on a small country road, the D 14, towards Monbazillac. As you drive over the wide Dordogne plain you can see in the distance the large rounded hill where most of the southerly vineyards are situated. The Moulin de Malfourat, an old sail-less windmill, provides a superb viewpoint over the sloping vineyards, the Dordogne valley and the distant town of Bergerac.

There is not much of interest in Monbazillac itself, an unassuming cluster of grey stone houses around a small square. But stop at the adjacent château, an elegant and successful mixture of Renaissance and military architecture dating from the sixteenth century. It has *caves* you can visit, and a restaurant. Now you are in the heart of vineyard country. Leave the wine road for a short detour to the nearby fifteenth-century Château de Bridoire. Then continue through the small villages of Rouffignac-de-Sigoulès and Pomport on a small winding country road towards Sigoulès, which holds an annual wine fair in July. Next to it is the tiny village of Monbos with its miniature grey-stone, turreted château. Little more than a rough track leads to the village. This route includes the quietest and most scenic small roads wherever possible.

The countryside becomes flatter and more open now, and the vines alternate with meadows and woods. The small road continues to the hamlet of Thénac; you can taste the local wines at Château Thénac. A sequence of minute villages follows: La Bastide, Monestier and Gageac-et-Rouillac, where there is a fourteenth-century château. Saussignac, the next village, is rather larger, with an imposing château. Now you head back towards the River Dordogne to the busy

ABOVE TOP: VINEYARDS NEAR THE MEDOC WINE VILLAGE OF ST JULIEN.
ABOVE: THE GRAPE PICKERS' REFECTORY AT CHATEAU LASCOMBES
IN THE MEDOC.
OPPOSITE: A VIEW OVER THE ROOFTOPS OF ST EMILION.

market town of Ste-Foy-la-Grande, an ancient *bastide*. Here the route crosses the river to Port-Ste-Foy, where it turns left on to the D 32 E 2 towards Vélines in the region of Montravel. The village has a lovely Romanesque church and mellow, grey stone houses.

The route continues to Moncaret and Lamothe-Montravel, where there is the large *cave co-opérative* of Montravel. The small village of St-Michel-de-Montaigne is the next place of interest on the route; there is an old Romanesque church here and a château where you can buy the wines made in the surrounding vineyards. The circuit continues along a small scenic road through woods and meadows towards Montpeyroux, which also has a fine old church and a château, the Manoir de Mathecoulon. You are in the Côtes de Bergerac region now – the western limit of the Bergerac vineyards and close to the wine-producing area of St-Emilion and the Côtes de Francs. Next is the *bastide* town of Villefranche-de-Lonchat with an old church, a pretty square shaded by plane trees, and a *cave co-opérative*. The lake of Gurson, a peaceful spot where there is a restaurant under the trees, is nearby; it has camping, picnic and boating facilities, and is over-looked by the ruined Château de Gurson.

From here the Route des Vins continues back towards Ste-Foy-la-Grande through some small, unremarkable villages. After passing St-Méard-de-Gurçon on the main road (the D 708), it turns left on to a small, country road leading to the hamlet of Ponchapt. Towards the town of Le Fleix, as the road descends to the river, there are occasional views through the trees of the valley below. From here it returns to Bergerac along the D 32.

The regions of Pécharmant and Rosette lie to the north and east of Bergerac and, although not part of the signposted route, are well worth exploring. Take the main road, the N 21, towards Périgueux from the centre of Bergerac. After the village of Lembras you will find the D 21 to the right leading to the little village of Lamonzie-Montastruc, which boasts the Château de Bellegarde and the Manoir de Grateloup.

To the south-east of the riverside village of Mouleydier is Lanquais, where you can visit the very fine fifteenth-century château. There is another château in Bannes, and the medieval town of Issigeac is of interest too with a sixteenth-century church and a bishops' palace, le Château des Evêques, built a century later, as well as some picturesque old timber-framed houses.

If you want to extend you visit to Bergerac further you can follow the Circuit des Bastides, a shortish tour which takes you to many of the ancient *bastide* towns in the region, such as Beaumont, Villeréal, Eymet and, perhaps the region's greatest jewel, Montpazier, which is no great distance from the thriving vineyards of Monbazillac.

LANDES

THE WINES

THE REGION HAS relatively small areas of vineyards with just two appellations, VDQS Vin de Tursan and Vin de Pays des Terroirs Landais. The wines of Tursan were given VDQS status in 1958, and today the vineyards extend to about 400 hectares. The majority of production is by the co-operative at Geaune but there are also a handful of individual producers, including Michel Guérard – the master chef who began the wave of *nouvelle cuisine*.

White Tursan wines are made primarily from the region's special grape variety, the Barroque, with a small proportion of Sauvignon Blanc and Manseng.

Reds and rosés are produced from a blend of 90 per cent Cabernet Franc with Sauvignon together and Tannat.

Vin de Pays des Terroirs Landais is produced principally in the region known as La Chalosse, in Les Sables Fauves – the wild sands – to the east of Mont-de-Marsan. A small amount is produced along the coastal strip of the Landes forest near St-Julien-en-Born. The grapes used range from the Gascon variety, Colombard, to the Cabernets, Merlot, Sauvignon Blanc and the local varieties of Arriloba and Barroque.

Vins de Tursan

In the far north-eastern corner of the Landes, bordering on the Armagnac country, are the vineyards of Tursan, centred on the little town of Geaune, due west of Auch beyond the River Adour. They have existed for very many centuries and were part of the *domaine* of Eleanor of Aquitaine, the wife of Henry II of England. The wines were exported to England as early as the twelfth century, and later found markets in Holland and Germany.

THE VINEYARDS

The region of Tursan lies to the east of the main road, the N 134, and just to the south of Aire-sur-l'Adour, a lively market town set beside the broad brown River Adour. It has the impressive twelfth-century cathedral of Sainte Quitterie du Mas with a Roman crypt containing the remains of the patron saint of Gascony, and makes an ideal base from which to explore the region. The route through the countryside is clearly signposted as the Circuit du Tursan et de la Chalosse, and just after leaving Aire towards Pau you will see a large sign pointing to the route des Vins, on the D 2.

The vineyards are, by and large, quite small individual plots scattered through the countryside, some little larger than a modest suburban back garden; consequently, most of the wine is made in the *cave co-opérative* in Geaune. The rest of the countryside is planted with a variety of crops ranging from rape seed to maize, wheat and barley, and there is a considerable amount of grazing land, relieved by woodland and copses.

Travelling in an anti-clockwise direction from Aire-sur-l'Adour, the route winds through quiet lanes to the hamlets of Duhort-Bachen, where a few arcaded houses surround a pretty village green dotted with shady plane trees, and on to Renung, just a cluster of small houses and a church. Then it crosses a flat plain and the River Adour to Cazères-sur-l'Adour.

Here the route follows the main road, the N 124, for a short distance to Grenade-sur-l'Adour, a larger town that has an arena for *courses landaises*, the bloodless bull-fights peculiar to the Landes. The larger towns, including Aire-sur-l'Adour, tend to hold well-publicized bull-fights in the summer with professional matadors, but some of the small communities have makeshift arenas and often provide a more enjoyable and informal spectacle than the bigger centres. The Syndicat d'Initiative in Aire-sur-l'Adour has information on where and when these village events take place.

From here the route leads back into the depths of rural Tursan countryside to the genteel thermal resort of Eugénie-les-Bains, which is now more famous as the birthplace of *nouvelle cuisine* in the restaurant Les Près d'Eugénie than as a spa town. Michel Guérard's hotel-restaurant, in an elegant building set in a small park, has become a place of pilgrimage for gourmets. A large sign on the outskirts

ABOVE TOP: A SUMMER VINEYARD NEAR THE VILLAGE OF PREIGNAC IN THE SAUTERNES REGION.
ABOVE: A VINEYARD AND CHATEAU IN THE HAUT-BENAUGE REGION OF ENTRE-DEUX-MERS.
OPPOSITE: A HOUSE IN THE VILLAGE OF LABASTIDE-D'ARMAGNAC.

of the village proclaims it to be the '*Premier Village Minceur de France*' (France's leading village of slimness).

The next village, St-Loubouer, is one of the main centres of Tursan wine production, with a correspondingly high concentration of vineyards. From there the road climbs up on to higher terrain, where there are lovely views over the surrounding countryside and the snow-capped peaks of the Pyrenees are often visible in the distance. The views from Vielle-Tursan are staggering too, up on its hilltop terrace beside the church. The next villages are Sarraziet and Montsoué; the latter has a small *courses landaises* arena.

There is little to remark in most of the small villages through which the route passes; they are often nothing more than a cluster of houses and a small church. And many of the old farmhouses, despite their rather faded and derelict charm, are functional rather than picturesque. But the remoteness and peace of this countryside is very special.

Hagetmau is a largish town with a number of hotels and restaurants as well as the Roman crypt of Saint-Girons; a street festival is held here at the beginning of August. The next village on the Route des Vins, Samadet, has a museum with a collection of ancient regional pottery and a nearby shop sells reproductions of some of the pieces.

From here the route leads to Geaune, where you can taste and buy the region's wines at the *cave co-opérative*. The town has an arcaded square, a large Romanesque church and a small Maison du Vin; it hosts an annual agricultural fair at the end of July.

Terroirs Landais

The first of the three distinct areas of production of Vins de Pays des Terroirs Landais lies to the east of Mont-de-Marsan. This is the region known as Les Sables Fauves – the wild sands – and here the wines tend to reflect the grape varieties and characteristics of the Côtes de Gascogne.

I visited the prestigious Domaine d'Ognoas, near Arthez-d'Armagnac, renowned for its fine Armagnac and Floc de Gascogne – an aperitif made by fortifying white wine with *eau de vie*. An excellent Vin de Pays des Terroirs Landais is also made here from Colombard, as well as a small quantity of rosé from 80 per cent Cabernet Franc and Merlot.

A few kilometres to the north, the Domaine de Paguy near the village of Betbezer-d'Armagnac produces a red Vin de Pays from 100 per cent Cabernet Franc. The impressive old château is also a *ferme-auberge* listed with the Gîtes organization and also sells *confits* and *foie gras*.

Nearby is the village of Labastide-d'Armagnac, one of the prettiest of all the *bastides*. It has a particularly beautiful square, the Place Royale, bordered by ancient houses and stone arches, on which, it is claimed, the Place des Vosges in Paris was modelled (which, before the Revolution, was also called Place Royale). There is a fine fifteenth-century church overlooking the square and, in a street nearby, the picturesque Café du Peuple, which has now been turned into a private home.

At Parlebosque, a village to the north-west of Eauze, the Domaine de Laballe produces a white wine with a blend of Colombard and Ugni Blanc from 12 hectares of vines. Nearby, at the eighteenth-century Château of Lacaze, the Domaine du Comte produces another outstanding *blanc sec* Vin de Pays from a similar blend of grapes.

Coteaux de la Chalosse

The second area of the Terroirs Landais lies to the south-west of Mont-de-Marsan in a region known as La Chalosse between the Ardour valley and the Gave du Pau, on the edge of the Landes pine forest. It is a countryside of quiet charm, with gentle hills and shallow valleys where crops and meadows dominate and numerous small areas of vines are planted among them on the slopes.

The region is known for its gastronomy as much for its wines. Chalosse beef has an Appellation Contrôlée similar to that of Bresse chicken, and the *foie gras*, *confits* and *magrets* produced here are considered to be among the best in France. Every house and farm seems to have a muddy field with a pond in the centre, and the raucous cackle of geese and ducks echoes through the country lanes and villages.

The major part of the production of Coteaux de la Chalosse is from the *caves co-opératives* at Pouillon, Orthevielle and Mugron. The one at Mugron makes a basic red wine from Cabernet Franc, as well as a rosé from Tannat and a white wine from Barroque.

A superior red wine, called 'Cuvée du Vigneron', is made exclusively from Tannat with a longer period of maceration giving it the capability to be kept for some years. A 'Cuvée du Vigneron Blanc' is also made from a variety unique to the region called Arriloba, which is given a period of eight hours' maceration. This grape is also used to produce a Vin Blanc Moelleux.

There are just two independent wine-makers. I visisted the Domaine de Labaigt, where one of them, Dominique Lanot, farms about 6 hectares of vines near the village of Mouscardés, south-east of Pouillon. He makes a white wine from 100 per cent Barroque, a rosé from Cabernet Franc and a red from Cabernet Sauvignon. He told me that his Barroque vines were planted in 1920, and at the time of my visit was busy planting some Colombard in order to supplement his white wine production in the form of a blend. The other independent producer is Jean-Claude Romain at the Domain du Tastet near Pouillon.

A little to the south of Mouscardés, on the left bank of the Gave de Pau, is the town of Bellocq. At the *cave co-opérative* here they make a red Vin de Pays des Pyrénées-Atlantiques with a blend of Tannat and Cabernet. This departmental Vin de Pays is also made by the co-operative at Irouléguy in the foothills of the Pyrenees, but is only available *en vrac*.

Vin de Sable

To the north-west of the Ardour valley is the beginning of the great pine forest of the Landes, which reaches away westwards to the Atlantic and north almost to the vineyards of the Médoc on the left bank of the Gironde estuary. Vin de Pays des Terroirs Landais is also produced in this unlikely, sandy terrain and is called, appropriately enough, Vin de Sable. The main area of production is along the coastal strip between Messanges and St-Julien-en-Born. Many houses in this region have a small patch of vines nearby for '*consommation familiale*'; quite a few have front gardens planted with vines instead of a lawn and flower borders; but there are only a handful of *vignerons* making the wine on a commercial scale.

Mme Thévenin has a small vineyard of about 4 hectares, planted in the sand in the Quartier-Caliot, near the village of Messanges, where she produces a full-bodied red wine from a blend of Cabernet Sauvignon and Tannat. She supplies a number of restaurants in the region, including the atmospheric Auberge des Pins at Sabres, and also sells direct to the public, but only in cases of twelve bottles.

Mme Thévenin told me that she was one of only three 'official' producers of Vin de Sable. The second, the Domaine de Tutet, can be found about 4 kilometres south of the village of Lit-et-Mix on the D 652. Here Jean Biron makes red and rosé Vins de Sable from a small vineyard of Cabernet Franc and Cabernet Sauvignon, planted in the 1970s. When his roadside *caveau* is closed, M. Biron's wines can be bought in Le Tire de Bouchon, a small shop in the village. The third producer is the Domainé Point du Jour, on the outskirts of Lit-et-Mix, where M. Subsol's Vin de Sable can be bought in the village *charcuterie*.

A few kilometres to the south-east of St-Julien-en-Born is Lévignacq, with an attractive group of traditional Landais timber-framed houses and a fortified church built in the fourteenth century. From both Lit-et-Mix and St-Julien-en-Born there is access to the vast Atlantic beaches at Cap-de-l'Homy and Contis-Plage, and a little further to the north is the large resort of Mimizan-Plage.

LOT-ET-GARONNE
THE WINES

THE AOC APPELLATIONS to which Lot-et-Garonne is entitled are Côtes de Duras, Côtes du Marmandais and Buzet; there is also the VDQS appellation of Côtes du Brulhois and the Vins de Pays appellations of Agenais, Thézac-Perricard and Comté Tolosan.

Côtes de Duras

The vineyards of the Côtes de Duras are planted in the north-western corner of Lot-et-Garonne, sandwiched between those of Bergerac in the north, the Marmandais in the south and Entre-Deux-Mers and Bordeaux-St-Foy to the west. It is believed the vineyards of Duras were originally planted before the birth of Christ when vines were first brought by the Greeks to Marseilles. Records of their existence go back to the thirteenth century, when the inhabitants of the hamlet of St-Eylard paid tithes to the monks of the abbey of La Réole.

Today they cover about 2,000 hectares, three-quarters of which are used to produce white wines, both sweet and dry. The appellation was granted in 1937. The principal varieties for the whites are Sauvignon Blanc, Mauzac, Semillon and Muscadelle, while Cabernet Sauvignon and Franc, Merlot and Malbec are used for red and rosé wines. Some of the reds are made in the traditional way, needing to age for two years or so before drinking; others using carbonic maceration to produce a lighter, fruitier wine for drinking when young.

Set most attractively on a ridge above the valley of Dropt, the old town of Duras makes an ideal centre from which to explore the vineyards. An ancient *bastide*, it preserves a pretty château dating from the beginning of the fourteenth century and now houses a museum of local traditions, agriculture and life.

There are more than 40 individual producers together with the well-respected *cave co-opérative*, Berticot, which was established in 1965. The sign-posted Route des Vins leads through unspoilt countryside where meadows and fields of maize, wheat and sunflowers mingle with the vineyards planted between the villages of Loubès-Bernac in the north and Ste-Colombe in the west, Allemans in the south and Soumensac in the east.

Agenais

Vin de Pays de l'Agenais is an appellation given to wines produced over a wide area around Agen. It extends to the borders of Gascony in the south, to Quercy in the east, to Marmande in the west to Périgord in the north. In practice, however, the vineyards are to be found in three main areas: around the ancient *bastide* of Monflanquin, near Beaupuy and Cocumont in the Marmandais, and near the village of Mézin on the borders of Gascony and the Landes. Apart from a few small independent producers, the production is from four co-operatives based in these areas.

Monflanquin

The Caves des Sept Monts at Monflanquin, in the north of the region, was established in 1967 and, unlike the co-operatives in the Marmandais, produces only Vin de Pays. There are records of the vineyards in the Haut-Agenais dating back to the fourth century, and, like many French wine-growing regions, they reached their peak in the Middle Ages.

The onslaught of phylloxera, two world wars and the changing needs of agriculture almost brought wine-making to an end in this region. Now, however, it is enjoying a healthy revival, and today the co-operative vinifies and markets the wines produced from a total of about 220 hectares farmed in small plots by 200 *vignerons*. For most of the farmers the vineyard is only a small part of their agriculture.

The principal grape varieties used for the Haut-Agenais wines, which are limited to red and rosé, are Merlot, Cabernet Franc, Cabernet Sauvignon and Cot. The wine called 'Cuvée des Bastides' is produced from 80 per cent Merlot and 20 per cent Cot; another, called 'Vin des Sept Monts', is made from a blend of 50 per cent Merlot, 30 per cent Cabernet Franc and 20 per cent Cot.

The superior 'Prince de Monségur' is made from Cabernet Franc and Cabernet Sauvignon and aged in oak casks for up to eight months. A rosé is also made from a similar blend of these two varieties, using the *saignée* method in which the juice for the rosé wine is bled from the vat during the early stages of fermentation, before too much colour has been extracted from the grape skins.

The Caves des Sept Monts is not the only reason to visit Monflanquin, for it is a village of considerable charm. Set on a hill above the valley of the Lède, the village was built in the thirteenth century by Alphonse de Poitiers in the typical *bastide* form of that period. The square is surrounded by covered arcades, and in one corner a fortified Gothic church soars above the rooftops. Narrow streets lead up the hill to the square and church, and from a terrace nearby there are splendid views of the surrounding countryside.

A short drive to the north-east leads to a winding stretch of the Lède valley and to the village of Gavaudun, where the keep of a feudal castle dating from the twelfth century is set behind on an outcrop of rock.

About 10 kilometres to the north is the Château de Biron, a great mass of towers rising from a steep domed hill. It was the home of Charles de Gontaut, who was made a baron of Biron by Henry IV in 1598 but beheaded for treason just four years later. The castle roof was extensively damaged in 1972 by a violent hailstorm, but after a period of dereliction the building has been restored and can now be visited.

Monflanquin is one of a trio of *bastides*, and a short distance to the north of Biron is perhaps the most enchanting of them all, Monpazier. Its construction was begun in 1264 on the orders of Edward I, King of England and Duke of Aquitaine, with the aid of the then lord of Biron, Pierre de Gontaut. The original grid pattern of the *bastide* construction has been preserved to a remarkable degree, and three of its original fortified gateways remain, together with the ancient grain measures in the covered market hall on one side of the square.

If you are at Monpazier it would be a great pity not to visit Montferrand-du-Périgord, just a little further to the north. It is one of the least visited of the region's many picturesque villages and has retained a quiet, almost hidden ambience. A steep main street rises from the floor of the valley to the ruins of a château set on the summit of the hill from which there are sweeping views of the Couze valley. It has an ancient covered market hall, a church and many old houses, farms and *pigeonniers* hidden among the apple and walnut trees.

Villeréal, 15 kilometres south-west of Monpazier, is the third village in the *bastide* triangle. Like Monflanquin, Villeréal was founded by Alphonse de Poitiers in 1269 but was held by the English during the Hundred Years War. There is a fine fortified church dating from the thirteenth century, a number of old houses and a covered market hall in the centre of the arcaded square.

Thézac-Perricard

A short distance to the south-east of Monflanquin is the River Lot, flowing towards its confluence with the Garonne, and just beyond is one of the forgotten vineyards of France, Thézac-Perricard.

Once upon a time, the story goes, in the reign of Napoleon III, the President of the French Republic, Armand Fallières, entertained Nicholas III, Tsar of Russia, during a state visit. Being a native of the Agenais, and a strong supporter of his local gastronomy, M. Fallières served the wine of the region and the Tsar was so impressed that he placed an order for 1,000 bottles. There was not enough to meet this request and M. Fallières was obliged to tell the Tsar that it was 'sold out'. The Tsar would probably be luckier today, for the vineyards have been revived and now extend to over 50 hectares which are dotted around the countryside in small plots and farmed by 16 individual growers. Planted with Merlot and Cot, the vineyards produce only red and rosé wines, with a base of around 80 per cent Cot.

Thézac-Perricard is in fact two villages about 4 kilometres apart. In 1991 the *vignerons* opened an attractive modern *caveau* near Thézac where you can taste and buy the wines as well as local specialities such as *foie gras* and *pruneaux*. The hamlet of Perricard is very attractive, with its cluster of old stone cottages, farm buildings and a small château.

Pruneaux d'Agen are the region's most important and famous crop, and the harvest was in progress at the time of my visit. Laid out in shallow trays inside a large wooden barn, with warm air wafted by large fans, the fat purple plums are dried to a lesser degree than most prunes and are delicious enough to eat raw, like rich, honeyed candies.

A dozen kilometres or so south-west of Perricard is the ancient hilltop village of Penne-d'Agenais. It was a fief of the English Kings during the Hundred Years War, but was almost completely destroyed during the Wars of Religion. Although extensively restored, it still has a medieval atmosphere, and the old buildings and narrow lanes can be explored. Two of the fortified gateways have survived, including the Porte de Ricard, named after Richard the Lionheart who first fortified the village.

A short distance to the south of Penne, in the midst of peaceful countryside, is the tiny fortified village of Frespech, where a château, church and ramparts of silvery grey stone make a particularly pleasing group.

Côtes du Marmandais

The vineyards of the Côtes du Marmandais, which were promoted to Appellation d'Origine Contrôlée in 1990, are planted largely around the villages of Beaupuy, on the right bank of the Garonne, and Cocumont, on the left: these are also the locations of the two co-operatives mainly responsible for the wine's production, along with Vin de Pays de l'Agenais.

Known once as the wines of the Bordeaux 'upper country', the vineyards here are effectively an extension of those in the Gironde and there are records of the wines of the region being exported to London at the beginning of the fourteenth century. After the phylloxera destruction in the last century they all but disappeared, but were revived in 1948 by a small group of *vignerons* who were granted a VDQS appellation in 1955. The vineyards are planted largely with Merlot, Cabernet Franc, Sauvignon, Gamay, Syrah, Malbec, Arbourieu and Fer-Servadou for the reds and rosés, while Sauvignon Blanc, Semillon, Ugni Blanc and Muscadelle are used for white wines.

The Beaupuy vineyards extend to about 650 hectares, of which about 20 per cent are used to make Vins de Pays. They encompass 17 villages and stretch northwards along the pretty valley of the Gupie to the point where they almost merge with the vineyards of the Côtes de Duras. At Cocumont, to the south, the co-operative vinifies the grapes from nine communities which have about 800 hectares under cultivation, extending southwards in the attractive rolling farmland around the village of Romestaing. A scenic road leads from Cocumont to St-Sauveur-de-Meilhan and then to Meilhan-sur-Garonne, with splendid views along the Canal Latéral and the wide River Garonne which runs alongside.

In this area you will see large plantations of what appear to be jumbo grape vines but are in fact the famous Marmande tomatoes; they are odd to see, planted in the same way as vines, in long orderly rows and trained on stakes and wires.

Vin de Mezinais

Vin de Pays de l'Agenais is also produced from a little vineyard about 60 kilometres due south of Marmande in the furthermost corner of Lot-et-Garonne, close to the village of Mézin in a region known as the Pays d'Albret. The wine is produced by a small co-operative with a winery at Poudenas, in the Gélise valley. The vines were first planted at the beginning of the 1980s, and the first harvest was in 1984 from a total of 25 hectares. Now 21 producers farm a total of around 70 hectares, making exclusively white wine from a blend of Colombard, Gros Manseng and Ugni Blanc.

I first tasted the wine at La Belle Gascogne, a hotel restaurant set in a sixteenth-century mill house astride the river. It proved a little more complicated to buy, however, since the winery is used only for production and has no sales facilities. This aspect of the co-operative is handled by Alain Conte, one of the *vignerons* who lives near Mézin. You can find his farmhouse, Le Not, by following the sign to La Ferme de Gagnet from the road which skirts Mézin.

M. Verzéni, the president of the co-operative, told me that they have recently succeeded in having a new Vin de Pays appellation, Mézinais, created especially for them since their grape varieties and style of wine are very different from those around Marmande and Monflanquin in the Haut-Agenais.

The village of Poudenas is delightfully picturesque, with a Roman bridge spanning the river by the mill house, a cluster of old stone cottages and a large

ABOVE TOP: THE CHATEAU OF DURAS.
ABOVE: THE BRIDGE SPANNING THE RIVER DORDOGNE AT STE FOY-LA-GRANDE.
OPPOSITE: THE PILGRIM VILLAGE OF ST-JEAN-DE-PIEDPORT IN THE PYRENEES.

château set on the hill behind. It was built in the thirteenth century by the lords of Poudenas, who were fiefs of Edward I, Duke of Aquitaine, to defend the valley of the Gélise, and was further fortified in the sixteenth century. There is an especially fine *pigeonnier* in a field near the village on the road to Mézin.

The Pays d'Albret takes its name from the powerful family which ruled the region for many centuries. In the nineteenth century it was an important centre for the production of bottle corks, and there is a museum in Mézin recording this industry and its history, together with the life of Armand Fallières, President of the French republic between 1906 and 1913, who was born and buried here. His home is near the village of Villeneuve-de-Mézin, where there is a remarkable fortified church dating from the twelfth century.

Vins de Buzet

The wines of Buzet were granted their Appellation d'Origine Contrôlée in 1973 but their origins go back more than two thousand years. Nurtured by the abbeys and the feudal lords of the Middle Ages, the vineyards and their popularity grew to the point where they began to be seen as a serious rival by the *vignerons* of Bordeaux. Then, in 1189, Eleanor of Aquitaine gave the merchants of Bordeaux the exclusive right to trade with northern Europe. In order to survive, the Buzet vineyards became, effectively, an extension of those of Bordeaux, a situation which lasted until the beginning of the twentieth century when the privilege was abolished.

The *cave co-opérative* was established in 1955, two years after the VDQS appellation was granted to eight villages – it was extended to 27 in 1967. Today the co-operative produces 95 per cent of the Buzet wines from a vineyard of 1,600 hectares farmed by over 250 individual producers. The permitted grape varieties are Cabernet Franc, Sauvignon, Merlot and a little Malbec (or Cot) for the reds. The white wine is produced from Sauvignon Blanc, Semillon and Muscadelle.

It is known as the wine of the Musketeers: indeed one of the most important wine villages, Xaintrailles, is named after a captain who was a companion of Joan of Arc. The countryside here is quintessential Gascony, with big rounded hills, sweeping views and a sky which seems to go on for ever. Nérac lies at the heart of the region, set astride the River Baïse. On the right bank is the old part, known as Petit Nérac, with narrow cobbled streets and numerous old houses, joined to the newer part of the town by a Gothic bridge.

On the left bank, beside the modern bridge, you can see the surviving wing of the magnificent Renaissance château which was once the palace of Marguerite of Navarre and the home of her grandson, later Henry IV. His amorous escapades are commemorated by a statue of a reclining lady in the gardens of the Promenade de la Garonne, on the right bank. She was Fleurette, the daughter of a palace servant, who after being seduced and abandoned by young King Henry, committed suicide by drowning herself in the pool beside the statue.

A tour of the vineyards can be made by following the country roads from Nérac to Barbaste, with its fortified mill and old stone bridge over the River Gélise, and then to Lavardac, a small town on the banks of the same river, and Vianne. This small *bastide*, complete with very well preserved walls and fortified gateways on the banks of the Baïse, was established in 1284 and has a very pretty church with a large bell tower. A few kilometres to the west is Xaintrailles, set on the summit of a hill with extensive views over the valley of the Garonne. It retains the château, dating from the twelfth century, which belonged to Joan of Arc's companion, Jean Poton de Xaintrailles. A short distance further west is another interesting old *bastide*, Durance. To the east are the wine villages of Montesquiou, Espiens and Montagnac-sur-Auvignon.

PYRÉNÉES-ATLANTIQUES
Jurançon

ON THE LEFT bank of the river, almost in the suburbs of Pau, is the small town of Jurançon which gives its name to an AOC wine produced from vineyards of about 600 hectares on the hillsides between the Gave de Pau and the Gave d'Oloron. Records show the existence of the wines of Jurançon in the year 988 and that Henri II of Albret bought a vineyard there in 1552. The wine was placed firmly on the map the following year, however, when Henri IV was born; it is said that at his christening his lips were rubbed with a clove of garlic and moistened with a drop of Jurançon wine.

The Appellation d'Origine Contrôlée was granted in 1936, the area being one of the first in the country to receive it. This was exclusively for a sweet wine, however, and the AOC for Jurançon Sec was not approved until 1975. The principal grape varieties are Gros Manseng for Jurançon Sec and, for the younger sweet wines, Petit Manseng and smaller proportions of Courbu, Camaralet and Lauzet. The progressive *cave co-opérative* of Jurançon is based in the village of Gan, where they vinify the grapes from 530 hectares of vines.

Béarn-Bellocq

The development of the vineyard of Bellocq was largely due to the establishment of the *bastide* and its château in 1281 and the influence of Gaston Phebus and Henri IV, princes of Béarn, who were great admirers of the wine. Later, in the seventeenth century, the Protestants who were expelled from the region carried its fame to England and the Low Countries.

A VDQS appellation was granted in 1934, and an AOC for Béarn in 1975 which was extended to Béarn-Bellocq in 1990. Red and rosé wines are made from Cabernet Sauvignon and Franc with Tannat, which provides the distinctive body and strength. White wine is produced from Gros and Petit Manseng together with Raffiat de Moncade, which is grown only on the terrain of Bellocq. The vineyards, of about 160 hectares in total, are planted on the right bank of the Gave de Pau between Orthez and Labatut and in the triangle of land west of Salies-de-Béarn between the Gave de Pau and the Gave d'Oloron.

The salt springs of Salies-de-Béarn have been known since the eleventh century, and the old houses of the salt merchants create an attractive riverside scene. To the south, Sauveterre-de-Béarn is set above the Gave d'Oloron with remains of ramparts, towers and a bridge which once spanned the river. To the north-west of Salies is the riverside town of Peyrehorade, where the impressive ruins of the medieval Château d'Aspremont, built on the site of an earlier fortress, overlook the Gave; nearby is the sixteenth-century Château de Montréal. A few kilometres further west, on the left bank of the river, is the little hilltop *bastide* of Hastingues, founded at the end of the thirteenth century and named after Lord Hastings of Guyenne.

Irouléguy

The village of Irouléguy is situated in the foothills of the Pyrenees between St-Etienne-de-Baïgorry and St-Jeane-Pied-de-Port. The vineyard was cultivated by the abbey of Ronceveaux during the Middle Ages but almost disappeared after the destruction of phylloxera at the end of the nineteenth century. The revival began in 1943 with the formation of a producers' association and was recognized by the award of a VDQS appellation ten years later; the present AOC classification was granted in 1970. Today the vineyard extends to over 150 hectares, and there are plans to increase this to 200 by the end of the century. Like the wines of Béarn-Bellocq, Tannat is the principal variety for the exclusively red and rosé wines, with additions of Cabernet Franc or Acheria.

From St-Etienne-de-Baïgorry a scenic road leads through the red-rock Vallée des Aldudes across the border towards Pamplona. A more famous route leads off in the same direction from the old pilgrim town of St-Jeane-Pied-de-Port, on the banks of the Nive. This is the region's most visited place – deservedly so, as behind its fifteenth-century ramparts is a network of narrow cobbled streets dominated by a massive citadel. Its name derives from the fact that the village offered a resting-place to pilgrims before they began their climb over the Pyrenean pass (Port) of Roncesvalles which leads into Spain and on towards the holy city of Santiago de Compostela.

THE CUISINE

As may be expected in such an extensive region, there is a rich diversity of food. A speciality of Bordeaux, in the Gironde, are dishes served 'à la bordelaise' in a sauce of red wine and meat stock with tomatoes, shallots, herbs and seasoning. Cèpes, large, brownish wild fungi with a firm meaty texture, are often served in this way; so too is lamproie, an eel-like, freshwater fish (lamprey). Another freshwater delicacy is alose (shad), which has a firm white flesh with an almost buttery texture and a distinctive flavour. The oysters for which the region is famed are often stewed gently in white wine with small sausages called crépinettes; while gravettes, oysters found only in the Arcachon Basin, a little to the south of the Médoc, have a unique, delicate flavour, reminiscent of hazelnuts.

Tourin, a rich onion soup, is thickened with egg yolks and cream and served over garlicky bread; often it is enriched with red wine. Steaks grilled over the glowing embers of vine prunings are very much a speciality of this region, the aroma of the wood imparting a wonderful flavour to the meat; and the delicately flavoured milk-fed lamb from the low-lying meadows around Pauillac on the Gironde estuary is highly prized. Walnuts are in important crop in the Dordogne; walnut oil is used as a dressing on salads, and you'll often see walnut bread served with the cheese.

A popular dish in the Basque region is poulet basque, chicken cooked with white wine, tomatoes, peppers, lardons and mushrooms. Jambon de Bayonne is a raw, cured ham served in paper-thin slices as an hors d'oeuvre, either on its own, with melon, or as part of a salade composée with foie gras. In piperade eggs are scrambled lightly over stewed peppers, onions, garlic, tomatoes and ham. For dessert, you will find gateau basque on many menus in the south of Aquitaine, it's a deliciously light, eggy cake baked to a golden crust. The Pyrenean cheese called Brebis is one of the most distinctive of France; made from the milk of two types of sheep, it has a rich creamy texture and a strong earthy flavour.

MIDI-PYRÉNÉES

THE REGION OF Midi-Pyrénées occupies the southern central section of France, its northern extremity bordering with the Massif Central and the mountains of the Auvergne while to the south lies the great range of the Pyrenees. Westwards is Aquitaine and the Atlantic, and to the east, Languedoc and the Mediterranean. It encompasses eight *départements*: Lot, Aveyron, Tarn, Gers, Haute-Garonne, Tarn-et-Garonne, Hautes-Pyrénées and Ariège, of which only the last two possess no delimited vineyards. Corrèze in Limousin has been included as its two small areas of vineyards are convenient to tour in addition to those of Lot. The most important wine production is to be found in the *départements* of Lot, Tarn and Gers. Toulouse is the region's capital and France's fourth largest city. Built of red brick, it has earned the title of 'Ville Rose' (pink town).

LOT

THE *DÉPARTEMENT* OF Lot is the most northerly of the Midi-Pyrénées region, and the river after which it is named provides the terrain for its most prestigious wine, Cahors, named after the capital of the *département*. This appealing town is situated in the valley of the River Lot, which threads its way through the countryside in a series of winding loops and curves. Once the thriving capital of the old kingdom of Quercy, Cahors is situated in one of these loops, which almost encircles the city in the shape of a horseshoe. Its fortifications and dominant

position made it virtually impregnable, so much so that during the Hundred Years War, when the British took possession of all the other towns in Quercy, only Cahors resisted. Today it is an elegant town with broad streets lined with trees shading the pavement cafés, and here you begin to feel some of the Mediterranean atmosphere.

The town has a fine old quarter with magnificent medieval buildings and ruined ramparts. Of particular note is the Maison de Roaldès, sometimes called the Mansion of Henri IV because the king was reputed to have stayed there during the siege of 1580, and also the twelfth-century cathedral of Saint-Etienne. The medieval Pont Valentré is Cahors' *pièce de résistance*, however. This fortified bridge spans the River Lot, supported by three towers, and is considered to be one of the finest examples of French military architecture. The bridge is the recommended starting point for the wine route.

THE WINES

Much of Cahors' wealth during the Middle Ages came from trade and banking, but wine has always been an important part of its commercial life, and the region has long been famous for its vineyards. During the Roman occupation, the Emperor Dolmitian ordered the wines to be uprooted as a penalty for an attempted uprising, and for two centuries no wine was produced. Later the deep-red wine of Cahors became very popular in England, where it was often preferred to Bordeaux wines, despite that region's attempts to prevent it being shipped. Legend has it that the Popes insisted on its use for the celebration of Mass.

The best wines of Cahors are made from the vineyards in the lower Lot valley beside the river between Cahors and Fumel to the west. The rich red soil, often scattered with limestone pebbles, is planted primarily with Malbec, Merlot and Jurançon grapes. The deep red wines which they produce, classified Appellation Contrôlée, are often matured for three years or more in oak casks, improving further with age in the bottle.

The lesser wines, such as the red, white and rosé Coteaux de Quercy and Coteaux de Glanes, are produced from a wider area away from the river, and this countryside is also well worth exploring.

THE VINEYARDS

The official Route des Vins is clearly signposted, and starts and ends in Cahors although it can, of course, be picked up from any point. Cross the bridge to the south bank of the river and follow the signs to the first wine village of Pradines. The next small community is Douelle; in earlier times this was where the Cahors wines were loaded on to flat-bottomed boats to be transported down river to Bordeaux. Nearby is the ruined Château de Cessac. At this point the valley is quite wide and the vineyards lie between the road and the river.

There are several important growers in the next village, Parnac, which is almost beside the river, and you can walk on a track that runs along the river bank. Close at hand, near the main road, is the large, highly-regarded *cave co-opérative* of the Côtes d'Olt, where you can taste the local Appellation Contrôlée wines. You can also buy Vin de Table and Vin de Pays in large plastic containers (*en vrac*).

Take a short detour to St-Vincent-Rive-d'Olt (Olt is the old name for the river), then go on to Luzech. Here, the river forms a characteristic loop, this one so dramatic that it almost seems as if the town is an island. Luzech's old buildings include a twelfth-century chapel, and there are remarkable views over the river towards the vineyards, which can be reached by a small road that ascends out of the village to the hilltop called Impernal.

The road curves round to Albas dominated by its church and with tiny red-tiled houses built on a large rock beside the river. The hills get steeper now and the valley narrower, and from the winding road there is an inspiring succession of views. At Grézels, a small wine village, there is another detour up and out of the valley through a wooded hillside towards the village of Floressas, where the Château Chambert is situated; you can taste and buy some wine at the château. After returning to Grézels, follow the Route des Vins through small communities such as Pescadoires, often no more than a cluster of small stone houses and a church. The landscape begins to change: fruit trees and meadows with fields of sunflowers and maize are scattered among the vineyards, and gentle hills are crowned with copses.

Puy-l'Eveque, on the north bank, is the next large town. Tiers of mellow old houses tumble down the steep hillside to the water's edge. The church stands on the summit; it has a fortified belfry and a doorway decorated with statues. There is a spectacular view of the Lot valley from the esplanade beside the remains of a thirteenth-century castle. At this point the Route des Vins crosses the river and continues through Duravel, a village of mellow stone houses topped by a small château.

From here the wine road winds up and away from the river through a wooded hillside to St-Martin-le-Redon, which is little more than a cluster of crumbling, yellow stone houses surrounding a small church, and makes few visible concessions to the twentieth century. The next village, Cavagnac, is situated high up the hillside and is full of rather curious little houses with porches and eaves. The vineyards are not so evident here, and the land is quite densely wooded. It has a tranquil quality, and a much sparser population than the region closer to the river.

Follow the wine route to the Château de Bonageuil, a splendid example of fifteenth-century military architecture; it was strongly fortified with no less than three lines of defence. Strangely, it looks rather romantic set on a hilltop overlooking a small wooded valley and could easily be the setting for a fairy story or a Gothic novel. If you walk along a little road that winds through the wooded hillside to the east of the château to a small clearing you will get a sudden and spectacular view of the building. This is just 6 kilometres from the industrial town of Fumel, which marks the western limit of the circuit.

The return route follows the main road (the D 911) for a short distance past Soturac, then crosses back over the river to the wine village of Touzac. At Vire-sur-Lot the route turns south on to the D 58 through a quiet valley patterned with vineyards and then back to Puy-l'Evêque and the north bank of the river. On the return journey to Cahors, it stays near the river, passing through Prayssac and Castelfranc, then follows the D 9 to Caix, Crayssac and Caillac. It then rejoins the main road, the D 911, at Mercuès, with its imposing thirteenth-century château. Once the property of the counts of Cahors, the château was rebuilt in the last century and is now a luxury hotel. From here the main road leads back into the centre of Cahors.

The total circuit is only about 120 kilometres long, but it would be easy to spend several days exploring the countryside and there are several other places in the region not on the official route which are well worth visiting. One of the

ABOVE: A FIELD OF SUNFLOWERS NEAR BEAUMONT IN GASCONY.
OPPOSITE TOP: THE CHATEAUX OF CASTELNAU NEAR BRETENOUX.
OPPOSITE BELOW: A COUNTRY LANE NEAR PARNAC IN THE LOT VALLEY.

most important vineyards in the region is that of Georges Vigouroux near Lalbenque (off the N 20, south of Cahors), a village renowned for its truffle market as well as its wine.

Although it is not in the wine-growing area, it would be almost unthinkable to visit the Cahors area and not see the village of St-Cirq-Lapopie, about 30 minutes' drive east along a beautiful scenic road through the upper Lot valley. St-Cirq-Lapopie is the showpiece of France's tourist industry: it has quaint old brown-tiled houses, narrow hilly streets, a fifteenth-century church and a ruined château. What more could you want?

Coteaux du Quercy

The AOC Cahors wines are exclusively red and made from a blend of Malbec, Merlot and Jurançon grapes. But there is also a Vin de Pays appellation, Coteaux du Quercy, which was created in 1976 and under which white and rosé wines are also produced.

The Vin de Pays vineyards are found mainly on the terrain of the *causses* which lie to the south of the River Lot. The region is known as Quercy Blanc because of the silvery stones and outcrops of rock which typify the countryside. The vineyards extend over a wide area totalling over 400 hectares, from the truffle village of Lalbenque in the east to Montaigu-de-Quercy in the west.

In the heart of the Vin de Pays region is Castelnau-Montratier, set on a hill overlooking the valley of the Barguelonne. A *bastide*, constructed in the thirteenth century, it derives its name from the fact that it was built by Ratier, a lord of Castelnau, on the site of a previous village which had been destroyed by Simon de Montfort during the Albigensian crusades. It has an unusual triangular 'square' surrounded by arcades which, on Sundays, is the location of a lively country market with stalls laid out in the shade of plane trees.

Here I met Mme Dieuzade, whose family farm 6 hectares of vines, planted in 1980, at the Domaine de la Combarade in the countryside to the north of the village. They make a red wine called 'Tradition', which is a blend of Cabernet Franc, Merlot, Auxerrois and Gamay, and another, 'Clef de St Pierre' which is produced from 60 per cent Merlot, 30 per cent Cabernet Franc and 10 per cent Auxerrois. A 'Rosé d'une Nuit' is made from a blend of Cabernet Franc and Gamay in which skin contact is allowed for just 12 hours or so, creating a very pale and delicately coloured wine. A less expensive red wine, 'La Rapiette', is also produced from a similar blend of grape varieties

A short distance to the south-east is Montpezat-de-Quercy, with an arcaded square, many old houses and the fourteenth-century collegiate church of Saint-Martin, which contains a number of large Flemish tapestries woven in the sixteenth century. Near the village on the main road, the N 20, is a *caveau* belonging to the Vignerons de Quercy, a co-operative formed from 65 individual producers who farm a total of 120 hectares in the surrounding countryside and make red and rosé wines from Cabernet Franc, Merlot, Tannat and Gamay.

About 10 kilometres east of Montpezat-de-Quercy is the little hill village of Puylaroque, which looks out over the valleys of the Candé and Lère. A *bastide* built in the twelfth century, it has a number of old houses along its narrow streets, a fine church with a large clock tower and sweeping views over the surrounding countryside from the village walls. In the hills to the south, M. Pierre Belon farms 12 hectares of vines at the Domaine d'Ariés. President of the Coteaux du Quercy, he makes a notable rosé from Cabernet Franc as well as a fine oak-aged red wine, Cuvée du Marquis des Vignes, which have won an impressive succession of medals between them.

The Coteaux du Quercy is a very extensive and progressive Vins de Pays appellation with a total of 20 producers. M. Belon told me the association was pressing for an elevation to VDQS status, which they fully expect to be realized in the near future. The proposal is to specify the varieties grown for the new appellation to be 50 per cent Cabernet Franc, which is known locally as Bouchy or Oeil de Perdrix, and a maximum of 20 per cent each of Auxerrois (Cot), Merlot, Gamay and Tannat.

Other notable producers of Coteaux du Quercy include the Domaine de Caille at Labastide-de-Marnhac, Fernand Carles near Puylaroque, Domaine de Lafage at Montpezat-de-Quercy and the *cave co-opérative* at Parnac on the banks of the Lot. Since 1992, to aid their cause, the Vin de Pays association have staged an annual wine fair at Montpezat-de-Quercy. Here, along with the local wines, gourmet appetites are indulged with such delicacies as roasted wild boar, *cassoulet* and *fondue du tomme*, accompanied by ballads, music and minstrels.

There is no official Route des Vins through the Vin de Pays vineyards and villages, but you can see the best of the countryside by following the signs for the Route de Quercy Blanc and the Route de Chasselas, the desert grape for which the region is also renowned.

The little hill village of Lauzerte is one of the prettiest *bastides* in the region with a picturesque arcaded square. It was built by the Count of Toulouse in 1241, and you can still see many old timber-framed houses of silvery stone along the narrow streets surrounding the central square. A few kilometres to the northeast is Montcuq, set on a promontory above the valley of the Barguelonette, with the tower of a twelfth-century castle soaring above it.

Coteaux de Glanes

This small Vins de Pays appellation is centred on the small village of Glanes, high on the *causse* above the left bank of the River Cére, near its confluence with the Dordogne, a few kilometres to the east of Bretenoux. This hilly country has supported plantations of vines for many generations; as early as the seventeenth century it was recorded that the wines of Glanes were greatly appreciated by the lords of the great fortress of Castelnau. As with many of France's lost wine regions, however, phylloxera and two world wars left only a few small plots for personal consumption.

The present commercial vineyard was founded by George Vidal in 1976 with a planting of just 6 hectares. At first the wines were known as Vins de Pays du Lot but a special appellation was created in 1981 which covered an area incorporating six adjacent villages. Glanes has remained the centre of production, however, and today there are about 25 hectares which are farmed by a group of eight *vignerons*. They all tend their vines independently, but the vinification, bottling and marketing are carried out as a joint enterprise in a modern custom-built winery at the edge of the village. Red and rosé wines are made from a blend of 45 per cent Gamay, 45 per cent Merlot and 10 per cent Ségalin, which is a cross between Jurançon and Portugais Bleu. The grapes are de-stalked and vinified together in stainless steel vats for a period of up to one week and bottled at the end of April or the beginning of May.

The village occupies a beautiful site on a steep hillside with fine views to the south over the Ségala countryside. The vineyards are scattered in small planta-

ABOVE TOP: THE WEEKLY MARKET IN THE TOWN OF EUZE.
ABOVE: THE VILLAGE OF PERRICARD NEAR PENNE D'AGENAIS.
OPPOSITE: THE OLD VILLAGE OF PUY-L'EVEQUE OVERLOOKING THE RIVER LOT.

tions between orchards of peaches, apples, plums and walnuts. An enjoyable scenic drive through the Ségela can be made by following a winding country lane through the villages of Creyssac and Teyssieu to Laval-de-Cère, on the banks of the river.

If any one small area of France could be singled out for having more than its fair share of picturesque villages then this region would have to be the choice. About 10 kilometres south-west of Glanes is Autoire, a collection of houses, manors and small châteaux which bristle with towers, turrets, gables and dove-cotes. Built of a honey-coloured stone with steeply pitched roofs covered by earth-brown tiles, many of the houses have small balconies which are reached by flights of stone steps. The village is set in a deep ravine on the north-eastern edge of the Causse de Gramat, at the narrowest part of which a small river drops dramatically for more than 30 metres in a series of waterfalls to the valley floor.

A short distance to the north Loubressac, a fortified village set on the edge of an escarpment overlooking the Dordogne valley. It can be seen from a long way off, its ramparts, spires and towers ranged along the ridge like a cockscomb. In the thirteenth century the village was a dependency of the Baron of Castelnau, but was largely destroyed during the Hundred Years War and rebuilt in the fifteenth century. The privately owned château dates from this period, and there is a thirteenth-century church.

The views from the village walls are stunning: east to the valley of the Cère, north to the distant castle of Castelnau and west towards the Cirque de Monvalent on the Dordogne. The small hôtel-restaurant of Lou Cantou shares this view and offers both comfortable accommodation and good food. Nearby, almost hidden by apple orchards and walnut trees, the picturesque hamlet of St-Médard-de-Presque occupies a tranquil spot on a hillside overlooking the Bave valley.

To the north west, the village of Carennac lies along the left bank of the Dordogne in one of its most attractive reaches alongside the Île Barrade, where tall trees shade the water. In medieval times, when the village was a dependency of the abbey of Cluny, a priory and church dedicated to Saint Pierre were built here on the site of a tenth-century chapel. The priory was badly damaged during the Revolution, but a hexagonal tower and a fortified gateway remain, together with the beautiful carved doorway which decorates the church of Saint-Pierre. There are many fine old village houses with gardens reaching down to the water's edge, and the whole place has an atmosphere of great tranquillity.

CORRÈZE

Branceilles

ABOUT 10 KILOMETRES north of Carrenac is the village of Branceilles, in the *département* of Corrèze, in Limousin. At the end of the nineteenth century there was a thriving vineyard in this region, whose wines won a medal in the Universal Exposition of 1878. Phylloxera spelt the end of these vineyards, like so many others, but just over one hundred years later a group of *vignerons* banded together to replant them. The first *cuvée* was produced in 1990 with just 8,000 bottles; by the following year the figure had more than tripled. With the appellation Vins de Pays de la Corrèze, the small *cave co-opérative*, representing a dozen producers, produces its Vin de Mille et une Pierres (wine of a thousand and one stones) from a total vineyard area of 30 hectares. The red wine is made from a blend of Merlot and Cabernet Franc, the rosé from Gamay. The *caveau* is open from 10.00 to 12.00 am and from 3.00 to 6.00 pm each day except Sundays and holidays.

In the hamlet of St-Julien-Maumont, a few kilometres north of Branceilles, M. Paul Delmas makes a tiny quantity, just 200 bottles each year, of Vin de Paille which he likens to a Muscat de Rivesaltes, to be drunk as an aperitif or dessert wine. A similar quantity of Vin de Paille is reported by Rosemary George, in her book *French Country Wines*, as being made by Mme Soursac in the village of Queyssac-les-Vignes, a few kilometres south of Branceilles.

Branceilles lies in the midst of some of the region's loveliest countryside, which is dotted with photogenic villages. About 4 kilometres to the south-east, the village of Curemonte is strung out along a wooded ridge overlooking the valley of the Soudoire with three castles, three churches, many fine old houses and ancient stocks beside the timbered market hall. The writer Colette lived here for some years. A short drive to the south-west, surrounded by meadows, the village of Martel thrusts a forest of spires and towers into the skyline. In the centre is a delightful square with a beautiful timber-framed market hall fenced in by tall, narrow houses. The town hall, the Hôtel de Raymondie, once housed the law courts and was built originally by the Viscount of Turenne in the thirteenth century. Nearby is the twelfth-century Maison Fabri, which was the home of Henri Court-Mantel, Richard the Lionheart's brother.

A dozen kilometres or so to the north of Martel are two more villages which deserve a detour. Turenne is set on a steep, domed hill with the ruins of a castle jutting from its crest, and to the east of it is Collonges-la-Rouge, with houses and manors built of rust-red stone and decorated with towers and turrets, like a collection of miniature castles.

Coteaux de Vertougit

Vins de Pays de la Corrèze, established in 1991, is also made from two minute vineyards about 40 kilometres further to the north-west of Branceilles, beyond Brive-la-Gaillarde, in the tiny hamlet of Vertougit, just east of the ancient hill village of Voutezac. Here Madame Léon Chauffier of the Domaine de la Méganie farms 3 hectares of vines and produces around 20,000 bottles each year of red wine made from a blend of Cabernet Franc/Sauvignon and Merlot. Vines have existed here since the fourteenth century and you can see, carved in stone over the door of the ancient *caveau*, the emblem of the Knights Hospitallers, dated 1542. In those times it was known as the wine of La Vinadière and was, according to legend, appreciated by such connoisseurs as Louis XIII and Henri IV. Nearby, from an even smaller vineyard of just one hectare, M. Cessac also produces a red wine from Gamay.

The countryside around Voutezac is delightful, a peaceful rural backwater where hidden river valleys, steep rounded hills and tiny stone hamlets allow you to escape the busier, more touristy aspects of the Dordogne a short distance to the south. Don't miss seeing St-Robert, a hill village, and the imposing castle of Juillac to the west, or the beautiful Vézère valley, a short drive to the north-east, near the hamlet of Estivaux. Linger in the medieval town of Uzerche, further up the Vézère, or, to the west of it, Ségur-le-Château, a fortified village on the banks of the Auvézère.

TARN-ET-GARONNE

THE WINES

ALTHOUGH BY NO means a major wine-producing region, Tarn-et-Garonne does produce some of the more interesting and lesser known wines of France.

The appellations to which it is entitled are the AOC Côtes du Frontonnais, the VDQS Côtes du Brulhois and Vins de La Ville-Dieu, and the Vins de Pays Coteaux et Terrasses de Montauban, St-Sardos and Comté Toloson. The Côtes de Brulhois also extends into the *département* of Lot-et-Garonne in Aquitaine, around the village of Goulens and its *cave co-opérative*.

Vins de La Ville-Dieu-du-Temple

To the south, the River Tarn flows towards its confluence with the Garonne near Moissac. In the centre of the triangle of countryside between the rivers is the village of La Ville-Dieu-du-Temple, which gives its name to a small VDQS appellation. As in many French wine regions, the wines were introduced here by the Romans and planted on terraces. Defences were constructed by Julius Caesar to protect them, for in those days this was the western border of the Narbonnaise Province.

In the ninth century the forest of Agre was cleared by order of the abbots, and the vineyards were extended. Two centuries later the land was given to the Knights Templars, who built the village of La Ville-Dieu. The wines of the Middle Garonne, as they were known, were transported by boat to Bordeaux and exported to England, where they enjoyed considerable popularity.

At that time the vines occupied about 1,200 hectares, about half of the tillable land. They were largely destroyed by phylloxera, but after determined efforts the vines were restored and in 1947 the Vin de La Ville-Dieu was awarded VDQS status.

The Ville-Dieu vineyards now extend to about 350 hectares and only traditional grape varieties are allowed: Negrette, the Cabernets, Syrah, Gamay and Tannat. The vines are grown in 13 communes around the town of La Ville-Dieu, where the *cave co-opérative*, representing over 600 growers, is responsible for the production. The premier wine, red only, is the 'Cuvée Capitouls', which is produced from a blend of 25 per cent each of Gamay, Syrah and Cabernet Franc, with 10 per cent Negrette and 15 per cent Tannat, and is matured in oak for six months before bottling. Two less expensive wines are also produced.

In addition to the VDQS wines, La Ville-Dieu is also the centre for the production of Vin de Pays des Coteaux et Terrasses de Montauban, which was granted an appellation in 1981. Of the total vineyard area about 80 hectares are devoted to the production of Vins de Pays, using a blend of 50 per cent Cabernet and 25 per cent each of Syrah and Gamay.

A Vin de Pays des Coteaux du Quercy is also produced at the co-operative with the label 'Jacques de Brion', from just over 100 hectares of vines planted in the countryside to the north of Caussade. A blend of 40 per cent Cabernet, 30 per cent Gamay, 18 per cent Tannat, 10 per cent Cot and 2 per cent Merlot is used to produce red wine only.

Comté Tolosan

Vin de Pays du Comté Tolosan is also produced at La Ville-Dieu, an appellation which can apply to a wide area of the Midi-Pyrénées and Aquitaine covering eleven *départements*. It is usually sold in bulk to restaurants and supermarkets, but here it is bottled and labelled 'Armand de Tolose', and is subject to the controls of this specific region. It is produced from about 30 hectares of vines around La Ville-Dieu. Red varietal wines are made from Cabernet and Syrah, together with a rosé from a blend of 80 per cent Gamay and 20 per cent Syrah.

Vins de St-Sardos

A short distance to the south of La Ville-Dieu, on the left bank of the Garonne, the village of St-Sardos has its own Vins de Pays appellation and a small co-operative which is responsible for all the production. The vineyards, in small plots, extend along the slopes overlooking the Garonne valley around the villages of St-Sardos, Mas-Grenier and Verdun-sur-Garonne.

There are about 200 hectares in total, with 150 individual producers. The 'Domaine de Tucayne' comes from an individual vineyard with 17 hectares of especially favourable terrain and is vinified separately from a blend of Cabernet Franc, Tannat and Syrah and matured in oak casks before bottling. Domaine de Cadis is also a separate production, from Syrah and Tannat, made only from vines with a yield of less than 40 hectolitres per hectare. Two other red wines are produced: 'Gilles de Morban', from Cabernet, Tannat and Syrah (together with a rosé from a similar blend of grape varieties), and a basic Vin Rouge de Pays from a mix of Cabernet, Tannat, Syrah, Gamay and Arbouriou.

Côtes du Brulhois

To the west of La Ville-Dieu-du-Temple, on the left bank of the Garonne, is a region known as the Brulhois, with a VDQS appellation which was granted in 1984. An area of 10,000 hectares distributed over 42 communes is allocated to the Côtes du Brulhois, but only about 200 hectares are actually cultivated at the present time.

Like those of Cahors to the north, the Brulhois wines were once known as black wines on account of their deep ruby-red colour. The vines are planted on terraces and slopes overlooking the Garonne, mainly on the left bank, but with a smaller area around the village of Puymirol in the hills to the north of the river. The permitted varieties include Tannat, Cabernet Franc, Cabernet Sauvignon and Merlot, together with some Cot and Fer Servadou. The wines are mainly red, but a small quantity of rosé is also produced.

Two *cave co-opératives* are responsible for the majority of production, one near the village of Donzac on the left bank of the Garonne a few kilometres west of Valence, and the other near the village of Goulens, in Lot-et-Garonne, on the N 21 to the south of Agen. Vins de Pays de l'Agenais is also made at the latter.

Don't miss seeing the delightful little *bastide* of Dunes, a few kilometres south-west of Donzac, with its small arcaded square and well-preserved ancient houses. About 10 kilometres south-east of Donzac, set on a hill overlooking the Garonne, is Auvillar. It was one of the many busy ports that developed along the banks of the river and was mentioned in records as early as the ninth century. It was largely destroyed during the Wars of Religion but was rebuilt and its prosperity restored under the influence of Colbert, Louis XIV's finance minister, who helped to establish factories making writing quills and pottery.

Built almost entirely of red brick, the village has a fine gateway and clock-tower, and a beautiful triangular 'square' surrounded by timber-framed houses and arcades, in the centre of which is a round market hall with a tiled roof supported on elegant stone columns.

To the north-west of Auvillar, beyond the right bank of the Garonne, the village of Puymirol looks out over the valley of the River Gandaille. A *bastide* built in the twelfth century, it retains a distinctly medieval appearance, with its many old houses, gateways and a pretty arcaded square. It is also the location of one of the region's finest restaurants, L'Aubergade, where leading chef Michel Trama presides over the cuisine.

AVEYRON
THE VINEYARDS

TODAY ONLY FOUR small pockets of vineyards remain in what was once an extensive wine-growing region, although small family plots can still be seen. Marcillac is the only AOC wine produced in the *département*, while those of Entraygues et du Fel and Estaing have a VDQS appellation and Gorges et Côtes de Millau is a Vin de Pays.

Entraygues et du Fel

From its source in the Cevennes near Bagnoles-les-Bains, not far from that of the Tarn, the River Lot runs an almost parallel course for much of its length before likewise flowing into the Garonne. At the confluence of the Lot and the Truyère is the attractive little market town of Entraygues, where a castle stands on the bank of the Lot and tree-shaded meadows run down to the water's edge.

The town is surrounded by steep rounded hills, which in late summer are tinted bright purple with heather, but once were covered with vines. The wine-making tradition of the region was greatly encouraged in the Middle Ages by the monks of the abbey of Conques, and remains of the stone terraces used to retain the soil on the steep slopes are still visible. Before phylloxera there were over a thousand hectares of vines on the hillsides, but now there are just a handful of producers and only about 20 hectares of vines. M. Walthus, whose 6 hectares of vines are grown on the steep hillside to the north of the village above the left bank of the Truyère, told me that the appellation is best known for its white wine, and that his own is made from a blend of Chenin Blanc and a local variety, Plantaganet. He also makes a red wine from 60 per cent Cabernet Sauvignon, 30 per cent Fer Servadou and 10 per cent Negret – for the colour, – and a rosé from 100 per cent Gamay. François Avalon, in neighbouring St-Georges, is also known for his white wine, made from pure Chenin Blanc.

The full name of the appellation is Vin d'Entraygues et du Fel, the latter referring to the hamlet of Le Fel, a cluster of old stone houses and farms set at the summit of a lofty, sheer-sided hill overlooking the Lot just west of Entraygues. This peaceful spot has a small *auberge* that provides a truly rural retreat with good simple food and accommodation. It belongs to the Logis network and also to a chain of similar small hotels linking walks through the Chataignerie, the high-ridge chestnut country of the region.

Vins d'Estaing

Estaing, one of the prettiest riverside villages in France, is to be found about 20 kilometres upstream of Entraygues. There is a château set up high above the village rooftops and an old stone bridge spanning the Lot. The castle belonged to François d'Estaing, Bishop of Rodez, who financed the construction of one of the great towers of its cathedral from his revenues, and whose statue can be seen on the bridge. A fête is held on the first Sunday in July when the villagers, dressed up in medieval costume, process through the narrow streets to the church, and the village is the subject of a *son et lumière* presentation.

Like Entraygues, the village has its own VDQS appellation, which was granted in 1965. A group of six producers have formed a small co-operative, the

Caveau de Viala, farming about 12 hectares of vines, which makes it the smallest co-operative and VDQS appellation in France. Its winery can be found in a small industrial estate a short distance to the north of the village, below the steep, terraced hills on which the vines are planted. A basic red wine is made here from 60 per cent Gamay with a balance of Pinot Noir and Negrette, while a 'Cuvée Prestige' is produced from 80 per cent Cabernet Sauvignon and 20 per cent Fer Servadou. A blend of 70 per cent Gamay and 30 per cent Jurançon Noir is used to make a rosé, and the white wine is produced from 70 per cent Chenin Blanc and 30 per cent Mauzac.

Up river from Estaing the D 920 leads to the atmospheric riverside town of Espalion, after which the valley route continues to the old walled village of St-Côme-d'Olt and over the hills to St-Geniez-d'Olt. Best known for its strawberries, the small agricultural co-operative in the village also sells the wines of Estaing.

A few kilometres downstream from St-Geniez is the twelfth-century village of Ste-Eulalie-d'Olt, with its old houses, a pretty church, modelled on that of Sainte-Foy at Conques, and two small châteaux. A festival and procession are held here on the second Sunday in July to celebrate the two thorns preserved in the church, which are said to be from Christ's crown and were brought here by the feudal lord on this return from the Seventh Crusade.

Vins de Marcillac

To the south-west of the Lot gorges, between the villages of Entraygues and Estaing, the steep, rounded hills, deep woods and plunging valleys are crisscrossed by numerous small streams, cascades and rivers, which run red with the sandstone soil carried along in their current. Ancient red-stone farmhouses are dotted here and there, and the quiet country lanes lead to a succession of villages, including the ancient *bastide* of Villecomtal, with its fortified gateways, while Muret-le-Château, Salles-la-Source and Bozouls – dramatically sited on the brink of a chasm – are well worth visiting.

Among the many pretty villages hidden within this region is Marcillac, a small market town which gives it name to an AOC wine made in the vineyards on the slopes surrounding the town. Although there are a number of independent producers, a couple of whom are based in the town, the bulk of production is from the co-operative, Cave du Vallon, which can be found near Valady, on the N 140 a few kilometres to the south-west. Formed in 1965, it currently has 55 members farming a total of 100 hectares. The appellation was granted in 1990 and there has been considerable progress since with new plantings, modernization of production and marketing efforts. The red wine is made from 90 per cent Fer Servadou, the local name of which is Mansois, together with Cabernet Sauvignon, Gamay, Merlot and Cot (Malbec).

Gorges et Côtes de Millau

The River Tarn rises in the Lozère mountains near Malpertus, and passes through immensely varied countryside on its way to join the Garonne beyond Moissac. Until it reaches Florac it is a mountain river fed by streams and underground springs, but as it descends it enters a great rift between the limestone plateaus of the Causses de Méjean and the Causse Noir, creating one of the great sights of France, les Gorges du Tarn.

Downstream of the gorges is the busy town of Millau, where the main industry is based on goat and sheepskins. Although, at first sight, there is little sense

ABOVE TOP: A SUMMER MEADOW IN GASCONY NEAR
THE VILLAGE OF CASTEX D'ARMAGNAC.
ABOVE: VINEYARDS OF THE FRONTONNAIS NEAR
THE VILLAGE OF LABASTIDE-ST-PIERRE.
OPPOSITE: VINEYARDS OF THE COTEAUX DU QUERCY
NEAR CASTELNAU-MONTRATIER.

of being in wine-growing country, the region has its own appellation of Vins de Pays. Formerly known as Aveyron, it is now called Gorges et Côtes de Millau. The *cave co-opérative*, based in the small town of Aguessac, a few kilometres north of Millau, is the driving force behind the commercialization of the local wines and has a *caveau* where they can be tasted before buying, both *en vrac* and in bottles.

Wine-making has a long tradition in this region. The ruins of the château in the neighbouring village of Compeyre once guarded a wealthy cave-dwelling community who, during the Middle Ages – when the valley was filled with vines – were responsible for the making, storing and selling of all the region's wines.

The Gamay de Beaujolais was the favoured variety in those days, and it still represents a large proportion of the planting. Here it is known as the Gamet du Pape. The neighbouring village of Mostuéjouls had an impressive château during the period of the popes of Avignon and one of its lords was made a cardinal in the Pope's court. Each year when returning to Avignon he would take with him a supply of the local wine. It is said that the Pope would have no other on his table and, as a result, for more than 600 years the vines have been known as Gamet du Pape.

During the Wars of Religion the village was destroyed, and it never regained its prosperity, but the caves remain and are still used today for storing wine. In 1850, before phylloxera, the vineyards covered 15,000 hectares, and there is evidence of an active export market between Compeyre and Rivière-sur-Tarn to New York, which continued until 1870. The onslaught of phylloxera was followed by the First World War, and the loss of more than 500 *vignerons* from the valley signalled the end of the region's wine industry.

Replanting of the vines began in 1960, and in 1966 the appellation was created. The co-operative, claimed to be the smallest in France – although this, as we have seen, is hotly contested – was established in 1980, and today the Gamet du Pape is supplemented by Syrah and Cabernet Sauvignon together with local black and white grapes varieties.

The co-operative makes a red wine from a blend of 40 per cent Gamay, 30 per cent Syrah and 20 per cent Cabernet Sauvignon, with the balance made up of the traditional varieties, Tanat, Cot, Duras and Negrette. A 'Cuvée des Affineurs' is also produced with 60 per cent Cabernet Sauvignon, 20 per cent traditional varieties and the balance of Syrah and Gamay. A rosé is made using 50/50 Gamay and Cabernet Sauvignon, and a white from 70 per cent Chenin Blanc and 30 per cent Mauzac. Considerable care is taken over quality control, and the yield is restricted to 60 hectolitres per hectare, less than many Vins de Pays. There are just three independent producers based in Rivière-sur-Tarn, to the north of Millau, and at Candas and St-Georges-de-Luzençon, to the west of it.

The vineyards extend along the narrow valley in small pockets for 80 kilometres between Peyreleau and Connac, to the west near Réquista, through some of the most spectacular scenery in France. From Compeyre to Peyreleau the vineyards can be seen along both sides of the valley, and the D 907 on the right bank provides splendid views. The alternative is a quiet road running along the left bank through vineyards and orchards from Millau via the pretty village of La Cresse to Peyreleau.

From Peyreleau there is a a truly breathtaking round trip through the Tarn Gorges to the villages of Les Vignes, La Malène and Ste-Enemie before crossing the Tarn and traversing the Causse Méjean to the riverside town of Meyrueis. From here the D 966 returns to Peyreleau through the beautiful Jonte Gorges.

Downstream from Millau the D 41 follows the river along the right bank, to the little wine village of Candas. A detour from here along the D 96 to St-Beauzély provides more stirring sights, including the village of Castelnau-Pégayrols, perched dramatically on a steep rocky escarpment.

From St-Beauzély the D 30 and D 993 lead back to the river at St-Rome-de-Tarn. The route continues to follow the river via the villages of Le Truel and Broquiès to Brousse-le-Château, a tiny village with a château and church surrounded by ancient houses, set on a steep rock at the confluence of the Tarn and the Alrance. Le Relais de Chasteau offers simple accommodation and good food at modest prices beside the river.

TARN
THE WINES

TO THE WEST of Albi, the *département*'s capital is the town of Gaillac, renowned for its AOC wines, which were recognized in 1938, and for its very well-known Vins de Pays, Côtes du Tarn. It is one of the oldest vineyards in France, originally planted during the first century. In the tenth century it was taken under the wing of the abbey of Saint-Michel de Gaillac and from the twelfth to the fourteenth centuries was exported to England, Holland and Belgium.

The communes of Broze, Cahuzac-sur-Vère, Castanet, Cestayrols, Fayssac, Lisle-sur-Tarn, Montels and Senouillac are entitled to the appellation Gaillac Premier Côtes, for an aromatic sweet white wine. Gaillac white wines can range from bone dry to sweet and are made as still wines as well as sparkling (*mousseux*) and slightly sparkling (*perlé* or *péttilant*).

The Mauzac variety dominates the white wines together with another local variety seldom found elsewhere, the Len de l'El. Muscadelle, Sauvignon Blanc, Semillon and Ondenc are also grown. Plantings of the black-skinned varieties include Duras, Braucal, Merlot, the Cabernets, Syrah and the increasingly popular Gamay. Red Gaillac wines are usually made as a blend of Duras, Fer Servadou and Syrah, or Duras, Merlot and Cabernet. A Primeur is also made from Gamay using carbonic maceration.

In addition to AOC Gaillac wines, the Vin de Pays des Côtes du Tarn has become a major export success and, like Côtes de Gascogne, done much to help create an identity for the more modestly-priced wines of France. It is, ironically, better known in the world market than its superior sister wine. Again, like the Côtes de Gascogne, the Côtes du Tarn largely owes its marketing success to one particular *cave co-opérative*, at the village of Labastide-de-Lévis, between Gaillac and Albi. It was created in 1949 by a group of 80 *vignerons* with the aim of restoring the ancient vineyards of Gaillac. Today it has 412 members, representing 10 per cent of the total area of vineyards, and is established as the largest producer of AOC Gaillac wines. In 1957 it created the co-operative at Cunac, a few kilometres to the east of Albi, and in 1974 incorporated the Cave du Pays Cordais near the village of Souel.

At the Labastide-de-Lévis co-operative, white Côtes du Tarn is produced from a blend of Mauzac, Len de l'El and Muscadelle. A rosé is made from 100 per cent Jurançon and a red from 65 per cent Jurançon and 35 per cent Portugais Bleu. At Cunac a Gamay red is produced using carbonic maceration as well as Primeur using the same variety. A Blanc Moelleux is also made from the Semillon variety. Most of the Vins de Pays wines are available in conventional 75cl bottles, screw-capped 1-litre bottles and *en vrac*.

I also visited the cave at Rabastens where basic red, white and rosé Côtes du Tarn are sold *en vrac*, as well as a superior red and rosé sold in bottles. These are made from a blend of Duras, Merlot, Cabernet Franc, Cabernet Sauvignon, Brancol and Syrah, with the label 'Henry de Cambourne'. At the Cave de Técou, a few kilometres south-east of Gaillac, a 100 per cent Jurançon red and rosé is produced, as well as a white from Mauzac and Muscadelle with a little Len de l'El.

THE VINEYARDS

The vineyards extend on both banks of the Tarn, as far as Cordes to the north, Rabastens to the west, Bellegarde to the east and Giroussens to the south, and encompass over 70 villages. The soil of the left bank is gravelly and is used largely to produce red wines, while the hillier country to the north harbours the more favoured vineyards.

A tour of the vineyards will also lead you to some of the most attractive countryside and picturesque villages in this part of France. From Gaillac the D 964 leads north-west to the little walled hilltop village of Castelnau-de-Montmirail. A *bastide* built in the thirteenth century, it has at its centre a very pretty arcaded square surrounded by narrow streets of timber-framed houses. The Gothic church contains a Byzantine cross studded with precious stones.

The road continues westwards into the valley of the Vère to another spectacularly sited hilltop village, Puycelci. Less extensively restored than Castelnau, its old streets contain numerous houses from the fourteenth and fifteenth centuries as well as a good Gothic church. There are stunning views from the battlements across the valley to the Forêt de Grésigne.

A few kilometres north-west of Puycelci is the fortified village of Bruniquel, set on a cliff above the River Aveyron. At the summit is a castle which was built more than seven hundred years ago and originally named after Brunehaut, a Carolingian princess, which is how the village got its present name. A few kilometres up river there is another dramatic sight, the fortress of Penne, surmounting a jagged crest of rock, with narrow village streets laid out below.

A little further upstream on the right bank of the Aveyron is St-Antonin-Noble-Val, a small spa town set beside the river, which is spanned by an old bridge. The atmosphere is distinctly medieval, with dark narrow streets and numerous ancient houses, some dating from the thirteenth century, together with a Romanesque town hall which was restored by Viollet-le-Duc.

From St-Antonin the D 19 and D 91 lead south-east to Cordes, 'the city in the sky', as it has dubbed itself. Built on a steep rounded hill above the valley of the Cerou, it is the quintessential medieval stronghold with steep cobbled streets, fortified gateways, battlements, towers and many fine old buildings. The village possesses an outstanding hôtel-restaurant, Le Grand Ecuyer, where master chef Yves Thuries offers his culinary skills daily.

A quiet scenic route back to Labastide-de-Lévis can be taken by following the D 30, just to the south of Cordes, to Noailles, Cestayrols and Fayssac.

HAUTE-GARONNE

BEYOND THE SOUTHERN limit of the Gaillac vineyards there is little vine culture until the Côtes de la Malapère are reached to the west of the city of Carcassonne. In the *département* of Haute-Garonne, however, there are two small outposts, one to the south of the city of Toulouse and another to the north.

The Domaine de Ribbonet is situated in a region of big rounded hills to the west of the valley of the Lèze near the village of Beaumont-sur-Lèze. Here, in the midst of a 220-hectare estate which surrounds a fifteenth-century château, 33 hectares of vines are under cultivation. The château was the home of Clémant Adler, an ingenious engineer and inventor of the last century who successfully completed a 50-metre flight in his single-engined aircraft named Eole 1. He lived at the Domaine de Ribbonet until 1923, giving much of his attention to its vineyards and cellar.

The property is now owned by Christian Gerber and his family, and the vineyards have been under his care since 1974. The title of Château de Ribbonet is not allowed on the labels since Haute-Garonne is only a Vin de Pays appellation. A vast range of noble grape varieties are grown here – Cabernet Sauvignon, Cabernet Franc, Merlot, Pinot Noir, Gamay, Sauvignon Blanc, Semillon, Chasselas, Sylvaner, Riesling, Gewürztraminer, Pinot Gris, Chardonnay, Aligoté and Marsanne!

The Domaine's current tariff lists varietal red wines from Cabernet Sauvignon, Pinot Noir and Merlot together with 'Cuvée Clémant Adler', which is blended from Cabernet Sauvignon, Merlot and Cabernet Franc and allowed to mature in oak casks for up to 15 months before bottling. Varietal rosés are made from Syrah, Merlot and Cabernet Franc, and white vins de cépage are produced from Chardonnay and Marsanne – both oak-aged – as well as a Riesling and Gewürztraminer.

Côtes du Frontonnais

The small market town of Fronton lies about 25 kilometres due north of the city of Toulouse in a triangle of countryside between the converging Tarn and Garonne. Vineyards were planted here as early as the Merovingian times, when part of the Agre forest was cleared to plant the vines which later, in the twelfth century, belonged to the Knights Hospitallers. It is claimed that such notables as Pope Calixtus II, King Louis XIII and Cardinal Richelieu enjoyed and appreciated the wines of Fronton.

The region received its Appellation d'Origine Contrôlée in 1975, which resulted in the amalgamation with the vineyards of neighbouring Villaudric, and both names can be added to the appellation. Today, the vineyard extends to about 2,000 hectares, which is expected to increase to 2,800 hectares by the end of the century. The vineyards are planted predominantly with Negrette, from which only red and rosé wines are produced, and this variety accounts for between 50 per cent and 70 per cent of the blend with a balance of Gamay, Cabernet Franc, Cabernet Sauvignon, Fer Servadou, Cot, Cinsaut and Syrah. In addition to nearly fifty individual producers there are two co-operatives, at Fronton and Villaudric. The vineyards extend north as far as Labastide-St-Pierre and south to Villeneuve-lès-Bouloc, while the River Tarn forms the eastern boundary of the vineyard and Canals is the most westerly commune.

GERS

THE WINES

GERS IS ENTITLED to the appellations of AOC Béarn, Madiran and Pacherenc du Vic Bilh, the VDQS Côtes du Brulhois and Côtes de St-Mont and the Vins de Pays Côtes du Condomois and Côtes de Gascogne and Gers. However, the region's most famous product is probably Armagnac.

If Cognac has a serious rival when the time comes for coffee and cigars, it can only be Armagnac. The two producing regions are relatively close geographically, yet there is a considerable difference between their wines. The distillation process is also slightly different: instead of the two-stage process used in Cognac, the thin, quite weak, white wine of the Armagnac region is brought up to a level of 50–55 per cent alcohol in one stage. The local oak from which the casks are made is a darker and more resinous wood than the Limousin oak used for the Cognac casks, giving the Armagnac a darker, stronger colour in a shorter space of time. Its more rustic character, however, means that it needs longer to attain the subtlety and smoothness of its rival. The wine is distilled immediately after fermentation, at the end of September or in early October, and by law all distillation stops on 30 April. On 1 April the following year that brandy is designated Compte 1, the minimum age at which it can be sold as Armagnac. Napoleon, or Extra Armagnac, must be at least Compte 5.

The wine-growing region of Armagnac is divided into three areas: Bas-Armagnac, Haut-Armagnac and Ténarèze. Bas-Armagnac is the smaller, more westerly region and the most prestigious; Ténarèze is in the centre, and Haut-Armagnac extends north to the *département* of Lot-et-Garonne and south to the Hautes-Pyrénées. As with Cognac, the final product is usually the result of blending, from different regions and different vintages. The grape types used are Folle Blanche, or Picpoul, Colombard and St-Emilion (Ugni Blanc). It is possible to get Armagnac made from one particular grape type. Unlike Cognac, the production of which is quite centralized, well organized and well promoted, Armagnac tends to be produced by individuals, making and selling their product in a smaller and more fragmented way. This may to some extend explain why Cognac has more impact on the world's wine-lists.

An aperitif or dessert wine is also made locally by combining the local white wine with the distilled spirit; called Floc de Gascogne, it is advertised extensively in the region. By and large, Vin de Pays des Côtes de Gascogne is produced from the same vineyard regions as Armagnac, but Madiran, Pacherenc du Vic Bilh and Côtes de St-Mont are produced in separate, isolated wine-growing areas. The other Vin de Pays appellation of Gers is Côtes de Condomois, which is widely produced in the region around its namesake town. The grape varieties and style of wine are very similar to Côtes de Gascogne, although the emphasis is more on red and rosé wines, in contrast to the Côtes de Gascogne which is predominantly white. The co-operative at Condom, for instance, makes a red wine from a blend of 80 per cent Tannat and 10 per cent each of Merlot and Cabernet, a rosé from Merlot and Cabernet, and whites from Ugni Blanc, Colombard, Gros Manseng and Sauvignon.

THE VINEYARDS

Although there are signs indicating Circuit d'Armagnac, these refer to a number of quite separate circuits and so are rather difficult to follow. The route suggested here combines the best of all these circuits, including the most significant towns and aspects of the countryside. The most logical starting point is the town of Condom. It is an easy drive from the A 61 autoroute between Bordeaux and Toulouse.

Condom is one of several towns which proclaim themselves to be the capital of Armagnac. It is certainly the capital of the Ténarèze and, being an important river port, has been a centre for the manufacture and distribution of the brandy for centuries. Its Gothic cathedral of Saint-Pierre has an unusually large cloister with exceptional ribbed vaulting. There is a small Armagnac museum in the adjacent town hall.

Follow the circuit in an anticlockwise direction to the little fortified village of Larressingle, set in the middle of quiet rolling land with a patchwork of vineyards. Its walls enclose a small cluster of old stone houses, a ruined château and a church, the whole place no larger than a modest château. An information kiosk sells local produce and the village's own brand of Armagnac. Just to the south of Condom is the Château de Cassaigne, where you are welcome to see the castle and taste the Armagnac. There is also an example of one of the copper mobile stills (*alembics*) which until quite recently were towed from village to village to distil the local wine. In a park close to Cassaigne, at the end of an avenue of trees, is the mellow stone Cistercian Abbaye de Flaran, which has a fourteenth-century cloister and contains ancient *chais* where the wine used to be stored. At Valence-sur-Baïse, a *bastide* with an arcaded square, there is an unusual church framed by two large belfries.

Continuing westward on the D 15 you come to the ruined château of Beaumont. Montréal, a fortified town built in the thirteenth century, is next along the route: this has the typical Armagnac central square surrounded by arcaded houses lining narrow streets built on a grid pattern. A kilometre or so to the north of Montréal is Fourcès, one of the most picturesque of all the *bastides*. Its ramparts are surrounded by a moat full of water-lilies, there is a small bridge leading through the fortified gateway into a little square shaded by plane trees and overlooked by old houses and arcades, and there is a pretty church situated by the bridge just outside the village.

Beyond the hill town of Castelnau-d'Auzan is the thermal resort of Barbotan-les-Thermes. Unlike many spa towns, this is a lively place with shops and pavement cafés; a curious fortified gate acts as an entrance to the town. Nearby is the lake of Uby, where you can go boating and fishing. The next town is Cazaubon, in the middle of some of the best vineyards of the Bas-Armagnac, and a little further to the west is Labastide-d'Armagnac.

Among the Côtes de la Jeunesse vineyards, a few kilometres south of the village, is the museum of the Vignerons d'Armagnac; it is clearly signposted from the D 626. Near the road to the south of Labastide, surrounded by vineyards, is an ancient chapel called Nôtre-Dame des Cyclistes, where there is a small collection of relics and memorabilia on display. The hamlet of Castex-d'Armagnac, a little further south of Labastide, was a château with an impressive *chais* lined with ancient casks. The *domaine* of the Samalens brothers, important producers who make visitors very welcome, is quite close by in Laujuzan.

The small town of Eauze also claims to be the capital of Armagnac; it has a Maison d'Armagnac and many mouth-watering food and wine shops. Market day is Thursday, where, centred in the small church square, it spills along the narrow streets towards an open space shaded by plane trees, under which some of the most delectable produce is displayed. The Armagnac dealers used to bring their samples and trade here, but modern marketing methods now seem to have done away with this old-fashioned pleasure.

The next town on the route is Nogaro, with its large Romanesque church, Saint-Austinde. There is a forest at Aignan, a few kilometres further south, signposted from the village church down a narrow lane. The nearby village of Lupiac sits in the middle of scenic countryside. Going north, there are sweeping

ABOVE: A GOOSE FARM NEAR THE VILLAGE OF GEAUNE
IN THE TURSAN REGION.
OPPOSITE TOP: THE MEDIEVAL FORTIFIED BRIDGE SPANNING
THE RIVER LOT AT CAHORS.
OPPOSITE BELOW: A VIEW OF THE RIVER LOT OVER THE
ROOFTOPS OF ST CIRQ-LAPOPIE.

panoramic views over the rolling hills on either side of the road, which are dotted with old stone windmills. Set back in the woods is the Château de Castelmaure, the birthplace of Charles de Batz, who is better known as the Gascon hero d'Artagnan, immortalized by Alexandre Dumas in *The Three Musketeers*. He is much honoured still, with varying degrees of dignity – from a statue in Auch to labels and posters advertising Armagnac.

Vic-Fézensac, the next large town, has a covered arena for the many Courses Landaises which it hosts throughout the year. It is also the place to stock up with the regional food specialities, such as *confits*, *foie gras* and fruits preserved in Armagnac; you will find a tempting assortment of such things at Chez Jeannot, a shop with irresistible displays.

Auch, the largest town of the region, is built on the banks of the River Gers. The cathedral of Sainte-Marie, one of the last great Gothic cathedrals, is clearly visible from quite a distance; you can approach it from the river via a magnificent flight of stone stairs. Inside, the Renaissance choir-stalls incorporate over 1,500 individual figures and sculptures carved in heart oak; the work took over forty years to complete. The stained-glass windows, in reds and purples, are the cathedral's most famous feature and date from the early sixteenth century. Outside, a large square is lined with elegant buildings and pavement cafés, and the Hôtel de France, the restaurant of André Daguin, one of the region's great chefs, is around the corner.

Just to the north-west of Auch is the village of Roquelaure, with good views of the surrounding landscape from its hilltop setting. Nearby, set in the midst of woods, is the Château de Rieutort, once the home of the Comte du Barry, whose wife became the mistress of Louis XV. In Lavardens the old stone houses are tiered up the hillside to an imposing château and an old church.

Continuing northwards along the main road, the N 21, you pass the town of Montestruc-sur-Gers, where there is a *cave co-opérative*, on the way to Fleurance and Lectoure. Fleurance has a strange, arcaded hall in the centre of its square and an equally unusual circular covered market. Lectoure is set on a hilltop high above the River Gers, encircled by medieval ramparts. On the route back towards Condom don't miss the spectacular fortified town of Terraube; its enormous château looks as if it is about to topple over the edge of the hill.

Madiran – Pacherenc du Vic Bilh

The AOC wines of Madiran are exclusively red, made chiefly from the Tannat grape, with a percentage of Cabernets Sauvignon and Franc and Fer Servadou also permitted. The region's AOC white wine is Pacherenc du Vic Bilh, because it is based on the Pacherenc grape, also known as the Arrufiac, with a proportion of Gros Manseng and Courbu. It is made as a dry white and a *moelleux*.

The Madiran wine circuit lies to the south of Aire-sur-l'Adour and can be most easily found by following the N 134 as far as the village of Garlin. Here the wine circuit is clearly signposted on to the D 16 towards the villages of Castelpugon and Diusse. The landscape of Madiran is subtly different from that of the adjacent Tursan, and you always seem to be crossing a river, climbing a hill or plunging down into a valley, while all around is a mixture of meadows, woods, fields of grain and other crops. You will see many maize stores, wire and wooden cages some 2 metres deep and often up to 60 metres long – quite a sight when filled with newly harvested yellow maize. In the main, the villages are quite small and there are many individual producers who invite visitors to taste and buy their wines. In the hamlet of Diusse, for example, there is a *cave* attached to a fine château surrounded by vineyards, and nearby is one of the *caves co-opératives* of Crouseilles.

From Diusse the wine road runs along the top of a ridge providing excellent views over the landscape to both east and west. Beyond Cadillon, from where you can see the distant Pyrenees, is Arricau-Bordes, actually an amalgamation of two villages. Here there is a quite spectacular château of golden stone perched on the hillside, and you can visit its *cave*, where a selection of Madiran wines of different vintages is available. The larger town of Lembeye is the southernmost point of the Madiran wine route, with a fortified gateway and a large square. The nearby hamlet of Corbère-Abères has a *cave* which you can visit; so too has Crouseilles to the north, which also has an old château.

Madiran has a fine church set in a small square surrounded by stone houses and an ancient covered market. The nearby hamlet of Aydie houses the well-respected domaine of Château Aydie, which produces both Madiran and Pacherenc de Vic Bilh. To the north-east, close to the main D 935, is Castelnau-Rivière-Basse where, from a terrace beside the quaint, crumbling church, there is a magnificent view over the countryside to the east.

Côtes de St-Mont

Les Producteurs de Plaimont, near the village of St-Mont, are the leading producers of Côtes de St-Mont and are also largely responsible for the production and marketing success of the Côtes de Gascogne. The co-operative, formed initially in 1974 by a small group of producers, became a fully-fledged union in 1979, with the aims of restructuring the vineyards, adopting strict quality controls and modern vinification techniques and expanding their market.

In 1850 the vineyards of the *département* of Gers covered over 150,000 hectares; today the figure is 25,000, of which the 1,350 Plaimont producers farm a total of 2,260 hectares. This is made up of 790 hectares for Côtes de St-Mont, 225 for Madiran, 45 for Pacherenc de Vic Bilh and 1,200 for Armagnac and Vins de Pays.

Côtes de St-Mont is a VDQS appellation granted in 1957 and incorporates nearly fifty communes around the River Adour and its tributaries in the cantons of Aignan, Euze, Marciac, Plaisance, Riscle, Montesquiou and Aire-sur-l'Adour. The village of St-Mont itself consists only of a few ancient houses and a church, and is dominated by the large *cave co-opérative* on its outskirts. Here red wines are made from a blend of 70 per cent Tannat, 10 per cent Pinenc or Fer Servadou, 15 per cent Cabernet Sauvignon and 5 per cent Cabernet Franc, and are aged from 8 to 15 months in oak casks. The white wine is produced from a blend of local varieties, 40 per cent Arrufiac, 30 per cent Gros Manseng, 25 per cent Petit Courbu and 5 per cent Petit Manseng. The *saignée* method is used to produce rosé wines from a blend of Tannat and Cabernet.

The Côtes de Gascogne red wines – by far the smaller percentage – are made from Tannat with a small proportion of Cabernet. The white wine, called Colombelle, is a blend of 70 per cent Colombard, 20 per cent Ugni Blanc and 10 per cent Listan, but a pure Colombard is also made. In Gascony, unusually, the Primeur wines are always white and a Colombelle Primeur is on sale from 1 November.

The majority of the Côtes de St-Mont production is by the co-operative, but there are a few independent producers, some of whom have broken away from the group. The Côtes de Gascogne, however, is produced over a much wider area and there are many other sources, both co-operatives and independent *vignerons*, spread between Montestruc-sur-Gers in the east and Crouseilles in the west and as far as Condom in the north.

THE CUISINE

The products of the numerous duck and goose farms of the region figure largely in the cuisine of the Midi-Pyrénées, and delicacies like *foie gras*, *confit d'oie* and *confit de canard* can often be bought directly from the farms. *Foie gras à la quercynoise* is goose-liver served in thin slices with a sauce made by simmering finely chopped vegetables and herbs in stock and white wine and flavoured with cognac and truffles. *Rillettes d'oie*, a creamy pâté made from shredded goose meat blended with its own fat, is another local speciality to look out for.

A slice from a whole, lightly-cooked *foie gras* is a wonderful way to start a meal; it is also served as a *galantine* or in thin slivers served on a *salade composée* along with perhaps some *jambon de canard* (smoked breast of duck thinly sliced and served like a Bayonne ham). André Daguin, of the Hôtel de France in Auch, combines a piece of *foie gras* with fresh scampi and cooks them *en papillotes*. *Confit d'oie*, or *de canard*, is made by cooking pieces of duck or goose slowly in their own fat to be preserved before re-heating under a grill, or in a hot oven, to a crisp, golden-skinned delicacy. *Cou d'oie* is a sausage-like pâté made by stuffing a goose neck with chopped meat, liver and herbs while *salmis de palombe* is a casserole of pigeon in a rich red-wine sauce which is spiked with wine vinegar and cooked slowly until the meat falls from the bones.

The small, round creamy goat cheeses called Cabecou, found especially in the Lot valley, are worth seeking out. They are delicious when flashed under the grill and served on a bed of mixed salad leaves with a tangy dressing.

LANGUEDOC-ROUSSILLON

HE REGION OF Languedoc-Roussillon encompasses five
départements: Lozère (which, officially, has no vineyards), Gard,
Hérault, Aude and Pyrénées-Orientales. Languedoc is widely
considered to be the birthplace of the French wine industry. The vine
is probably indigenous to the area, but its cultivation dates from the
Roman occupation in the second century BC. Then, wine was
imported from Italy through the Roman port of Narbo Martius, now
Narbonne; it was this trade which encouraged the Narbonnais to cultivate the vine and produce their own wine. Wine-making became so
important to the region that legend has it that when the Visigoths
invaded the city of Béziers in the fifth century they met no resistance
because everyone was out in the vineyards harvesting the grapes.

The area's Roman heritage is also evident in a wealth of architectural remains: there are ruined ramparts, aqueducts, amphitheatres,
bridges and churches throughout the region. The Roman amphitheatre in Nîmes, is the most perfectly preserved in the world.

The region's name is a reference to its mother tongue, literally the
Langue d'Oc – *oc* being the regional word for 'yes'; the northern part
of France, where 'yes' was *oil* (now *oui*), was at one time known as the
Langue d'Oil.

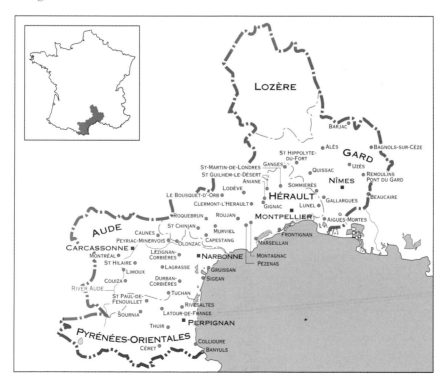

GARD

THE WINES

THE AOC APPELLATIONS to which the Gard is entitled are: Lirac – Tavel – Chusclan – Laudan – St-Gervais – Clairette de Bellegarde – Costières du Gard. The Vins de Pays appellations are: Coteaux de Cèze – Coteaux du Pont du Gard – Duché d'Uzès – Mont Bouquet – Cevennes – Coteaux du Salavès – Côtes du Vidourle – Vaunage – Sables-du-Golfe-du-Lion.

The vineyards fall into five main regions. Côtes du Rhône is an appellation granted to the most northerly vineyards on the west bank of the Rhône and in the valley of the River Cèze between Pont-St-Esprit and Comps. The Costières de Nîmes lies in the countryside to the south-east of the city between the A 9 autoroute and the Canal du Rhône et Sète. Clairette de Bellegarde is a separate appellation within these vineyards. Coteaux du Languedoc is an appellation applied to the vineyards to the west of Nîmes and extends beyond the River Vidourle into the *département* of Hérault. There are also a number of Vins de Pays appellations around this region which apply to vineyards beyond the limit of the AOC vineyards.

The grape varieties grown in the Gard are extremely diverse. While those permitted for use in the AOC wines are largely traditional Mediterranean varieties, such as Grenache, Cinsaut, Mourvèdre and Syrah for reds and Clairette, Ugni Blanc, Roussanne and Marsanne for whites, the Vins de Pays appellations allow a much wider choice and varieties like Chardonnay, Sauvignon Blanc, Cabernet Sauvignon and Merlot are quite widely grown.

Côtes du Rhône

An enjoyable tour through the Côtes du Rhône vineyards of the Gard can be made by beginning in the attractive old riverside market town of Pont-St-Esprit. It is named after its thirteenth-century bridge, built by the Frères Pontifs, which spans the wide, swirling Rhône. From here a small road, the D 23, leads off to the south-east through a wooded valley to the Chartreuse de Valbonne, where you can visit its fine thirteenth-century cloister and taste and buy the *domaine's* wine from a small *caveau*.

From here the road continues to the wine village of St-Laurent-de-Carnois in the valley of the Cèze. This lovely valley is well worth exploring, with its maze of narrow lanes leading through unspoiled countryside to a sequence of picturesque villages. La Roque-sur-Cèze is especially pretty, built on a rounded hill which rises above the surrounding vineyards, its web of narrow cobbled streets leading up to a Romanesque chapel and the remains of a château at the top of the hill.

Nearby is the Cascade du Sautadet, where the Cèze flows down over a series of saucer-like rocky depressions – an idyllic spot for a picnic. The neighbouring village of Cornillon is perched high on a cliff-like bluff with far-reaching views of the valley and the vineyards which reach away towards the horizon.

Bagnoles-sur-Cèze is just a short distance to the east, and from here you can travel along quiet country roads to a succession of the most southerly of the Côtes du Rhône wine villages: Chusclan, known for its rosé, Laudun and St-Victor-la-Coste, where there is a huge, partially derelict fortification called La Castella perched above the village. From here the route continues, via the old walled village of St-Laurent-les-Arbres, to the villages of Lirac and Tavel, both famous for their highly alcoholic, full-bodied rosés.

Costières de Nîmes

This appellation covers an area of 25,000 hectares in the vicinity of Nîmes, mainly to the south-east, although only about half of that is actually under cultivation. The production is mainly red wine, with some rosé and a very small quantity of white wine. The vineyards around the town of Bellegarde have a separate appellation for a white wine made exclusively from the Clairette variety. The principal communes are St-Gilles, Vauvert, Bellegarde, Beaucaire, Redessan, Manduel and Générac.

Coteaux du Languedoc

TO THE SOUTH-WEST of Nîmes the D 40 leads towards the beautiful valley of the River Vidourle, with villages and towns decorating its banks. Here, the vineyards are not intensively cultivated and the broad valley through which the road sweeps is chequered with vineyards, meadows and crops such as asparagus and rapeseed; the hills on either side, although quite steep, are not very high. As you travel westwards the land becomes more undulating and the distant mountains more dominant. The River Vidourle gives its name to the vineyards of the area which, as well as producing AOC Coteaux du Languedoc, also has a Vin de Pays appellation, Côtes du Vidourle, produced from the vineyards around the villages of Aspères, Crespian, Lecques, Souvignargues and Villevieille.

It's possible to buy wines directly from many of the smaller country *caves co-opératives* in the Languedoc, but not all have a *caveau* and some are open for sales to the public only once a week or less. However, the well-run *caveau* at Crespian, a short distance to the north of Sommières, is open during normal business hours and also represents the co-operatives of neighbouring Cannes and Montmiral. As well as AOC Coteaux du Languedoc, the *cave* also has an excellent selection of Vins de Pays. A white Côtes du Vidourle is made here from a blend of Ugni Blanc, Sauvignon, Grenache Blanc and Rolle, as well as a rosé from Syrah, Cinsaut and Grenache and a red wine from Syrah, Grenache and Carignan. *Vins de cépage* are also made with the Vins de Pays d'Oc label from Sauvignon, Chardonnay, Merlot and Cabernet Sauvignon.

The Vaunage is a region immediately to the east of Vidourle, near the charming old walled town of Sommières. In addition to producing AOC Costières de Nîmes and Coteaux du Languedoc, it gives its name to a local Vin de Pays. The appellation is largely disappearing under the Vins de Pays du Gard label; the region's main *cave co-opérative* at St-Côme gave up using the name a few years ago.

One notable upholder of the Vaunage appellation, is M. Dominique Robin of the Domaine Mas de l'Escattes on the stony hillside just to the north-east of Calvisson. He has 40 hectares of vines which are planted on three clearly defined types of terrain. Costières de Nîmes is produced on the well-drained alluvial soil of the steepest slopes, Coteaux du Languedoc on the higher, dryer limestone *garrigue*, while the lowest slopes, planted with 15 hectares of vines, are ideal for the Chardonnay, Viognier and Cabernet Sauvignon grapes used for the Vins de Pays.

Vins de Pays

ABOUT 20 KILOMETRES south-west of the Cèze valley as the crow flies, the peak of Mont Bouquet creates a dramatic shape on the skyline. A small road leads up to the summit, from where there are breathtaking views of the *garrigue*, the Rhône valley, the mountains of the Ardèche and the Cevennes.

ABOVE TOP: A VINEYARD SIGN NEAR THE VILLAGE OF FAUGERES.
ABOVE: HARVESTING GRAPES IN THE VALLEY OF THE CEZE NEAR ST MICHEL D'EUZET.
OPPOSITE: A VINEYARD NEAR THE OLD TOWN OF PEZENAS.

The mountain gives its name to a Vin de Pays grown in vineyards planted on its slopes. The main producer is the *cave co-opérative* at Brouzet-lès-Alès, but there is no *caveau*. Mont Bouquet is a name which seems destined to disappear under the mantle of Vins de Pays du Gard or Cevennes.

The medieval town of Uzès is a short drive to the south of the Cèze valley. It has a wealth of fine old buildings and towers, some of which are currently undergoing extensive restoration. The main square, Place aux Herbes, is the location of a lively country market on Saturday mornings which, in the winter months, includes the stalls of truffle dealers.

The impressive Ducal Palace is the legacy of the powerful family which ruled the area between the eleventh and eighteenth centuries and is now the location of a sound-and-vision exhibition of the region's history.

Duché d'Uzès

There are extensive vineyards in the countryside around the town which are used to produce Vins de Pays. They have a sound history, dating back over 2,000 years and gaining fame and honour by supplying wines to the popes of Avignon in the fourteenth century.

Recent changes have resulted in two new appellations, Duché d'Uzès and Cevennes. The former refers only to wines produced in the vicinity of Uzès, but the latter can also include wines produced in Mont Bouquet, Coteaux de Salavès and Libac, together with the previously-named Uzège and Coteaux Cévenols. In practice, Vins de Pays des Cevennes will probably spell the end of Mont Bouquet and Coteaux de Salavès; Libac has already disappeared.

The change is not just in name; the regulations too have been altered. The *cave co-opérative* at St-Quentin-la-Poterie, a few kilometres to the north-east of Uzès, was one of the main production centres of Vins de Pays de l'Uzège, and their premium wine, 'Marquise des Terres Rouges', is made from a blend of Grenache, Syrah and Merlot. But the regulations for the newly-forged Duché d'Uzès appellation do not allow the use of Merlot, so this particular wine has now had to become Vin de Pays des Cevennes. On the other hand their red and rosé wines, made from Syrah and Grenache alone, have become Vins de Pays de la Duché d'Uzès.

Cevennes

The Domaine de Gournier, south-west of Uzès near the village of Ste-Anastasie, has also suffered from the change in regulations and has been obliged to change the name of its highly-regarded Vins de Pays de l'Uzège to Vins de Pays des Cevennes. From a vineyard of 55 hectares the *domaine* produces varietal Chardonnay and Sauvignon together with a white wine blended from Ugni Blanc, Chasan and Rolle. A rosé is made from Grenache, Cinsaut and Mourvèdre, and a red wine from a cocktail of Merlot, Cabernet Sauvignon, Grenache, Syrah and Mourvèdre. Merlot and Cabernet Sauvignon are also used to make a superior red wine which is kept in oak for eight months before the wine is bottled.

Vins de Pays des Cevennes is also made at the *caves co-opératives* of St-Christol-lès-Alès, Quissac and St-Privat-le-Vieux in the suburbs of Alès. The *caveau* at the latter also contains a tempting selection of locally produced pâtés, olives, preserved fruits and jams. The wines made here include red *vins de cépage* from Merlot and Cabernet Sauvignon as well as a Syrah rosé.

Coteaux du Pont du Gard

Just before its confluence with the Rhône, the River Gard is spanned by the most remarkable aqueduct in Europe, the Pont du Gard, a magnificent three-storey construction with tiers of elegant arches. It was built in 19BC by Agrippa, the son-in-law of Augustus, to divert water from the River Eure near Uzès across the Gard to the Roman city of Nîmes. It fell into disuse in the tenth century, and the structure was plundered for its stone, but in the nineteenth century it was restored by Napoleon III. It's an immensely popular site and the best way to see it, especially in the summer, is to rise early when the golden stone is lit by morning sunlight and before the convoys of coaches begin to arrive.

The bridge gives its name to a Vin de Pays, Coteaux du Pont du Gard, which is produced by a group of seven *cave co-opératives* vinifying the grapes from a total of 1,000 hectares of vines. There are also about ten independent growers. The co-operatives' *caveau* is near the stone village of Vers, close to the quarry from where the stones used to build the Pont du Gard were hewn.

Here a basic red wine is produced, blended from Grenache, Carignan and Syrah, a rosé using Grenache, Cinsaut and Carignan, and a white from Ugni Blanc, Clairette, Bourboulenc and Grenache Blanc. In addition, *vins de cépage* are made from Merlot, Chardonnay and Sauvignon Blanc.

A kilometre or so to the south-east, Castillon-du-Gard is built on a knoll, rising like a small island amid a sea of vines. The nearby town of Remoulins is famous for its cherries, and in the springtime a stunning display of blossom appears among the vineyards.

Coteaux de Salavès

The wine-growing area of this part of the Gard extends further up the valley of the Vidourle to the foothills of the Cevennes. The vineyards around the villages of St-Hippolyte-du-Fort, Durfort, Pompignan, Corconne and Quissac produce a Vin de Pays called Coteau de Salavès. Sadly, it would seem that this is another long-established name that is likely to disappear under the Vins de Pays de Cevennes banner as a number of *cave co-opératives* are beginning to change their labels.

The co-operative at St-Hippolyte-du-Fort appears to be resisting the temptation, however, and still makes a red Coteaux de Salavès blended from Merlot, Cabernet Sauvignon, Syrah and Grenache and a white using Ugni Blanc, Clairette and Sauvignon. They also produce a Cevennes red using 80 per cent Merlot and 20 per cent Grenache, as well as a pure Sauvignon Blanc.

Sables-du-Golfe-du-Lion

The most southerly vineyards of the Gard are planted in the bleak landscape of the Camargue, where only Vins de Pays are allowed with the name Sables de la Golfe du Lion. The vineyards planted here date back to the fourteenth century and are unique in France in that the vines were not grafted on to American root stock. It was unnecessary here, as it was found that phylloxera could not survive on the sandy terrain.

The area of production is around the medieval walled town of Aigues-Mortes and Stes-Maries-de-la-Mer, famous for its gypsy festival. It also extends westwards along the narrow coastal strip from the marina resorts of Le Grau-du-Roi and La Grande-Motte to Sète and Cap d'Agde in the *département* of Hérault.

The largest producer is Listel, but there are two smaller cave co-opératives based at Aigues-Mortes as well as a number of independent producers. The Cave

THE PYRENEES AND THE MAURY VALLEY SEEN FROM THE CHATEAU DE QUERIBUS.

des Remparts make a basic red wine from Cabernet Sauvignon and Carignan, and a Gris de Gris using Grenache Gris with a little Carignan and Merlot. A white wine is made from 100 per cent Ugni Blanc, as well as a Chardonnay sold as Vin de Pays d'Oc.

The Cave Sabledoc can be found a kilometre or so from Aigues-Mortes, along the road towards Stes-Maries-de-la-Mer. Here they make a varietal Chardonnay and Sauvignon Blanc together with the region's speciality, Gris de Gris, and a basic blended red wine called 'Rouge Rubis'.

One of the most highly-regarded independent producers of Vin des Sables is the Domaine du Petit Chaumont, with a vineyard of 114 hectares situated 3 kilometres from the sea between Aigues-Mortes and La Grande-Motte. Records have been discovered which mention the *domaine's* existence as early as the end of the thirteenth century.

In the past Gris de Gris was responsible for their main production, and it is still of great importance; it is made here from Syrah, Grenache, Cinsaut, Merlot and Carignan. They also make conventional rosé, from Cabernet Sauvignon, Merlot and Syrah, an excellent white wine, from a blend of 50 per cent Sauvignon with 25 per cent each of Chardonnay and Clairette, and a red wine from 50/50 Cabernet Sauvignon and Merlot.

HÉRAULT
THE WINES

THE AOC APPELLATIONS to which the département of Gard is entitled are: Muscat de Lunel – Muscat de Mirival – Muscat de Frontignan – Clairette du Languedoc – La Mejanelle – Cabrières – St-Christol – Vérargues – La Clape – Montpeyroux – Picpoul de Pinet – Pic St-Loup – Quatourze – St-Drézéry – St-Georges-d'Orques – St-Saturnin – Faugères – St-Chinian – Minervois – Muscat de St-Jean-de-Minervois. The Vins de Pays appellations are: Coteaux de Murviel – Cessenon – Haute Vallée de l'Orb – Coteaux du Salagou – Mont Baudile – Gorges de l'Hérault – Val de Montferrand – Berange – Collines de la Moure – Vicomte d'Aumelas – Côtes du Ceressou – Caux – Côtes de Thau – Côtes de Thongue – Ardaillhou – Coteaux du Libron – Coteaux d'Enserune – Coteaux de Fontcaude Côtes du Brian.

The grape varieties predominantly grown in the Hérault are Carignan, Cinsaut, Grenache Noir, Mourvèdre and Syrah for reds and rosés, and Bourboulenc, Clairette, Grenache Blanc, Marsanne, Picpoul, Vermentino and Roussanne for whites. Other varieties, such as Chardonnay, Sauvignon Blanc, Cabernet Sauvignon and Merlot are also being increasingly widely grown for the production of Vins de Pays.

THE VINEYARDS

The Route des Vins of the Coteaux du Languedoc can be followed by beginning in the wine village of St-Christol, about 20 kilometres north-east of Montpellier. From here it leads to St-Genies and Vérargues where the hillsides are quite densely cultivated with vines. A few kilometres to the east is the small town of Lunel which has its own appellation for a sweet white dessert wine made from Muscat Blanc à Petits Grains. As the Route des Vins turns north-west towards the wine villages of St-Drézéry and Fontanès the landscape begins to change, taking on a wilder and more rugged character with steep, rocky outcrops and the dense, wiry *maquis* dotted with pine trees.

Soon the large, distant, conical shape of the Pic St-Loup appears to the west. The road continues northward to the small villages of Valflaunès, Lauret and Claret, on the D 17, which now winds its way through dense pine forests. This is a tranquil place in which to stretch your legs or have a picnic lunch. Corconne, the most northerly point of this part of the wine route, is a little village of old stone houses set at the foot of two cliffs in a ravine.

From here follow the same road back to Valflaunès, where a small road, the D 1, branches off to wind around the dramatic Pic St-Loup. This countryside is full of colour; the steep, rocky hillsides are covered with *maquis*, wild flowers and herbs and shaded by pine trees; it is popular with the local people, who come here to walk, climb and picnic at the weekends. In the nearby village of Nôtre-Dame-de-Londres is a small twelfth-century château.

The Route des Vins now leads to St-Mathieu-de-Tréviers, Cazevieille and St-Jean-de-Cuculles, the latter teetering on a hilltop. The quiet road through this region weaves through steep, rocky hillsides with pine forests and there are frequent beautiful views, with the Pic St-Loup constantly dominating the landscape. It's worth visiting the little medieval village of Les Matelles; its ramparts, fortified gateways, narrow, steeply winding streets, archways and tunnels are all in miniature.

The next important wine village, some way to the west, is Montpeyroux, which produces well-respected VDQS reds and rosés, as does nearby St-Saturnin. An essential detour here is to the Gorges de l'Hérault and the medieval village of St-Guilhem-le-Désert. Although these gorges are not as deep and extensive as those of, say, the Verdon or the Tarn, they are nonetheless very impressive. You can climb down to the riverside quite easily in many places and enjoy the solitude surrounded by majestic rocks. St-Guilhem is built along a deep cleft in the side of the gorge, its tiny, narrow, stone houses with their brown-tiled roofs nestling under a massive rock looming high above. Nearby is the Grotte de Clamouse, where it is well worth stopping.

The most northerly area of the Coteaux du Languedoc vineyards lies in the beautiful hidden valley of the Buèges to the west of the River Hérault. The tiny walled village of St-Jean-de-Buèges is a gem. You can drive north up the D 4 from St-Guilhem to Brissac and then back along the Buèges valley through St-André, St-Jean and Pégairolles-de-Buèges and then continue over the heights of Mont St Baudille before descending to Arboras and back to Montpeyroux. About 10 kilometres or so to the south-east of Montpeyroux, on the *garrigue* to the east of the road between Aniane and Gignac, is the Mas de Daumas Gassac, a *domaine* which has become renowned for its fine red wine, a Vin de Pays de l'Hérault which now commands prices more in line with the excellent clarets with which it is frequently compared.

Coteaux du Salagou

Another worthwhile detour in this region is to the Lac du Salagou, where you can windsurf, sail and canoe; there are also camping facilities. The countryside on the western shore of the lake is planted with vines with their own Vin de Pays appellation, Coteaux du Salagou. Nearby is the Cirque de Mourèze, a place with strange dolomitic pinnacles which shelter a tiny village in the middle. There is also small *cave co-opérative* producing Coteaux du Salagou at Pégairolles de l'Escalette, to the north of Lodève. A very pretty small walled village, it is set amid dramatic scenery at the foot of the Causse du Lauzarc.

ABOVE: THE PONT DU GARD NEAR REMOULINS.
OPPOSITE TOP: VINEYARDS ABOVE THE VILLAGE OF CASSAGNES.
OPPOSITE BELOW: THE CANAL DU MIDI NEAR
THE WINE VILLAGE OF CAPESTANG.

ABOVE TOP: THE FISHING HARBOUR OF PORT VENDRES.
ABOVE: THE VILLAGE OF CARAMANY PERCHED ABOVE
THE VALLEY OF THE AGLY.
OPPOSITE: THE CHATEAU OF CASSAN NEAR ROUJAN.

with houses built of large, rough, white stones; the vineyards in this region are also covered with white, flinty stones, which at times create the illusion of a recent snowfall.

From here, the wine road continues through the villages of Agel and La Caunette towards Minerve, a village with a tragic history. During the Albigensian crusades, the inhabitants burnt themselves to death *en masse* rather than surrender to Simon de Montfort's forces. The Romanesque church at Minerve contains an altar dated 456 and supposed to be the oldest in France. There is an archaeological museum here and the remains of extensive medieval fortifications.

The route continues south to Azillanet, then west through Cesseras and Siran towards Caunes-Minervois. The vineyards here, in what is now a much flatter landscape, are very extensive and opportunities to stop and taste wine are frequent. The grottoes of Limousis are close by; they can be visited with a guide on Sundays and holidays only in the afternoons. The Minervois circuit is completed via the wine villages of Laure-Minervois, Rieux-Minervois (where there is an interesting octagonal church), Azille, Olonzac, Pouzols-Minervois, Argeliers – and back to Montouliers.

La Clape

The final part of this Route des Vins, which lies in the *département* of Clade, is concentrated in the Montagne de la Clape, a region very near the sea, between Narbonne and Narbonne-Plage. The Montagne de la Clape is a strange hump of a hill set on the flat coastal plain from which it rises quite dramatically. It is a quite curious landscape; on top it is rocky, rugged and even a little bleak, covered with *maquis* and dotted with pine trees. It has a rather remote and not-of-this-world atmosphere.

The circuit winds through Salles-d'Aude, Fleury, Gruissan, Armissan and Vinassan. There are some impressive views from the small road that leads to the village of Armissan, displaying the unusual nature of the landscape of la Clape. The wines here have an excellent reputation, particularly the white wine, with its dry but fruity character well suited to regional seafood dishes. The route is by the sea around Gruissan, an old circular fortified town which in fact stands on a lagoon, and there are lovely pine forests between the water and the mountain. Close by is the Château de Bouis, one of many places where you can taste and buy the local wines. A highly-regarded Vin de Pays is also made in this region, Côtes de Pérignan.

THE AUDE
THE WINES

THE AOC APPELLATIONS to which the Aude is entitled are: Minervois – Corbières – Fitou – Limoux. VDQS: Côtes de la Malapère – Côtes du Cabardèes et de l'Orbiel. Vins de Pays: Haute Vallée de l'Aude – Côtes de Prouille – Coteaux de Miramont – Hauts de Badens – Coteaux de Peyriac – Côtes de Lastours – Cité de Carcassonne – Vale de Dagne – Val d'Orbieu – Côtes de Pérignan – Coteaux de Narbonne – Val de Cesse – Hauterive en Pays de l'Aude – Côtes de Lézignan – Coteaux de la Cabrerisse – Coteaux du Termenès – Vallée du Paradis – Torgan – Cucugnan.

Corbières is the largest appellation in the *département* with a current production of over half a million hectolitres. This is made up of about 85 per cent red wine, 10 per cent rosé and just 5 per cent white. For red and rosé wines the varieties used are Grenache Noir, Cinsaut, Syrah, Mourvèdre, Carignan, Lladoner, Picpoul and Terret, while Grenache Blanc, Macabeau, Bourboulenc (Malvoisie), Terret, Picpoul, Rolle, Marsanne, Roussanne and Muscatel are used for white wines. In addition other varieties less typical of the region, such as Chardonnay, Sauvignon Blanc, Cabernet Sauvignon and Merlot, are used to make a Vins de Pays.

In 1948 the wines of Fitou became the first in the Languedoc region to be awarded their Appellation d'Origine Contrôlée. Today the Fitou vineyard extends to nearly 4,000 hectares in two separate areas, one beside the Mediterranean in the region of Leucate and the other about 30 kilometres to the west in the heart of the Corbière mountains between Paziols and Carcastel. Only red wine is entitled to the appellation, and it is produced from a blend of around 75 per cent Carignan and a balance of Grenache Noir and Lladoner, with Syrah, Macabeau, Cinsaut and Mourvèdre allowed to contribute no more than 10 per cent of the blend. The yield is limited to a maximum of 45 hectolitres per hectare and both carbonic maceration and traditional fermentation are used – the former for wines intended to be drunk young. AOC Fitou wines must be aged for at least nine months in the barrel.

Côtes du Cabardès et de l'Orbiel

This a VDQS appellation granted in 1973 to a designated area of vineyards to the north of Carcassone and west of the Minervois, in the hills bordering the valley of the River Orbiel. It covers about 40 communes and comprises a total of 2,200 hectares producing primarily red wine made from traditional Mediterranean grape varieties, although some south-western varieties are also permitted. A small amount of rosé is also produced. The Cabardès made by the co-operative at Pezens, for example, is made from 50 per cent Merlot, 35 per cent Grenache and 15 per cent Cabernet Sauvignon. The principal communes are Moussoulens, Villemoustaussou, Conques-sur-Orbiel and Pennautier.

Côtes de la Malapère

A VDQS appellation established in 1976, Côtes de la Malapère was the result of a bold experiment, initiated in the 1960s, to establish new grape varieties which could benefit from a climate which was influenced both by the Mediterranean and by the more moderate conditions of south-west France. The wines here, only red and rosé, are based mainly on a mixture of traditional Mediterranean varieties like Grenache and Syrah and a proportion of south-western varieties such as Merlot, Cabernet Sauvignon and Cabernet Franc. The vineyards are planted about 20 kilometres south-west of the Corbières in a region known as the Pays de Razès, a countryside of open undulating hills with meadows, woods and fields of grain.

Blanquette de Limoux

This wine claims to be the oldest sparkling wine in the world, with champagne just a young upstart by comparison. Produced in the upper valley of the Orb around the market town of Limoux, the wine owes its existence to the monks of the abbey of neighbouring Ste-Hilaire. The curious name of Blanquette, meaning white in the language of Oc, is attributed to the veil of fine white hairs which cover the undersides of the Mauzac vine leaves, the dominant variety from which the wine is made. The appellation, granted in 1938, covers 41 communes with

14,500 hectares of vines under cultivation. In addition to Blanquette, the appellation also covers Crémant, which has a higher percentage of Chenin and Chardonnay and is aged for longer in the bottle. Still white wines are also entitled to the AOC appellation and are made from the same three grape varieties but with Mauzac representing only 15 per cent of the blend.

In a region where the Appellation d'Origine Contrôlée decrees a single colour or type of wine there is often a Vin de Pays which fulfils the need for greater variety. Here the Vins de Pays de la Haute Vallée de l'Aude, also widely produced, provides an interesting range of alternative red and white wines made from a wider range of grape varieties.

THE VINEYARDS

The vineyards in the Aude are divided into 11 separate terrains, each with its own character and style of wine, and along with the AOC Corbières and Fitou wines there are a considerable number of Vins de Pays produced from within the same regions. Although some of these are similar, but inferior wines to the AOC product, many are quite different and compare well with those labelled AOC.

The Corbières vineyards are divided into a number of individual *terroirs* which also produce some very interesting Vins de Pays. The most southerly *terroir* is that of Queribus around the villages of Padern, Duilhac and Cucugnan, an ancient village strikingly situated on a rocky knoll in the valley of the River Verdouble, under the shadow of the ruins of the thirteenth-century Château de Peyrepertuse. The *cave co-opérative* of the village is the sole producer of wine from the surrounding vineyards. Only red wine is made here, with the Vin de Pays appellation of Cucugnan, from a blend of Carignan, Grenache and Syrah.

To the east of Cucugnan the River Verdouble enters the valley of the Torgan near the village of Padern, where the outline of another ruined castle shapes the skyline. Between Padern and Tuchan the road provides sweeping views over a wide, shallow valley which is filled with vineyards as far as the eye can see.

The *terroir* of Durban lies to the east where the Vins de Pays de Torgan are produced by the *cave co-opérative* in the village of Tuchan, at the foot of the 900-metre peak of the Montagne de Tauch. The neighbouring village of Paziols has a very progressive co-operative which has been selling direct to the public since 1946. Situated right in the south-eastern corner of the Aude, the co-operative has vineyards which fall within the Fitou and Rivesaltes appellations as well as the valley of the Torgan and Corbières.

The D 611 passes the hill-top castle of Aguilar on its way through a valley bordered by *garrigue*-covered hillsides to the village of Villeneuve-les-Corbières. This is the centre of production for the Vin de Pays de la Vallée du Paradis. From here an enjoyable scenic drive through the vineyards and *garrigue* can be made by following a quiet country road through the mountains to the villages of Embres-et-Castelmaure, St-Jean-de-Barrou and Fraissé-des-Corbières, where there is a restored thirteenth-century château.

From here the D 205 descends from the Col de Souil to Roquefort-des-Corbières on the coastal plain. This is the *terroir* of Sigean, and around the edges of the Etang de Bages and the villages of Sigean, Portel-des-Corbières, Leucate and Peyriac-de-Mer, is the production area for AOC Fitou and Vins de Pays des Coteaux du Littoral Audois. This wine is predominantly red and produced largely from the Carignan variety by a group of three *caves co-opératives*. One of them, based in Peyriac, has an especially good *caveau*.

A short distance to the south of Narbonne, the D 105 branches off the N 9 and leads through the vineyards planted around the edge of the lagoon. There is a succession of captivating views on the way to the villages of Bages and Peyriac-de-Mer. The little village of Bages is built on a rock overlooking the lake, and has a network of steep narrow streets rising up from a small quayside where fishing boats are pulled up on to the beach with their nets draped over rickety wooden causeways to dry.

The lake shore is a bird-watcher's paradise where all manner of water birds congregate along the water's edge, and large flocks of flamingos are a common sight. The small town of Peyriac has a quiet lakeside waterfront and a number of beaches which can be reached along a rough road. Although popular in the daytime during the summer months, the town has little hotel accommodation and has retained a quiet, unspoilt charm.

To the west of Villeneuve is the Terroir du Termenès, a road leads over the mountains through an attractive pocket of countryside to Quintillan and Palairac before descending into the gorges of the River Torgan and the village of Davejean, which has a twelfth-century church and fountain. To the north, amid spectacular scenery, are the remains of the castles of Termes and Durfort and the medieval village of Villerouge-Termenès, with a beautiful twelfth-century castle.

A medieval festival is held here in the summer to mark the death of the last of the Cathar zealots, Guilhem Bélibaste. He was burned at the stake in 1321 and his death signalled the end of the Cathar church. The celebrations held between July and September include a costume spectacular on Wednesdays and Sundays, a medieval banquet on Saturdays, and an exhibition which traces Guilhem's last days. The village has a *cave co-opérative* which produces the region's Vin de Pays, Coteaux du Termenès.

To the north of Villerouge is the *terroir* of St-Victor, where the landscape flattens out and becomes more open, with huge areas of vineyard reaching away towards the horizon. The small town of St-Laurent-de-la-Cabrerisse is the production centre for the local Vin de Pays, Coteaux de la Cabrerisse, as well as AOC Corbières, along with the villages of Montséret and Thézan-des-Corbières.

Nearby, at Château Caraguilhes, Coteaux de la Cabrerisse is also produced by an independent wine-maker with the label, 'Domaine de la Bouletière'. Here, Michèle and Lionel Favre use biological production methods to make red wines from 50 per cent Merlot with 25 per cent each of Carignan and Alicante, as well as a rosé produced from 50/50 Cinsaut and Carignan. A white from Bourboulenc and Carignan Blanc is also produced from time to time, but in limited quantities and not every year. Of the total of 128 hectares approximately one fifth is used to produce Vins de Pays. Château Caraguilhes dates from the sixteenth century, when it was a dependency of the Cistercian abbey of Fontfroide, a short drive to the east and surrounded by ravines. Close by is the thirteenth-century Château de Gaussan.

To the north of St-Laurent-de-la-Cabrerisse is the busy little market town of Lézignan-Corbières, the capital of the Corbières. Above the rooftops rises the imposing bell tower of a church which was constructed in the twelfth century on the site of an earlier Roman church. There is a large and varied collection of old wine-making equipment on display in the museum of wine at the Caves Saury-Serrès. The town's *cave co-opérative*, which was built in 1909 in a distinctly 'Belle Epoque' architectural style, contains an array of massive oak casks. It was the first co-operative to be established in the *département* of the Aude.

Further to the west along the valley of the Orbieu is the medieval walled village of Lagrasse, which was the capital of the Corbières until the middle of the nineteenth century. It has a web of narrow cobbled streets with many medieval houses as well as the fine fourteenth-century church of Saint-Michel. An ancient stone hump-backed bridge gives access to an abbey which was founded in the tenth century under Charlemagne. It is now occupied, and is being restored by a Byzantine Catholic order, but it can be visited. The village is known for its pottery market held during August and a more recently established leather market during July.

From Lagrasse the D 3 leads westwards through the gorges of the Alsou to a beautiful open valley patterned by vines and bordered by mountain slopes. Here, from the vineyards around the villages of Lagrasse, Serviès-en-Val, Montlaur and Monze, the Vin de Pays du Val de Dagne is produced. At Serviès-en-Val there is a seventeenth-century château with a lovely ochre façade flanked by towers and complemented by a terraced garden. The village has a small *caveau* in a cottage opposite the *cave co-opérative* named after Joseph Delteil, a well-known twentieth-century French writer from the region. A red Vin de Pays is produced here from Carignan and Merlot using carbonic maceration, and since 1992 a Chardonnay has been produced from a newly-planted vineyard of just 2 hectares. Nearby, the village of Villars-en-Val has an imposing château and a pretty eleventh-century church surrounded by cypress and olive trees. It is built on a terrace, from which there are sweeping views over the valley.

The city of Carcassonne, only a short distance from here, is perhaps Europe's most perfectly preserved fortified medieval town with a most unusual double circle of walls and elaborate entrance gates. Its present condition is largely due to the efforts of the architect Eugène Viollet-le-Duc, who restored the city in the mid-nineteenth century. The oldest parts date from Visigothic and Roman times.

A walk around the ramparts gives a strong impression of impregnability, although the city suffered badly at the hands of Simon de Montfort during the Albigensian crusades. Unfortunately, the medieval mood inside the old city is rather diminished by the presence of numerous souvenir shops selling suits of plastic armour and broad swords. Seen in the distance, on the other hand, from the vineyards which surround it, the city makes a much more atmospheric impression.

Vins de Pays de la Cité de Carcassonne is produced from the vineyards around a dozen or so villages which encircle the city: Trèbes, Villedubert, Pennautier, Montirat, Berriac, Palaja, Cazilhac, Cavanac, Couffoulens, Preixan and Rouffiac-d'Aude. A short distance to the north of Carcassone is the ancient village of Lastours, which is impressively sited beneath a monumental rock upon which stand the remains of four towers known as Caberet, Régine, Surdespine and Quéritinheux. They were built to protect the passage of valuable minerals mined in the neighbouring Montagnes Noir to the Mediterranean ports. Nearby are the fortified village of Conques-sur-Orbiel, the stalactite caverns of Limousis and the gorges of Clamoux. This is the production area for the VDQS Côtes du Cabardès et de l'Orbiel as well as the Vin de Pays Côtes de Lastours.

About 20 kilometres south-east of Lastours are the Minervois towns of Peyriac and Laure-Minervois; nearby, on the D 135, is the Château Gibalux, an ancient priory of the convent of Caunes-Minervois with a history dating back to the beginning of the twelfth century. Here Marie-Jean and Jean-Baptiste Bonnet produce AOC Minervois from a total of 50 hectares of vines and Coteaux de

Peyriac from 30 hectares. A varietal red Vin de Pays is made here from Merlot, as well as an oak-aged Chardonnay and one which is bottled directly from the vat.

A short distance to the south of Laure-Minervois is the little hill village of Badens overlooking the valley of the River Aude. The Vins de Pays des Hauts de Badens is one of the smallest appellations in the Aude, with just two independent producers. From the village of Badens you can see the Montagnes d'Alaric rising steeply beyond the opposite bank of the Aude valley. At the highest point of over 500 metres, the ruins of the château of Miramont can be reached from a road which leads up from the town of Barbaira.

The village of Routier, in the heart of the Pays de Razès, lies about 30 kilometres south-west of Carcassonne, and here the vineyards of the Côtes de Malapère are planted on the surrounding hills, mingling with woods, meadows and fields of grain. One of the main producers of this appellation is the Caves de Razès, a co-operative situated on the D 623. Routier has an attractive fifteenth-century château from which Michèle Lezaret produces Côtes de la Malapère from around 50 hectares of vines grown on the slopes around the village.

A few kilometres to the east of Routier is the tiny village of Malviès, with a château built at the end of the eighteenth century on the site of a Gallo-Roman settlement. Here, Mme Gourdou produces a fine oak-aged Côtes de la Malapère, with the label 'Cuvée Château Guilhem', from around 50 hectares of Merlot, Cabernet Franc and Cabernet Sauvignon.

The vineyards of Limoux begin only a short distance to the south-east of Routier and extend over a wide area, from St-Hilaire and Gardie, in the hills north-east of Limoux, south along the valley of the Aude to Quillan, close to the foothills of the Pyrenees. The fortified Benedictine monastery of Saint-Hilaire was founded in the eighth century, but the present building dates from the twelfth century and has a fine Gothic cloister which was built in the fifteenth. The hilly landscape on the western edge of the Corbières, around the villages of Pieusse, Puisse, St-Hilaire and Gardie, is particularly attractive and supports some of the most favoured vineyards.

PYRÉNÉES-ORIENTALES
THE WINES

THE GRAPE VINE flourishes in the warm climate of Roussillon and there is a long history of cultivation here: grains of vine pollen were found in the grottoes of Tautavel, where the first Europeans lived 500,000 years ago. The vineyards are often established on steep hillsides, where they are extensively terraced.

The vineyards have two regional Appellations d'Origine Contrôlée. Côtes de Roussillon, which includes red, rosé and white wines, covers the wide area from the coastal plain between the Etang de Salses and the mouth of the Tech to the valleys of the Agly, Tet and Tech. Côtes de Roussillon Villages is an appellation for red wine only, produced in the north of the *département*, between the valley of the Tet and the Corbières. The vineyards in the mountains to the south of the mouth of the River Tech have a separate appellation, Collioure. Vins Doux are a speciality of the Roussillon region and there are a number of separate appellations for these sweet fortified wines: Banyuls, Maury, Riversaltes and also Muscat de Rivesaltes.

In addition there are six Vins de Pays appellations: Pyrénées Orientales, which covers the whole *département*; Catalan, which includes the region to the south of Perpignan; Val d'Agly, which covers the upper valley of the Agly around

ABOVE TOP: THE MEDIEVAL WALLED VILLAGE OF MINERVE.
ABOVE: THE OLD VILLAGE OF PUECHABON.
OPPOSITE: VINEYARDS IN THE MOUNTAINS ABOVE THE VILLAGE OF BANYULS.

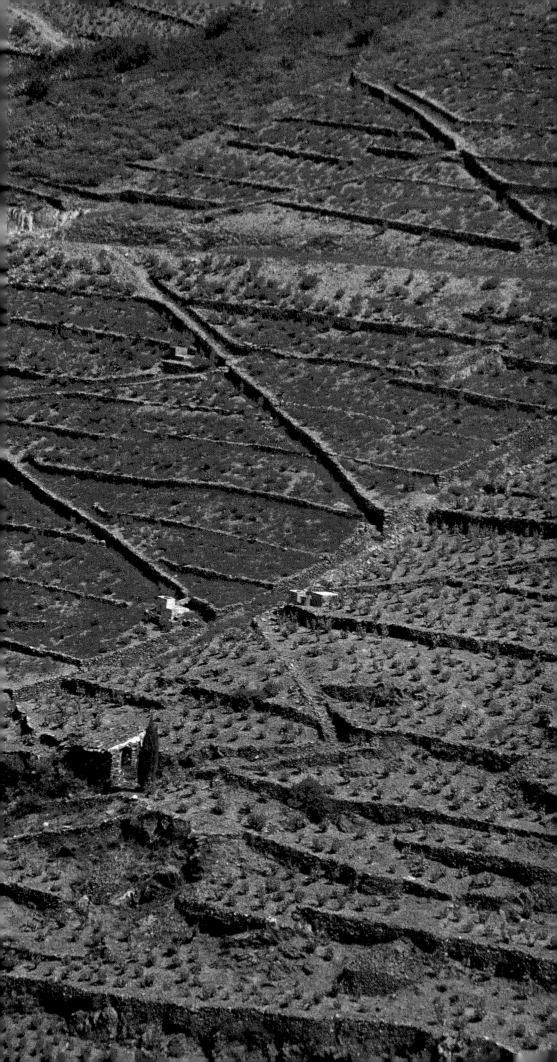

the villages of St-Paul-de-Fenouillet and Latour-de-France; Côtes Catalanes, which is granted to the villages in the lower valley of the Agly and the coastal plain to the north of Perpignan; Coteaux de Fenouillèdes, which encompasses the vineyards in the mountains to the south-west of St-Paul-de-Fenouillet. Côte Vermeille, an appellation which covers the area defined by the AOC of Collioure, is primarily red wine which is sold largely in bulk by co-operatives to *négociants* and local supermarkets.

The Vins de Pays are interesting here, since the appellation permits a far wider variety of grapes to be used than the more traditional restrictions of the AOC regulations allow – including Chardonnay, Chenançon, Cabernet Sauvignon and Merlot. White Appellation Contrôlée Côtes de Roussillon is a light, dry wine made chiefly from the Macabeo grape, with additions of Muscat and Grenache Blanc. AOC Collioure is a red wine made primarily from Mourvèdre, Grenache and Syrah.

Côtes de Roussillon Village consists of red and rosé wines made pre-dominantly from the Carignan grape to which other varieties, such as the Grenache Noir, Cinsaut and Syrah, are added according to the soil and location. The Vin Doux Naturel wines of Rivesaltes, Maury and Banyuls are produced mainly from Grenache Noir with additions of Grenache Gris and Blanc and small quantities of local varieties like Cinsaut, Carignan and Mourvèdre. A character-istic of these wines is the deliberate encouragement of oxidation to create the tawny, fruit-and-nutty flavour known as *rancio*. In addition the white Muscat de Rivesaltes is made from Muscat d'Alexandrie and Muscat Blanc à Petits Grains.

THE VINEYARDS

Ideally, the Route des Vins of Roussillon should be explored from a central base such as Perpignan; it is not really a circuit, but rather a series of excursions into different regions. On the inland parts of the route in the north, hotel accommodation is quite limited; however, you are never more than an hour or so away from the coast and its resort areas.

Perpignan is the capital of the *département* and the centre of the Roussillon wine industry. It is a city of wide, tree-lined boulevards, leafy squares, smart shops, stately old buildings and monuments and a lively social calendar. The Palace of the Kings of Majorca is a magnificent thirteenth-century building in the old centre of the city, the cathedral of Saint Jean is fourteenth-century, while the Rue des Mercaders contains many medieval houses. The Castillet, a crenallated fourteenth-century, red-brick fortress, houses the Casa Pairal, the Catalonian Museum of Popular Arts and Traditions; from its terrace there are fine views of the city, the sea and the mountains.

The first part of the Route des Vins explores the Aspres region. The small town of Thuir is the centre of this wine-producing area; it has the largest wine cellars in Europe. Beyond the pretty hilltop village of Camélas nearby, there is a tenth-century retreat hidden in the hillside. Also close by is Castelnou, a pic-turesque medieval village in a wonderful hilltop setting, surrounded by vine-yards, against a backdrop of mountains. There is a château and ramparts here dating from the tenth century, the thirteenth-century church of Sainte Marie, which has been restored, and a centre for arts and crafts, where exhibitions and concerts are held.

A number of small wine villages on the plain, including Banyuls-dels-Aspres, Trouillas, St-Genis-des-Fontaines (which has a ruined Benedictine abbey) and

Bages, all have *caves* where the local wines can be tasted. Continue towards the coast to Argelès, a lively fortified town with many ancient remains; it is also a busy summer resort with an extensive beach.

Along the valley of the River Tech is the busy town of Céret, where a fourteenth-century bridge, the Pont du Diable, spans the river, and there are old town gates and a fourteenth-century church. Céret's museum of modern art contains works by painters who have lived here, most notably Dufy, Picasso, Chagall, Gris, Braque and Matisse. The town is also known as the cherry capital of France, as its orchards produce the first fruit of the year, and there is a *sardane* festival here every August. At the nearby Château d'Aubiry you can taste and buy local wine.

The second section of the wine route is centred around Banyuls-sur-Mer. Although quite small, this region has a spectacularly varied landscape. The lure of the warm climate, sea, wines and food could tempt you to linger here. Collioure is the first town on this route. You approach it along a road that winds around the steep hillsides lining the coast. The vineyards here are planted precariously on the terraced slopes, some of which plunge straight down to the sea.

Collioure is a lovely town, one of the most attractive seaside villages on the Mediterranean. Henri Matisse and André Derain spent the summer of 1906 painting here, at the high point of their Fauvist collaboration. In spite of the obvious tourist appeal, Collioure has lost little of its charm or character. Be warned, however, that in July and August it can become very crowded. It has a tiny, turreted church overlooking a small shingle beach, which is populated by a small fleet of coloured fishing boats and café tables and chairs spilling over from the small cobbled promenade. High above the other side of the harbour is the majestic Château Royal, a former residence of the kings of Majorca.

The spectacular coast road continues winding its way round the hills to Port-Vendres, the ancient Port of Venus. Now a busy town with a bustling harbour and many sea-front cafés and restaurants, it has a large *cave* called the Cellier des Templiers. Continue along the coast to the small town of Banyuls-sur-Mer. Noisy and colourful, with a busy harbour, it has its own appellation for a highly regarded red Vin Doux Natural. In the town itself and along the roadside there are many opportunities to taste the wines. From here the Route des Vins continues, with views that constantly surprise and delight, to the town of Cerbère, almost on the Spanish border.

The Banyuls wine route follows the small roads that climb up into the mountains beyond the coastline; although they are signposted, they are quite easy to miss (the Michelin map 86 shows them clearly). The first is just before you reach Collioure; the second a kilometre or so south of Port-Vendres at the top of the hill, and the third starts in Banyuls, at the Grande Cave des Templiers: these roads all link up, however, so you only need to find one of them. Be prepared for some stunning scenery as you climb higher, both towards the sea and inland to the mountains. There are vineyards covering every useful piece of land, held up by dry-stone terraces, and there is a network of drainage ditches originally developed by the Knights Templars. Soon you will be deep into a landscape that seems far removed from the busy Mediterranean towns a few kilometres away. The air is full of bees, butterflies and birds, and when you drive along the tiny road, scarcely wider than a car, through the wild and remote landscape, you see only the vineyards and an occasional small barn or hut. Stop at the *table d'orientation* on the road between Port-Vendres and Banyuls; from here you have a panoramic view from Narbonne-Plage in the north to Cerbère and Spain in the south.

The road climbs higher still, to the tower of Madeloc. Unless you have nerves of steel, get out and walk at this point, as the road is nothing more than a track and is very steep and narrow, with tight hairpin bends and a sheer drop on one side. Another place of interest on the road between Collioure and Port-Vendres is Nôtre-Dame-de-Consolation where there is a seventeenth-century hermitage and chapel.

The most northerly section of the Route des Vins, around Salses, north of Perpignan, also has some scenic delights in store. It is not a neat circuit and the signposted route is convoluted, but the distances are not very great and it is perfect countryside in which to meander. Salses itself is an unremarkable wine village set between the Etang de Salses and the hills. However, its impressive fifteenth-century fortress, the Fort de Salses, is a fine example of military architecture, guarding the route Hannibal took in 218BC. Its pinkish stone and domed construction seem to belong more to the Sahara desert than to rural France.

Nearby Rivesaltes is the birthplace of Marshall Joffre and an important wine community with many *caves* for tasting. It is known particularly for its Vin Doux Naturel, Muscat de Rivesaltes. In the small town of Baixas are ruined ramparts, fortified gateways and many old buildings, including a Gothic church. I was walking through the village with my camera when I was accosted by a little old lady, apparently the custodian of the church, who insisted that I see inside it, and then tottered off for the key. Once inside she showed me, with great pride, the magnificent gilded baroque *retable* (altarpiece) which dates from the seventeenth century. At Espira de l'Agly, close by, there is another notable church with beautiful interior features, including twelfth-century furniture and carved wood reliefs.

At the village of Cases-de-Pène, with its Hermitage de Nôtre-Dame de Pène, a small road (the D 59) climbs out of the valley of the River Agly towards the small wine village of Tautavel. The road winds around the top of an escarpment and you can look down on the floor of the valley, far below, carpeted with neatly patterned vineyards. This route now becomes even more spectacular as you twist down through the gorge of the River Verdouble. Tautavel has a *cave co-opérative*, Les Maîtres Vignerons de Tautavel, and is known also for its museum of prehistory. Many important anthropological finds have been made in the area: the most famous is the skull of the Caune de l'Arago man, believed to be 500,000 years old. The wine road continues to the head of the valley, to Vingrau, a village surrounded by vineyards and mountains, and with a thirteenth-century Romanesque church at its centre.

Returning to the main road, the D 117, the next town is Estagel, the birthplace of Dominique François, the nineteenth-century astronomer and physicist, who is honoured with a monument in the square. There is an exhibition of Catalan history here. A very worthwhile short detour is to the Château de Quéribus, an imposing grey fortress set, quite improbably, on the ridge of the sheer, rugged mountain; it appears to be carved out of the rock. There is a narrow road, winding up to the castle, from which there are superb views over the valley of Maury and the distant Pyrenean peaks.

The Route des Vins continues through the village of Maury, known for its Vin Doux Naturel, to St-Paul-de-Fenouillet, the centre of this region. About 5 kilometres from the town are the Gorges de Galamus – vast, jagged clefts in the rock, surrounded by sheer cliffs and chasms, while the silvery thread of a river is visible way below. In the summer there is a *caveau* at the entrance to the gorges, and you can visit the tiny hermitage of St Antoine de Galamus, tucked into the side of the gorge about half-way down.

From St Paul-de-Fenouillet, follow the wine road into the mountains to the south, along a small scenic route through the villages of St-Martin-de-Fenouillet, Ansignan and Sournia to the wine village of Caramany. There is a Roman aqueduct-viaduct near Ansignan which is still in use, carrying water to the vineyards in the valley, and the tunnel bridge below it allows people to cross the small river.

Caramany is curiously situated, its small red-tiled houses stacked up like a house of cards. The route continues through remote countryside, where the tranquil atmosphere is disturbed occasionally by quail and partridges fluttering across the road. Montalba-le-Château is a beautiful village perched on top of the mountain, surrounded by vineyards, with views of the distant often snow-capped Pyrenean peaks in the background; there is a wine museum in the small château here. This part of the route is completed by returning to the coastal plain via the villages of Bélesta, Cassagnes, Latour-de-France, with its AOC Côtes de Roussillon Villages, Montner, with the nearby chapel of Forca Réal, and Corneilla-la-Rivière.

THE CUISINE

Perhaps the best-known dish of the Languedoc region is *cassoulet*, named after the covered dish in which it is cooked, the *cassolle*. It is a very rich combination of meats such as lamb, duck or goose *confits*, pork or bacon and sausages, baked with onions, garlic and tomatoes and white beans. Then there are the famous Toulouse sausages, *anchoide* (anchovy paste) from Nîmes, game and pâtés and the famous *petit pâtés de Pézenas*, small raised pies made with sweetened and spiced minced lamb. Fresh and saltwater fish are found in abundance, but the people of Languedoc are still fond of dried salt cod; in *morue à la minervoise* it is cooked with the red Minervois wine, onions, olive oil, garlic, anchovies and olives. *Pelardon* is a favourite goat's-milk cheese of the region; it is sold in small discs and has a soft texture and a delicate nutty flavour.

Roussillon cuisine includes specialities such as *sanglier de Fenouillèdes*, a wild boar stew, *perdreau à la catalane*, wild partridge cooked in the Catalan style with onions, tomatoes and peppers, and *bolas de Picolat*, meatballs flavoured with garlic, green olives and parsley. The anchovies of Collioure are also a regional delicacy and are often served as a first course, as part of a *salade composée*. In the rich, fertile plains of Roussillon, many varieties of fruit – apricots, cherries, strawberries, lemons and peaches – are ripe much earlier than in other parts of France. A local temptation for the sweet-toothed is *touron*, a confection made from candied fruits, pistachio nuts, hazelnuts and almonds.

RHÔNE-ALPES

THE REGION OF Rhône-Alpes encompasses eight *départements*: Loire, Rhône, Ain, Haute-Savoie, Savoie, Isère, Drôme and Ardèche. The region extends from the Massif Central in the west to the borders of Italy and Switzerland in the east. As its name suggests, the region is dominated by two main topographical features, the River Rhône, which flows southwards in the west, and the massive range of high Alps in the east. Between these two extremes of wide river valley and snow-capped peaks there is an enormous variety of landscape, industry and agriculture, but the cultivation of the vine is a common factor throughout.

LOIRE
Cotes du Forez

BETWEEN THE MONTS du Forez and the wide valley of the Loire a range of hills harbours the most southerly of the Loire vineyards, the VDQS Côtes du Forez. They lie at altitudes ranging from 400 to 550 metres above sea level between the small town of Boën in the north and Montbrison, 17 kilometres to the south.

THE WINES

The production of Côtes du Forez is almost exclusively from the co-operative near the village of Trelins, just to the south of Boën. Before phylloxera there were more than 5,000 hectares of vines planted on the hillsides, but now there are

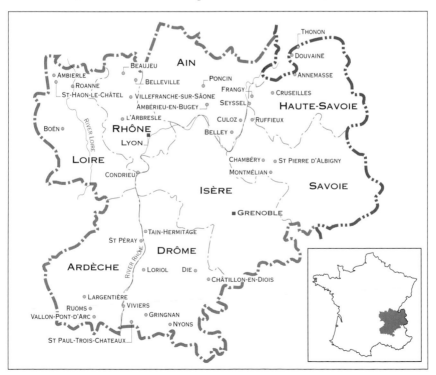

ABOVE TOP: A FARMHOUSE NEAR THE VILLAGE OF RUFFIEUX.
ABOVE: HARVESTING GRAPES NEAR THE VILLAGE OF VAUX-EN-BEAUJOLAIS.
OPPOSITE: THE VINEYARDS OF THE COTE ROTIE ABOVE THE VILLAGE OF CONDRIEU.

just 200 hectares divided between 21 communes, which produce in the region of 8,000 hectolitres each year.

Only red and rosé wines are produced here, solely from Gamay, the variety of the Beaujolais region which lies only 60 kilometres or so to the north-east. The Côtes du Forez was granted VDQS status in 1956 and the co-operative was established six years later. It now has over 200 hundred members, of whom only a few make a living exclusively from their vines. It is a very fertile region and the valley floor, if not pasture land, is planted with orchards and cereal crops.

Five grades of wines are produced: a red Primeur, which is on sale from 1 December; 'Cuvée Traditionelle', which is made as red, rosé *sec* and rosé *demi-sec*; a special *cuvée* made with the grapes from vines grown on volcanic soil and named after a different selected writer each year; 'Cuvée Prestige', which is made with grapes from the oldest vines; and 'Cuvée Pierre Dellenbach', which is produced from one particular vineyard on especially favoured terrain and vinified separately.

The co-operative also makes a red Vin de Pays d'Urfé, from Gamay vines grown outside the delimited areas for the Côtes du Forez, and a small quantity of white Vin de Pays is also produced from relatively recent plantings of Chardonnay.

THE VINEYARDS

The principal wine villages are Trelins – with the sixteenth-century Château de Goutelas nearby – Marcoux, Marcilly – where there is a thirteenth-century château perched on a hill above the vineyards, Pralong and Champdieu, a pretty walled village with ramparts, gateways and a fourteenth-century fortified church.

A tour of some of the most scenic parts of the Monts du Forez can be made by following the D 946 south-west from Montbrison to St-Anthème, where the D 139 leads north to the Col des Supeyres. From here the road descends again to Ambert, famous for its blue cheese, Fourme d'Ambert. En route you pass the ancient mill of Moulin Richard de Bas where you can still see paper being made.

An alternative, or additional, scenic route involves taking the D 44 north from Verrières-en-Forez, which lies about halfway between Montbrison and St-Anthème. This quiet road leads through a succession of attractive valleys and hillsides to St-Bonnet-de-Courreau, from where there are stunning views over the Forez landscape, before descending either to Marcoux or Pralong.

From Ambert you can follow the River Dore downstream to Vertolaye, where the D 268 and D 40 lead eastwards through splended scenery over the Col du Béal to the old village of Chalmazel; here you can see the impressive Château des Talru-Marcilly, which dates from the thirteenth century.

From here, the route descends into the valley of the Couzan, where the remains of another ruined château can be seen on a pinnacle of rock over 600 metres high, before returning to Boën. A few kilometres south-east of Boën is the Bastie d'Urfé, a medieval castle which was rebuilt in the sixteenth century in the Italian Renaissance style.

Côtes Roannaises

The vineyards of the Côtes Roannaises extend along the foothills of the Monts de la Madeleine from the left bank of the Loire at Villerest and St-Maurice to Chagny, about 20 kilometres to the north-west. Like many French vineyards, these were first established by the monasteries during the Middle Ages, and between the thirteenth and sixteenth centuries they continued to expand vigorously with the navigable Loire providing a ready means of transport to Paris.

THE WINES

Today there are around 130 hectares of vines distributed between 24 communes, but unlike the Côtes du Forez all of the wines are produced by individual growers and there is no *cave co-opérative*. Red and rosé wines are produced exclusively from a variety of Gamay, which is known here as St Romain à Jus Blanc. A small quantity of white wine is also produced from Chardonnay with the appellation Vin de Pays d'Urfé.

THE VINEYARDS

The leading wine villages are St-Maurice-sur-Loire, Villerest, Villemontais, St-André-d'Apchon, Renaison, St-Haon-le-Châtel, St-Haon-le-Vieux and Ambierle.

I visited Robert Chaucesse, whose vineyards high on the slopes above the village of Renaison have been in his family since the beginning of the seventeenth century. It is one of the oldest *domaines* of the region. In addition to his award-winning red and rosé Côtes Roannaises, M. Chaucesse also makes a Vin de Pays d'Urfé from a small plot of Chardonnay.

The village of St-Haon-le-Châtel still retains part of its ramparts, a fortified gateway and number of fine old houses. There is a *caveau* here where the Côtes Roannaises wines can be tasted and bought. At Ambierle, a short distance to the north, there is a fine Gothic church with a beautiful multicoloured roof of mosaic tiles, and a museum of folk art and local traditions.

The tiny walled village of Le Crozet, a little further to the north, was the property of the viscounts of Macon in the tenth century and became the domain of the counts of Forez in the thirteenth century when it was fortified. Entered by a gateway flanked by towers, it has narrow winding streets and numerous old houses, one of which has been made into a museum of local history. The town hall is situated in the fifteenth-century Maison du Connétable, a beautiful timber-fronted building with arcades which was in earlier centuries the shoe-makers' hall.

The best of the Monts de la Madeleine countryside can be explored by following the quiet country roads which link the villages of Le Crozet, Arfeuilles, Châtel-Montagne, Le Mayet-de-Montagne, St-Nicholas-des-Biefs, St-André-d'Apchon, Renaison and St-Haon-le-Châtel. The road from St-André-d'Apchon towards Arcon has some especially fine views over the Roannais countryside and the valley of the Loire. Beyond Arcon is the curious outcrop known as the Rocher de Rochefort, from where there are stunning views over the Rouchain valley.

To the south-west of the Côtes Roannaises is the Pays d'Urfé, from which the local Vin de Pays takes its name. A few kilometres south-east of St-Just-en-Cheval are the remains of the Chauteau d'Urfé. It takes about half an hour to walk up to the site, but on a clear day you can see the Alps. A short distance to the west, set on a hill, is the charming walled village of Cervières, which retains some of its ramparts, a number of fine old Renaissance houses and a church dating from the fifteenth century.

RHÔNE

THE GREAT CITY of Lyons, set at the confluence of the Saône and Rhône, is the capital of the *département* of Rhône; to many it is also the gastronomic capital of France. It is said that three rivers run through Lyons – the third being Beaujolais, perhaps the most famous wine in the world after champagne.

Beaujolais

Beaujolais is such a perfect name for a wine, suggesting ruddy-cheeked joviality and a hearty lust for life, that it might have been thought up by a poetic advertising executive. In fact, the name is derived from the town of Beaujeu, which lies in the heart of the countryside to the west of the *Autoroute du Soleil* near Villefranche. The landscape is almost alpine in character, with miniature, rounded mountains jostling together, while the country roads wind and climb through them, offering stunning vistas at every turn.

Protected by the foothills of the Massif Central to the west, the Beaujolais has a mild climate which is ideal for the cultivation of wines, although the mountainous nature of the landscape tends to encourage sudden storms and hail. It is quite a large area, extending from just south of Macon to the outskirts of Lyons, and produces a considerable volume of wine – over 11 million cases annually.

THE WINES

The most important vineyards are situated to the north of Villefranche, where the ten great wine villages of Beaujolais are grouped. In addition to the Crus, much of the Beaujolais-Villages wine is also produced from these vineyards. The less geographically favoured communes further south are largely responsible for the production of the basic, unnamed Beaujolais. Essentially, Beaujolais is a red wine produced from the Gamay grape, and is best drunk young; it is often served slightly chilled. There is also a rosé from the same grape and a white Beaujolais made from the Chardonnay grape. There are five basic types of red Beaujolais. The most common is known simply as Beaujolais; Beaujolais Supérieur merely denotes a higher alcohol content: 10 per cent instead of 9.

Beaujolais-Villages is an appellation given to about forty villages in the northern sector of the area and is generally of superior quality to the basic Beaujolais. Recently Beaujolais Nouveau has become something of a major event in the wine calendar: fermentation is specially controlled so the wine can be bottled and sold – amid great publicity – before the end of November. The most prestigious Beaujolais wines are those bearing the name of one of the ten communes: Saint-Armour, Juliénas, Chénas, Moulin-à-Vent, Fleurie, Chiroubles, Morgon, Brouilly, Côte de Brouilly and Régnié.

THE VINEYARDS

The Route du Beaujolais is signposted in a somewhat random fashion, and as you travel the maze of tiny roads you can easily be led into circles of confusion. But it is a very agreeable way of becoming confused, and the distances between the villages are small enough for it not to matter if you become temporarily lost. If you pinpoint exactly where you want to go with the aid of the Michelin map, you can then follow the local signposts to each place. This is very much a region through which you should meander slowly to appreciate it fully.

It is best to start the Route des Vins at the village of Crêches, near where the autoroute crosses the N 6, virtually on the border of the Mâconnais and Beaujolais. The division between the two regions is a little blurred here. But look at the vines and you'll know that you are in true Beaujolais country: the tall, gangly vines of the Pinot Chardonnay, from which the white Mâcon wines are made, have given way to the knee-high Gamay vines. Although in other regions the Gamay sometimes produces inferior wines, it is ideally suited to the soil and climate conditions found here.

St-Amour-Bellevue is the first village on the wine route. It has a *cave*, called the Caveau du Cru St-Amour, where you can taste and buy the local wines. From here the wine route leads through a succession of the Cruis wine villages. By and large, they are unremarkable, neither particularly quaint nor picturesque; however, they do have a certain quiet, rural charm and are situated in beautiful settings. They also provide countless opportunities to sample the wines.

In Juliénas, one of the local *caves* is in a deconsecrated fifteenth-century church; the other, just outside the village, is in the Château du Bois de la Salle, headquarters of the local wine co-operative. At the wine-tasting centre in Chénas, the Cellier de Chénas, there is a sculpture by Renoir depicting workers cutting down a forest of oak trees in readiness for planting the vines. There is scarcely an oak tree to be seen here now. Moulin-à-Vent, where one of the greatest Beaujolais wines is produced, has its tasting cellar close to the vaneless windmill after which the town is named and which is a famous symbol of Beaujolais. In Fleurie there is a fine restaurant, L'Auberge du Cep, serving local food, as well as an excellent *cave co-opérative*.

Of the ten Crus villages, Chiroubles occupies the highest ground, and its vineyards reach to an altitude of over 400 metres. If you climb – or drive – up this hill, past the vineyards, to its summit, you can sample the wines at the tasting centre and eat the regional specialities in the restaurant while enjoying a panorama over the Haut-Beaujolais. The cellars of Villié-Morgon, to the south, are also well worth visiting. Here the tasting is done in the huge vaulted rooms of a fifteenth-century château.

Brouilly, south of the D 37, boasts two wine châteaux – Château de la Chaize and Château de Pierreux – and two Crus: Brouilly is made in six different villages, while Côte de Brouilly comes from the vines that grow on the sunny southern slopes of Mont Brouilly. On the first Sunday in September a procession winds its way up the mountain to the small chapel of Nôtre-Dame du Raisin on the summit, where they pray for a successful harvest.

Between Chiroubles and Brouilly you can make a detour via the Col du Truges and the Col du Fût to Beaujeu. The route is one of the most spectacular in the Beaujolais, with narrow tracks winding along the hillsides by steep plunging valleys, at times reminiscent of the roads of Austria and Switzerland. Further south, beyond Brouilly, is Vaux-en-Beaujolais, the village where Gabriel Chevalier set his novel *Clochemerle*. An *auberge* and a tasting cellar honour the connection.

The charms of the Beaujolais region are not limited to the northerly vineyards and the famous ten Cru villages. The region to the south of Villefranche mainly produces ordinary Beaujolais; but it has much else to offer the traveller. There is a signposted route, called the Route des Pierres Dorées, which leads through beautiful unspoilt countryside to a succession of enchanting golden-stone villages. It begins at Limas, a small suburb of Villefranche. From here the D 70 climbs up along the ridge of a hill towards the village of Charnay; there are wide, sweeping views to the east over the Saône and north towards Beaujeu. A little further along is Belmont, which in spring and summer is always bedecked with flowers. These villages look very different from those of the more affluent communes not many kilometres north. There are plenty of places along the route where you can stop to taste and buy the simple wines produced here by an apparently limitless number of individual growers.

Châtillon, Chessy and Bagnols, three more small villages, are quiet, unspoilt and apparently completely unaware of their charm – always an endearing quality, making them worth a detour. The road north from Le Bois-d'Oingt towards Oingt is another route with beautiful views of the diverse landscape. Oingt is walled and has narrow cobbled streets and honey-coloured houses; there are a number of craft workshops in the streets, a wine-tasting cellar, an old tower and a terrace beside the church with fine views of the surrounding countryside. More obviously 'picturesque' than many of the other villages, it is also rather more self-conscious. Another detour will take you a short distance to the north-west of Oingt to the medieval hill village of Ternand, set amid a sea of vines.

Coteaux du Lyonnais

The vineyards of the Coteaux du Lyonnais lie between those of Beaujolais and the Côte Rôtie in the hills between the valley of the Gier and the Monts du Lyonnais. Vines have been planted here for more than 25 centuries, before the Roman occupation, and in the late eighteenth century there were over 13,500 hectares under cultivation. Today the production area is very much smaller with under 250 hectares of vines, less then just one of the Beaujolais Crus. The general style of wines and the grape varieties, however, are similar, with Gamay used for red wine, which is by far the greatest output, and Chardonnay and Aligoté for white.

The co-operative in the small town of San Bel, created in 1956, is the largest single producer, making 7,500 hectolitres of red wine and just 300 of white. They also produce some Beaujolais from vineyards within the boundaries of the appellation. There are a number of individual producers with vineyards in quite small, fragmented parcels, scattered between the communes of L'Arbresle, St-Genis-Laval, Givors, Mornat, Limonest and Vaugneray.

Côte Rôtie

Running south from Lyons – between the Savoie Alps to the east and the Massif Central to the west – towards the sprawling estuary beyond Avignon where it spills into the Mediterranean, the powerful Rhône traverses a wide variety of landscape, from ruggedly dramatic, steep-sided valleys to flatter pastoral farm and meadowland. For over 200 kilometres the banks of the Rhône are lined with vineyards, some teetering on precarious terraces high above the river, others spread flat and wide as far as the eye can see.

Just 30 kilometres south of Lyons is Vienne, the starting point for the wine tour down the Rhône. The main wine road is the N 86, which follows the course of the river for about 70 kilometres. The first village on the Route des Vins is Ampuis, which produces the rare Côte Rôtie, a full-bodied, deep red wine that benefits considerably from ageing. The hillsides here rise sharply from the river, almost like cliffs, and the vines are grown on narrow terraces, many of which date from Roman times. Ampuis itself was founded in 600 BC by the Phoenicians.

The Syrah grapes grown on these steep slopes which face south-west, are bathed in sunshine all day long, hence the name Côte Rôtie (literally, 'roasted slope'). A tiny road, the D 615, twists its way up the hillside behind the village and from it you get an excellent view over the terraced slopes to the Rhône.

The slopes are divided into La Côte Brune and La Côte Blonde, names which are more likely to be derived from the different coloured soils than from the often-quoted romantic legend of two maidens, one with flaxen hair, the other with dark. Although the red wines of this region are almost exclusively made from Syrah, a small percentage of Viognier is allowed in Côte Rôtie.

Condrieu & Chateau-Grillet

The wines produced in the next two villages, Condrieu and Château-Grillet, in contrast, are heavily scented whites made from the Viognier grape. They are produced in relatively small quantities, Château-Grillet particularly so as it is one of the smallest appellation areas in France, with only about 3 hectares of vineyards. The reputation and cost of Château-Grillet consequently depend as much on its rarity as on its character and quality. The vineyards rise in steep terraces behind the village of Vérin, and Château Grillet, a relatively unassuming building, looks out over them towards the fast-flowing Rhône.

HAUTE-SAVOIE
THE WINES

THE WINES OF the Haute-Savoie are almost exclusively white, with the Chasselas being the dominant grape variety for the AOC wines. However, Chardonnay is widely grown for Vins de Pays, and in the valley of the Arve white wines are produced from Gringet, a very interesting aromatic variety not found elsewhere in France and originally introduced from Cyprus in the thirteenth century. The appellations to which the *département* is entitled are AOC Crépy, AOC Savoie (with the Crus of Marignan, Ripaille and Ayze) and Vins de Pays d'Allobrogie.

THE VINEYARDS

The principal vineyards of the Haute-Savoie are to be found on the southern shore of Lake Geneva. The largest are those of the appellation of Crépy, with about 90 hectares of vines under cultivation by six *vignerons* around the villages of Douvaine, Loisin and Ballaison. The vineyard can be traced back to the fourteenth century, when it was established by the monks of the Abbey of Nôtre-Dame de Filly. Their methods of vinification are still used today, and the wines have a good reputation for improving with age.

One of the prettiest medieval villages in France, Yvoire, lies only a few kilometres to the north of Douvaine on the very edge of the lake. Its ramparts, fortified gateways, cobbled streets, ancient houses and a château rising up from the water are not to be missed.

For the Cru of Marignan, there are just 12 hectares of vines shared between two producers near the village of the same name which lies between Thonon-les-Bains and Douvain. One, M. Canelli-Suchet, is based at the Tour de Marignan, where there are fascinating ancient cellars in a fortified house dating back to the eleventh century. The Château of Ripaille, a magnificent fifteenth-century building on the eastern outskirts of Thonon-les-Bains, has vineyards reaching down to the lake shore and produce a highly acclaimed white wine from a vineyard of 21 hectares.

The Cru of Marin has vineyards of around 24 hectares in total, planted high on the hillsides overlooking the lake near the village of Marin, between Thonon and Evian-les-Bains. The wines are sold mainly to *négociants*, and there are only two producers who market their own wines. In addition to his 6 hectares of Chasselas M. Delalux also has a new planting of 2 hectares of Gamay from which he makes a small quantity of red wine.

Not far from the shores of Lake Geneva are the vineyards with the Cru of Ayze, these are to be found around the villages of Ayze and Marignier, which lie in the valley of the Arve near the town of Bonneville, between Geneva and Mont

ABOVE: THE VILLAGE OF MYONS BELOW THE TOWERING MASS OF
MONT GRANIER.
OPPOSITE TOP: A WINTER'S VIEW OF MONT GRANIER.
OPPOSITE BELOW: THE ABBEY OF HAUTCOMBE ON THE SHORES OF
LAC DU BOURGET.

Blanc. The vines are planted high up on a steep-sided valley at the foot of Le Môle. There are a total of 48 hectares, with six producers making a living from wine alone. Most of the production goes to local hotels and individuals who track the wine down after having tasted it in a restaurant. The unusual grape variety of Gringet grown here produces a white wine with a very aromatic bouquet reminiscent of jasmin; a *méthode champenoise* version is also produced.

Vins de Pays d'Allobrogie is produced by a single *vigneron* from Chardonnay vines near Contamine-sur-Arve lower down the valley, and another at the village of Fechy just to the south of Cruseilles on the steep slope of the Usses valley in view of the impressive Ponts de Caille which span it. Before phylloxera there were nearly 100 hectares of vines planted around the village but, apart from a few family plots, they had disappeared until 1976 when Jean-François Humbert planted 3 hectares of vines. His white wines consist of a pure Chardonnay and another with 90 per cent Chasselas and 10 per cent Chardonnay, while a red is produced from a blend of 70 per cent Gamay and 30 per cent Pinot Noir. This is just one more example of how many of the lost wine regions of France are gradually being restored, thanks to the effort and enthusiasm of one or two people.

SAVOIE
THE VINEYARDS

THE SAVOIE WINE route is not a true circuit, although if you use either Aix-les-Bains or Chambéry as a base you can make two separate circuits taking in the entire route. Most of the route I suggest is signposted; it goes from north to south with the town of Frangy (which is close to exit 11 on the A 40 autoroute) as the starting point. Frangy is a lively small town astride the N 508 in the valley of the River Usses, and is known for its appellation Roussette de Savoie. Take the small D 310 road out of the town towards the hamlet of Designy (this part of the route is not signposted). The quiet country lane leads through a peaceful, hilly landscape of vineyards and cornfields, woods and meadows. From here continue along the D 31 to Clermont, a village set on the hillside with views towards the Alps, where you can visit the large thirteenth-century château.

The route now continues along the D 57 through Droisy and then descends into the valley of the Rhône. The next stop is the little town of Seyssel, which is bisected by the river and famed for its Roussette de Savoie; it received its appellation in 1930 – late recognition for a town mentioned in eleventh-century records for its wine growing. *Méthode champenoise* white wine is also made here from Altesse (or Roussette) and Molette grapes.

Leaving Seyssel, the wine road continues beside the Rhône along the D 981 for a few kilometres until it meets the D 56, a small road that climbs up away from the river through vineyards towards the wine village of Motz. Continue through the hamlet of Chevigny to Ruffieux, where there is a *cave co-opérative* run by the Chautagne producers; there is another one in the neighbouring village, Serrières-en-Chautagne, beside the main road. Detour a little from Ruffieux up a narrow winding road to the summit of Mont Clergeon, where you can look out over the Rhône valley from the peaceful alpine meadows; just beyond the summit there are wonderful views of the snow-capped Alps to the east.

The next village, Chindrieux, is another commune within the Chautagne appellation; it is immediately to the north of the Lac du Bourget, in marsh-like terrain with brooks, slender trees and reed beds. The Route des Vins now follows the course of the Canal de Savières to Portout, a little village on the canal's bank.

Leave the wine route here and follow the D 914, which winds round the side of the mountain above the lake: you will be rewarded with frequent dramatic glimpses, through dense woods, of the blue-green lake far below.

From the terrace of the café high in the hills you can see the lake and the Abbaye de Hautecombe far below on its shore: you can reach the abbey via a small road. It was built in the twelfth century by Cluniac monks but was heavily restored in the eighteenth and nineteenth centuries, in a somewhat extravagant style. The lakeside road now joins the main road. Turn off for the Col du Chat and begin to retrace your path along the wine route to the north of the lake. When you reach the top of the Col du Chat, the Route des Vins follows a small road, the D 210, leading off to the right to the wine villages of Monthoux and Billième. The small villages here are quiet and undistinguished but have a rugged charm, the crumbling stone walls of the ancient houses and farms contrasting strangely with the gleaming stacks of shrink-wrapped, virgin wine bottles awaiting use. The vineyards cling to the steep hillsides, and there are frequent signs along the road, particularly in Billième, inviting you to stop and sample the local wines. The road descends now to the valley floor towards Lucey and the meadows of maize (which is used as cattle feed).

The Route des Vins continues along by the river on the D 921 to Chanaz. Like its neighbour, Portout, it is situated beside the Canal de Savières and has a number of waterside restaurants and cafés. Take the main road, the D 991, along the eastern shore of the Lac du Bourget to the small but important wine-growing community around Brison-St-Innocent. The village is, in fact, a residential suburb of Aix-les-Bains and the vineyards are cultivated between the gardens of the smart villas: the local climate is ideal.

There are no vineyards of significance now until you reach those south of Chambéry; to get there it is easiest to take the N 201 into the centre of the town. It would be a pity, however, not to linger a while in the elegant resort of Aix-les-Bains. It has a long tree-lined lakeside promenade with cafés and restaurants. All the usual seaside facilities are available here, from sunbathing on the beach to windsurfing, swimming and boating, and the modern thermal centre is renowned for the treatment of rheumatism and sciatica.

Jean-Jacques Rousseau lived at Chambéry for a while, and you can visit Les Charmettes, the house he stayed in and described in his *Confessions*; it is set in a quiet wooded hillside on the edge of the town. The wine route is signposted again from the suburb of Barberaz along the D 201, a quiet road which leads through the wine villages that nestle below the peak of Mont Granier. The two appellations in this region are the white wines of Apremont and Abymes; the five communes of St-Badolph, Les Marches, Myans, Apremont and Chapareillan are the centres of production. There are many places where you can taste and buy the local wines, and visitors are welcomed at the *caves*.

The appeal of these wine villages, small, rather haphazard collections of old stone houses and farms criss-crossed by narrow streets, lies mainly in the wines they make and their beautiful mountain settings: it is worth taking one of the many roads that climb up into the vineyards above the villages, from where there are rewarding views of the distant valley of the Isère and the mountains beyond.

To enjoy the mountain scenery to the full you should also visit the top of the very dramatic Col du Granier. You get to it via a narrow road that literally hugs its way around the side of the mountain providing a constant display of staggering views over the sheer side to the valley below and distant Chambéry.

ABOVE TOP: THE WALLED VILLAGE OF LARGENTIERE IN THE ARDECHE.
ABOVE: HARVESTING GRAPES IN THE VINEYARDS OF ST JOSEPH.
OPPOSITE: VINEYARDS ON THE SLOPES NEAR THE VILLAGE OF ST PIERRE D'ALBIGNY.

From Les Marches the Route des Vins crosses the A 41 autoroute and the main road, N 90 to the town of Montmélian. There is a large *cave co-opérative* here where you can taste and buy a variety of Savoie wines, including red wine from Mondeuse. The next stops are the wine villages of Arbin and Cruet, known for their red Mondeuse. The road follows the Isère valley, climbing higher as it nears the villages of St-Jean-de-la-Porte, St-Pierre-d'Albigny, Miolans and Fréterive, the latter marking the limit of the wine route. The silvery Isère shimmers below you and the dramatic snow-capped peaks of the Massif de la Vanoise are clearly visible in the distance. An essential small detour here is up a small road to the Château de Miolans, perched high up on the hill.

If you retrace your steps to Cruet, another narrow road, the D 11, winds up through the vineyards to the secluded lake of Thuile, an oval of limpid blue-green water surrounded by gentle sloping meadows and ringed with reeds. From here there is a pleasant drive through a series of valleys back to the wine villages of Chignin and finally St-Jeoire-Prieuré on the N 6, which will take you back into Chambéry or south to Grenoble and beyond.

Coteaux de Grésivaudan

The River Isère carves a winding valley westward from the high Alps towards Montmélian, where it takes a more southerly course towards Grenoble. Here the Massif de la Chartreuse and the Mont de Granier tower above its right bank, with the Chaîne de Belledonne dominating the left. Between Pontcharra and Grenoble, on the steep slopes beneath the sheer rock walls of the Chartreuse, are the vineyards of the Coteaux de Grésivaudan.

There are about 80 hectares of vines in all, with the greatest concentration around the villages of St-Ismier and Bernin. There are *caves co-opératives* here, and also at Barreaux, further north near Pontcharra. The co-operative at Bernin makes both red and rose wines from Gamay as well as a Pinot Noir and a white from Jacquère. A red is also made from a local variety called l'Etraire de la Dui and a white from another rather obscure traditional grape, Verdesse.

There are the three independent producers in the countryside around the village of Bernin, of whom Daniel Zégna is the largest with about 5 hectares of vines. He lives only a few hundred metres from the co-operative at Bernin. In addition to the grape varieties used at the co-operative, M. Zégna also grows a vine called Persan from which a red wine is produced. He told me that it is very astringent and tannic when young and must be kept for at least four years. Like his Etraire and Pinot Noir, it is kept in oak casks for six or seven months before it is bottled.

The Etraire variety originated from some vines discovered growing near a spring at the end of the eighteenth century, and Verdesse used to be widely planted in the region but was largely abandoned after the Second World War in favour of the more productive Jacquère. M. Zégna's most favoured vineyard of Pinot Noir is planted near the hamlet of Craponoz, below a cliff down which an impressive waterfall cascades. Traces of vines planted here by Benedictine monks in the eleventh century have been found, and the wines now produced from this vineyard are called Domaine de Craponoz.

Between Bernin and St-Ismier a road leads via the Col du Coq on to the Massif de la Chartreuse, a landscape of wooded slopes, fast-flowing rivers, waterfalls and bare-rock peaks. In the heart of the region is a deep valley crowded by the peaks of the Chamechaude, the Dent de Crolles and the Grand Som, each rising to over 2,000 metres. Here, near the village of St-Pierre-de-Chartreuse, is the monastery of La Grande Chartreuse, famed for its liqueur as much as for its religious order. The ruins of the original distillery, built in 1860 but destroyed by a landslide in 1935, can still be seen. The secret concoction is now made in Voiron, some 20 kilometres to the west.

Vins de Pays d'Allobrogie

To the west of Chambéry the River Isère flows through a very beautiful valley from its source in the high Alps. On its northern slopes are some of the most prestigious of the Savoie vineyards around the villages of Chignin, Cruet, St-Pierre-d'Albigny and Fréterive, where vines seem to cover every inch of the tillable land. However, on the southern slopes of the valley, among fields of maize, walnut trees, orchards and pastures, are much smaller plantations of vines, from which are produced Vins de Pays d'Allobrogie.

You can follow a spectacular route by taking the D 923 northwards from Pontcharra and, at Les Molettes, heading north-east along the D 29 to the villages of St-Pierre-de-Soucy, Villard-d'Héry and Châteauneuf. It is a tranquil region with stunning views to the north across the valley of the Isère to the mountains behind. To the west the great granite mass of Mont Granier dominates the scene.

The Vins de Savoie were elevated from VDQS to AOC status in 1973, and the Vin de Pays d'Allobrogie was created to allow the vineyards outside the delimited areas to produce less expensive quality-controlled wines with a local identity. In 1991 a total of 79 hectares of vines producing Vin de Pays were recorded, of which 59 were within the *département* of Savoie.

The wines are primarily white, with the Jacquère being the main, and most characteristic, variety. But Chardonnay, Chasselas and Mollette are also grown, as well as Gamay, for red and rosé wines. There are a total of 21 individual producers in the Savoie, of whom most have vineyards in the region I've described.

I visited Phillipe Chevrier near Les Mollettes, who has a relatively new vineyard of just 4 hectares. He makes varietal white wines from Chardonnay, Altesse and Jacquère, as well as a small quantity of red from a blend of Merlot and Cabernet Franc. It was the end of October and, sadly, he did not have a single bottle left from last year's harvest for me to try. He told me that about 65 per cent of his wine was sold directly to the public and the remainder to local restaurants.

At EARL Beauregard, in a big old farmhouse near the village of St-Pierre-de-Soucy, Pierre Dufayard has a more traditional approach, making only Jacquère from his 2 hectares of vines. He sells some of his pressed juice to the co-operative in Montemélian, but produces about 13,000 bottles on average each year with his own label. The harvest had just finished when I visited in October, and the new wine was bubbling away merrily in the vats to be ready for bottling during December. M. Dufayard gave me the opportunity to taste the previous year's wine alongside the newly pressed juice and the partially fermented wine, with a handful of his own fresh walnuts, the farm's other main crop, to accompany them. While the finished wine and fresh grape juice are both good, the new wine is also delicious. Known as Bourrou, and tasting both sweet and sharp, its intense fruit flavour and slight sparkle goes well with fresh green walnuts

AIN

TO THE EAST of the plain of Bresse and the city of Lyons, a tight loop in the River Rhône contains a landscape of steep rounded hills, wooded valleys and fast-flowing trout streams called the Pays de Bugey. The capital of the region is the small cathedral town of Belley, which lies about 10 kilometres west of the Lac du Bourget as the crow flies.

'A hundred square leagues of English garden' was how Brillat-Savarin described the region. Lawyer, philosopher, musician and gourmet, Brillat-Savarin was born in Belley in 1755 and became the mayor of the town at the time of the French Revolution. The region is known today as Le Pays de Brillat-Savarin, and a foundation in his name actively promotes the food and wines of the region.

THE WINES

The wines of Bugey were given VDQS status in 1958, and the vineyards contain one of the largest cross-sections of grape varieties to be found in any French wine-growing region; Burgundian vines such as Pinot Noir, Aligoté and Chardonnay are grown alongside Savoie varieties like Roussette, Jacquère and Mondeuse. The vineyards date from Roman times and were revived in the Middle Ages by the monasteries.

THE VINEYARDS

The 500 or so hectares of vineyards encompassed by the appellation are planted in the countryside around Belley. Scattered between cereal crops, orchards, walnut plantations and meadows dotted with brown and white cows, they support about 150 producers.

The village of Vongnes, a few kilometres north of Belley and sheltered by Le Grand Columbier, is the home of three producers, one of which, the Caveau Bugiste, offers an entertaining audio-visual guide to the history of wine production in the region. Here six producers have grouped together farming a total of about 40 hectares around the villages of Vongnes, Ceyzérieu and Flaxieu. They produce varietal white wines from Chardonnay, Aligoté, Roussette and Jacquère, red and rosé wines from Gamay and Pinot Noir, and a red from Mondeuse.

The ancient village of Cheignieu-la-Balme in the north of the region maintains a traditional Cru of Bugey – Manicle. Here, André Miraillet produces a red Pinot Noir and a Chardonnay together with a small amount of Gamay from 3 hectares of vines planted at the foot of a sheer cliff to the north of the village. I visited M. Miraillet at the end of October, just after the harvest, and his vats were bubbling away merrily in a cellar dating back centuries warmed by a wood-burning stove.

At the western edge of the Bugey vineyards on the steep hillsides overlooking the Rhône is the village of Montagnieu, another of the traditional Crus of the region. Here the father-and-son partnership of Franck and Jean Peillot farm 5 hectares of vines to produce mainly sparkling wines from Chardonnay, Altesse, Pinot Noir and Mondeuse. They also produce a smaller quantity of still wine from Chardonnay and Pinot Noir, together with a pure Rousette made from a plot of 60-year-old vines. It is labelled as Altesse, the variety's alternative name, because Roussette du Bugey is obliged to contain at least 20 per cent Chardonnay which this wine does not.

Rosé de Cerdon

The Bugey region has another appellation, Rosé de Cerdon, with the vineyards centred around the village of that name in the hills to the north of Ambérieu-en-Bugey. It is a sparkling wine, made in what is described as the ancestral way, from

Gamay or Pinot Noir. It is sweetish and very fruity with a relatively low alcohol level of 8 or 9 degrees. Many producers make a *méthode champenoise* which is usually much drier. A considerably inferior wine is also made by carbonating still wine, but it is clearly labelled 'Vin Pétillant Gazéifié'. The appellation also allows still wines to be made, mainly from Chardonnay, Gamay and Pinot Noir.

The countryside from which Rosé de Cerdon is produced has country lanes threading their way between steep, rounded hills to a succession of sleepy villages such as Le Poncieux, Jujurieux, Breignes, Mérignat and Vieillard.

In the more southerly vineyards there are two signposted circuits beginning in Belley which encompass the most interesting places and important wine villages. To the east of Vongnes, which has a beautiful eleventh-century church, is an area of marshland called the Marais de Lavours. It has been made into a nature reserve with an extensive boardwalk built on piles (the largest in Europe) constructed to enable visitors to view the wildlife at close quarters.

A few kilometres to the south of Vongnes is the Lac du Barterend, a secluded and peaceful lake surrounded by wooded hills, and to the north is Culoz which lies at the foot of Le Grand Columbier. It has a medieval château and a beautfiul garden, Le Clos Poncet, which contains a memorial to Gertrude Stein, the American writer who made the region her home at the beginning of the century. From here a road leads into the Valmorey region and to the summit of Le Grand Columbier providing sweeping views of the Alps and the lakes of Geneva, Le Bourget and Annecy.

To the south of Vongnes the wine route crosses on to the left bank of the Rhône where there are views over the Belley basin near the village of Parves. To the south of Belley the route leads to the villages of Arbigneu, in the Furans valley, and Premeyzel, in the valley of the River Gland – two renowned trout streams. Most of the villages and hamlets in the region have large communal bread ovens which are still periodically used for fairs and festivals. They are roofed with large flaked flat stones called *lauzes* and have a façade framed by flights of stone steps and a decorated gable.

A few kilometres south-west of Prémeyzel, in the village of Glandieu, is one of the most spectacular waterfalls in France, where the River Gland drops from a lofty rock shelf for 30 metres or more. The route continues to the north-east to Groslée, Lhuis and Montagnieu, along a steep ridge overlooking the Rhône, and then to the villages of Seillonez, Benonces and Ordonnaz to Chegnieu-la-Balme, where there is a small wine museum and a house which was once the home of Brillat-Savarin.

ISÈRE
Balmes Dauphinoise

ABOUT 20 KILOMETRES south-west of the Pays de Bugey is a Vin de Pays called Balmes Dauphinoise, the only appellation of the *département* of Isère. They are very small and localized vineyards dotted throughout a region of which the main town is Bourgoin-Jallieu. The vineyards are distributed in small parcels totalling about 30 hectares among nine producers in the villages of Sermérieu, Vézeronce, Veyrins, Corbelin, Granieu, Salagreux and St-Chef. The largest concentration is around the village of St-Savin, where there are two producers.

St-Savin is at the head of a pretty valley bordered by steep hillsides where meadows, vineyards and fields of maize are shaded by chestnut and walnut trees. I visited Marc Bonnaire, who farms about 6 hectares of vines on the slopes above the village. He makes a pure Chardonnay which represents three-quarters of his production and a red wine from 60 per cent Pinot Noir and 40 per cent Gamay. In the neighbouring village of St-Chef, Noël Martin specializes in a sparkling wine made by the *méthode champenoise*.

Perhaps the most interesting producer of Vin de Pays des Balmes Dauphinoise is the Domaine Meunier in Sermérieu, a peaceful hamlet of old stone houses in the countryside just west of Morestel. The vineyard was started by M. Meunier's grandparents, and now he and his wife manage about 5 hectares of Gamay, Pinot Noir and Chardonnay on the stony slopes at the edge of the village.

The majority of Vins de Pays are made to be drunk quite young, but M. Meunier has a different approach; the walls of his cellars are stacked four deep and ceiling high with bottles going back ten years or more. He claims that the unique quality of his soil, the vineyard's exposure and the way in which he makes his wines give them the capacity to improve with ageing.

ARDÈCHE
Côtes du Vivarais

UP RIVER FROM St-Esprit is Viviers, which has a well-preserved old quarter of cobbled streets and ancient buildings. The town gives its name to the mountainous region between the Cevennes and the Rhône valley known as the Vivarais. The region has a long history of wine growing: Pliny reported on the wines of ancient Gallo-Roman province of Helvie, as it was then known, and commented on the vine called Le Carbonarit which flowered for just one night.

The countryside, which ranges from luxuriant valleys to stony *garrigues* and wooded mountains, is also densely cultivated with vines. The Côtes du Vivarais has been a VDQS appellation since 1962 and covers the terrain around the following 14 villages: Barjac, Bidon, Gras, Issirac, Labastide-de-Virac, Lagorce, Larnas, Le Garn, Montclus, St-Privat-de-Champclos, Vinezac, Organac-l'Aven, St-Montant and St-Remèze. The final three of these are also entitled to the appellation of Cru.

THE WINES

The main permitted grape varieties are Grenache Noir, Syrah, Cinsaut, Auban and Carignan for red and rosé with Marsanne, Clairette, Bourboulenc, Macabeo, Mauzan, Picpoul, Ugni Blanc and Grenache Blanc for white wines.

There are numerous independent producers, of whom nearly 70 belong to the organization of Caves Particulières, which provides each member vineyard with distinctive brown and white signs depicting a *vigneron* carrying a barrel on his shoulders. In addition nearly 40 *caves co-opératives* are also distributed throughout the region.

The Vignerons Ardèchois, based at Ruoms, some 25 kilometres south of Aubenas, incorporates twenty of the co-operatives and has a very progressive approach to commercialization and marketing. It represents over three thousand *vignerons* farming nearly 6,000 hectares of vines with a total *cuverie* capacity of 700,000 hectolitres, 36,000 of which are at the Ruoms co-operative. Côtes du Vivarais red and rosé is made here from a blend of 50 per cent Grenache Blanc, 30 per cent Syrah and 10 per cent each of Cinsaut and Carignan, using 80 per cent traditional fermentation and 20 per cent carbonic maceration. The white Côtes du Vivarais is produced from about 30 hectares of vines planted on the stony terraces of the lower Vivarais and from a blend of Grenache Blanc, Clairette and Ugni Blanc.

Coteaux de l'Ardèche

In addition to VDQS wines the region also has a Vin de Pays appellation, Coteaux de l'Ardèche. Although a proportion of these wines are made using a blend of the same grape varieties as the AOC wines, many producers take the opportunity to make *vins de cépage* from varieties not permitted by the VDQS regulations.

At Ruoms, for example, they make a red using a blend of Grenache, Syrah, Cabernet Sauvignon, Cinsaut and Merlot, as well as *vins de cépage* from Syrah, Merlot, Cabernet Sauvignon and Chardonnay. They also produce a Vin de Pays du Comté de Grignan from Grenache, Syrah and Cabernet Sauvignon together with a small proportion of Cinsaut, as well as a similarly constructed Vin de Pays des Comtés Rhodaniens, which is produced using biological methods.

The vineyards

Near the village of Vallon-Pont-d'Arc, just above the gorges of the Ardèche, is the Domaine du Colombier, where Philippe and Alain Walbaum farm 27 hectares of vines along the banks of the River Ardèche. The terrain falls just outside the area defined for the VDQS appellation, so only Vin de Pays is made here. M. Walbaum makes what he calls a 'Rouge Tradition' from a blend of Syrah, Grenache Noir and Carignan, a 'Cuvée Spéciale' from just Grenache and Syrah, together with a rosé from pure Syrah.

The vineyard was planted by his grandfather in 1860. Now, in the cottages and outbuildings near the fine old farmhouse there are seven well-appointed gîtes for holiday-makers.

From Vallon-Pont-d'Arc a road leads north along the valley of the River Ibie to the picturesque villages of Les Salelles and St-Maurice-d'Ibie. It's a quiet secluded valley sheltered by low hills, covered in *garrigue*, with the small river winding between outcrops of rock over a bed of white stones. In the middle of the valley is the Mas de la Bégude, a very attractive old farmhouse where Gilles Azzoni and his wife produce both Côtes du Vivarais and Vins de Pays de l'Ardèche from 8 hectares of vines planted on the valley floor and the surrounding slopes. M. Azzoni told me that he was the first to introduce Viognier into this part of the Ardèche and has enjoyed considerable success with it.

Between Les Salelles and St-Maurice-d'Ibie a small road leads eastwards over the steep, *garrigue*-covered hills before descending, with sweeping views, into the valley of Valvignères. This is a much larger and wider valley than that of the Ibie and is carpeted with vines as far as the eye can see. Its name is derived from the Latin, Vallis Vinaria – valley of the vines – and wine-making was going on here 2,000 years ago, when the region was the centre of the Gallo-Roman province of Helvie. The wines were transported as far as Lyons, Rome and the Low Countries, where an amphora was discovered bearing the name Helvorium.

The little walled village of Valvignères has a pretty church and clocktower, and many old stone houses in small squares linked by narrow streets and passages. The valley has its own *cave co-opérative*, formed in 1951 and today supported by nearly 120 *vignerons* making both Côtes du Vivarais and Vins de Pays. In addition to the traditional grape varieties used for the VDQS wines, recent plantings include both Chardonnay and Viognier for *vins de cépage*.

Above: The château of Suze-la-Rousse, which houses
the University of Wine.
Opposite Top: The distant Rhone and vineyards above the
Bugey wine village of Montagnieu.
Opposite Below: The valley of the Ibie, near Vallon-Pont-de l'Arc.

Diverge a little from the prescribed route here to visit the hill villages in the countryside near Valvignères: St-Montant, St-Thomé, Alba-la-Romaine, Aubignas and Rochemaure – beside the Rhône.

The essential excursion here, though, is to the Gorges of the Ardèche, the reach of the river between Vallon-Pont-de-Arc – named after the pinnacle of rock through which the river has tunnelled – and St-Martin-d'Ardèche. The D 290 leads westwards from the N 86 a few kilometres to the north of Pont-St-Esprit and follows the left bank of the river. There are numerous spectacular viewpoints along the route, and in some places you can walk down to the water's edge.

There are a number of smaller but equally dramatic gorges in the region. From the town of Ruoms the D 4 crosses the Ardèche and leads north-west along the right bank for a few kilometres, revealing stretches of the river winding between steep, jagged cliffs. A short distance to the west of Ruoms is the small village of Labeaume, built in the gorges of the River Beaume. About 10 kilometres south-west from there is a region of eroded limestone rocks called the Bois de Païolive. From Labeaume follow the D 208 to Chandolas and Maison-Neuve on the D 104. A short distance to the south a small road leads through this strange landscape to Les Vans. Don't miss seeing the ancient village of Naves, a few kilometres to the west; this little cluster of crumbling stone houses looks as if it has hardly changed at all for several hundred years.

The village of Balazuc is another sight worth seeing. Balanced on the edge of a sheer cliff above a bend in the River Ardèche, a short distance to the north-east of Ruoms, its harmonious group of grey limestone houses, together with a four-teenth-century Romanesque church and the remains of ramparts make for a memorable view. During the Middle Ages the village was a stronghold for the silver-mine lords of neighbouring Largentière. This old walled village is also worth a visit; with its castle perched above and fortified entrance gates it retains a strong medieval ambience. Ten kilometres or so to the east is Vogüé, another impressively sited village on the banks of the Ardèche, with a row of old houses surmounted by a castle.

St-Joseph, Cornas & St-Peray

In the north of the *département* of the Ardèche is the wine-growing region of St-Joseph, which incorporates an area along the right bank of the Rhône between St-Peray outside Valence, and Chavany, about 60 kilometres to the north. The old riverside town of Tournon is the heart of this region and the vineyards which are entitled to the St-Joseph appellation, granted in 1956, amount to about 500 hectares producing a red wine made exclusively from Syrah.

In addition to numerous individual producers there are also a number of *caves co-opératives* where, along with the AOC St-Joseph wines, Vins de Pays des Collines Rhodaniennes are also produced. This appellation can apply to wines which originate from vineyards in the neighbouring *départements* of Rhône, Drôme, Isère and Loire. These include white wines made from Marsanne and Roussanne, together with red and rosé wines from Gamay.

I visited the excellent co-operative at St-Désirat during the harvest in late September, and there were long lines of tractor-drawn trucks waiting to disgorge their grapes into the winery. In just a few weeks the Vin Primeur, made from Gamay using carbonic maceration, would be on sale, and already the fermenta-tion vats were bubbling away vigorously. Primeurs are widely made in the Rhône valley, and since they are on sale on the third Thursday in October they offer an opportunity to sample the new wine some weeks before the more widely marketed Beaujolais Nouveau is available at the end of November. A Primeur is designed to be consumed by Christmas, or thereabouts, while a Nouveau can be expected to remain sound for about one year after bottling.

To the south of the St-Joseph region are the wine villages of Cornas, where they make red wine from Syrah, and St-Peray, which is known for its white wines, sparkling and still, produced from Marsanne and Roussanne. There is a scenic detour at Cornas, up a small road that climbs towards St-Romain-de-Lerps, where there is a ruined tower. You can return to the N 86 either by doubling back a little via the village of Plats and taking the D 219 into Mauves, or by turning left on to the D 287 and driving down into St-Peray.

DRÔME

THE VINEYARDS OF the *département* of Drome are to be found in five areas: around the village of Tain-l'Hermitage on the banks of the Rhône; adjacent to the town of Brézème where the River Drôme meets the Rhône; in the region around Die in the valley of the Drôme; in the countryside to the east of Montélimar; and on the slopes surrounding the small country town of Nyons.

The AOC appellations to which these vineyards are entitled are Hermitage, Crozes-Hermitage, Clairette de Die, Châtillon-en-Diois, Côtes du Rhône and Coteaux de Tricastin. In addition there are the Vins de Pays appellations of Collines Rhodaniennes, Coteaux des Baronnies, Comté de Grignan and Drôme.

Tain-l'Hermitage

On the left bank of the Rhône, opposite the old town of Tournon, you can see a huge granite rock towering above the village of Tain-l'Hermitage, named after a knight crusader who 'retired' here and made wine. Its vineyards of Hermitage and Crozes-Hermitage produce a strong and full-bodied red wine from Syrah grapes, which seem to thrive in the rough, rocky soil, as well as white wines from Marsanne and Roussanne. The vineyards of Crozes-Hermitage extend to just over 1,000 hectares, while those of Hermitage only cover 120 hectares.

From Tain you can follow a signposted route which takes you around the wine-growing communities of La Roche-de-Glun, Pont-de-l'Isère, Beaumont-Monteux, Chanos-Curson, Mercurol, Crozes-Hermitage, Larnage, Serves-sur-Rhône, Gervans and then back to Tain.

In a lay-by outside Mercurol I met a jovial Frenchman with a huge, black greasy machine called an *alambic* (a still); it looked like an ancient traction engine and had a Heath Robinson air about it. He told me that he spent three months of the year towing it around the local communes and converting grape must, apples, plums and pears into *eau de vie*. On a good day he could produce up to 500 litres, he said. I tasted a sample of his work – and it was fiery indeed. He showed me, with some pride, a picture of a beautiful copper and brass still on cart-wheels. He used it until fairly recently, but is keeping it safe now. It's his pension, he explained wrily. The right to own and operate these stills was passed down from generation to generation, but recent legislation means this will no longer happen and they are decreasing in numbers each year.

The Diois

The little town of Die, which lies in the heart of the Drôme valley, is known for its Appellation Contrôlée wine, Clairette de Die, a sweetish sparkling wine made in a traditional way. The existence of the Clairette de Die was recorded as early as 77 BC, when it was known as Aigleucos and unkindly described by Pliny the Elder as the least sophisticated wine of the Roman Empire. By 1380 laws were being passed to prevent any other wines being imported into the region.

The traditional Clairette de Die, which obtained its AOC title in 1942, is the only naturally sparkling wine made from the Muscat grape, but a *brut* version is also made from Clairette. There is a separate appellation for Châtillon-en-Diois, where about 50 hectares of vines around the village are used to produce still red wines from Gamay and whites from Chardonnay and Aligoté.

THE VINEYARDS

The vineyards extend along the valley of the Drôme, in some places planted high on the steep hillsides which border the valley. They cover about 1,200 hectares and encompass 32 villages, the greatest concentration being between Aoste-sur-Seyre, the picturesque riverside town of Seillans and Luc-en-Diois as well as around the villages of Pont de Quart and Châtillon-en-Diois in the valley of the River Bez. The main villages of production are Aurel, Barsac, Saillans, Vercheny Barnave, Châtillon, Menglon and St-Roman.

The valley of the Drôme carves a deep swathe into an impressive mountain landscape, and there are spellbinding vistas at every turn. From Die the D 518 leads north along the valley of the Comane via the picturesquely perched village of Chameloc to the Col du Rousset, a tortuously winding pass which provides stunning views of the Diois as the road climbs to its summit. Beyond is the Parc Régional du Vercors, a countryside of alpine-like meadows, racing rivers, gorges and bare-rock peaks.

A round trip encompassing some of the loveliest corners of the Vercors can be made by following the road northwards to La Chapelle-en-Vercors and Villard-de-Lans and returning via the Gorges de la Bourne to the pretty riverside town of St-Jean-en-Royans, and then driving south over the Col de la Croix to Vassieux-en-Vercors before returning via the Col du Rousset to Die.

An enjoyable drive can be made into the countryside to the south-west of Die by following the Drôme downstream to Saillans. This takes you past the village of Pontaix, which is built in a narrow defile, with old stone houses rising sheer from the river bank and a ruined château perched on the cliff above. From Saillans the D 156 climbs through impressive mountain scenery to the Col de la Chaudière before descending to the ancient town of Boudeaux in the valley of the River Roubion.

About 20 kilometres to the south-west in the valley of the River Jabron is the medieval hilltop town of Le Poët-Laval, established in the twelfth century by the Knights Hospitallers. Among the maze of steep cobbled streets is the ancient commander's residence, which has been converted into a comfortable and atmospheric hotel with a good restaurant. A few kilometres to the north-west is Châteauneuf-de-Mazenc, another tiny community of crumbling stone houses on a hill overlooking the valley of the Jabron.

Coteaux des Baronnies

The little town of Nyons, built astride the River Eygues, is set in a crescent of mountains bordering the Tricastin plain which reaches away to the west. It has an arcaded square and an unusual covered street leading to a gateway which was once the entrance to a castle. Nyons is the centre for a Vins de Pays, called the

Coteaux des Baronnies. The majority of the production is by the co-operatives, the Union des Producteurs in Nyons and nearby Les Pilles, with a small quantity being produced at Vaison-la-Romaine, Puyméras and the Cave du Prieuré at Vinsobres.

The grape varieties used for the reds and rosés are similar to those for the AOC Côtes du Rhône – Grenache, usually representing about 50 per cent, with the balance made up of Cinsaut, Carignan and Syrah. Red wines of a single grape variety are also made from Syrah, Cabernet and Merlot, and a white wine from pure Chardonnay. There are a total of about 1,200 hectares farmed by nearly 500 *vignerons*.

The co-operative at Nyons is something of an Aladdin's cave for gourmets since it also represents many of the region's olive producers. They have one of the finest cold-pressed virgin oils, as well as the delectable Appellation d'Origine Contrôlée black olives, harvested from a special variety, the Tanche, for which Nyons is famous. Other goodies include grape-seed and walnut oil, honey, truffles, preserved fruits and jars of *tapénade*, the pungent Provençal paste made from olives, capers and anchovies.

The greatest concentration of vineyards lies along the valley of Eygues to the south-west of Nyons and around the villages of Buis-les-Baronnies, Puyméras and Mirabel-aux-Baronnies. One of the few independent producers of the Coteaux des Baronnies is Yves Liotaud, of the Domaine du Rieux Frais at Ste-Jalle, a tiny community of old stone houses beside the River Ennuye, a tributary of the Eygues. M. Liotaud makes red wines from pure Syrah and Cabernet Sauvignon as well as a blended red from 50/50 Grenache and Syrah. A rosé is made from a blend of 70 per cent Grenache and 30 per cent Syrah, and a white from pure Chardonnay, which is kept for three to four months in oak barrels.

From Ste-Jalle a scenic road climbs over the Col d'Ey and then descends into the valley of the Ouvèze. One option now is to go east on the D 546, which follows the river upstream through the most beautiful part of the steep-sided valley to a junction with the D 65. From here a detour can be made over the Col de Perty, where you can see lavender terraces, before descending into the valley of the River Céans, the medieval village of Orpierre.

Alternatively, at the foot of the Col d'Ey you could turn south on the D 546 to the little market town of Buis-les-Baronnies and then west along the valley of the Ouvèze towards Vaison-la-Romaine. Another very beautiful detour can be made a few kilometres after leaving Buis-les-Baronnies by taking the D 72 and following the valley of the Derbous before climbing over the Col de Fontaube and the Col des Aires.

A few kilometres further east, beyond the little walled village of Reilhanette, is the Roman spa town of Montbrun-les-Bains, where the houses are tiered giddily up the side of a steep hill. It lies at the confluence of the Rivers Anary and Touroulenc, and a pleasant way of returning to Vaison-la-Romaine is to go west on the D 40 along the valley of the Touroulenc; you will pass below the alarmingly perched village of Brantes, now partially deserted.

Coteaux du Tricastin

The vineyards of the Coteaux du Tricastin are planted on the left bank of the River Rhône between Montélimar and Bollène. The region was granted its Appellation Contrôlée in 1973 and today the vines extend to 2,400 hectares, encompassing 21 communes. Vins de Pays du Comté de Grignan are also produced in this area. The red and rosé wines are made primarily from Grenache

Noir with a smaller proportion of Syrah, Carignan, Cinsaut, Mourvèdre and Picpoul, while whites are produced from Grenache Blanc, Clairette, Roussanne, Marsanne, Ugni Blanc and Viognier.

The principal wine villages are St-Paul-Trois-Châteaux, Suze-la-Rousse (famous for its imposing château which houses the university of wine), Chamaret, Réauville and Grignan, which is dominated by a massive eleventh-century fortress. The community was made famous in the seventeenth century by the writer Madame de Sévigné, who made frequent visits to her daughter, the resident Comtesse de Grignan.

THE CUISINE

The *charcuterie* and meat products of this region are particularly rich in both variety and flavour. *Rosette de Lyon* is an air-dried salami-style sausage of a bright pink colour made using the pig's large intestine as a case. *Caillettes*, found in the Ardèche, are round sausage-like parcels of chopped veal or pork meat and liver with spinach or blette leaves encased in caul. *Poulet de Bresse*, from the Ain, is considered to be the very best chicken and has its own *appellation contrôlée*.

Some of the great French cheeses originate from this region of the country. In the Alpine *départements* cow's milk is used for Tomme de Savoie and Beaufort, described by Brillat-Savarin as the prince of gruyères. Bleu de Gex is a blue-veined cheese known as *fromage persillé* because it has a similar marbled appearance to the *jambon persillé* of Burgundy. Reblochon is a creamy but firm yellow cheese – so named as it was made from an illicit second milking held back by the diary hand as a perk, or *rebloché*, to produce a richer creamier cheese for his own consumption – while St-Marcellin is milder, softer and ivory-coloured cheese once made from goat's milk but, commercially, now largely from cows, although farm-produced goat's-milk versions can still be found called Tomme de St-Marcellin.

Cream and cheese are also used in cooking. *Pommes de terre dauphinoise* is a wickedly rich dish of thinly sliced potatoes baked slowly in a shallow dish with butter and cream and a sprinkling of Beaufort. In *pommes de terre à la savoyarde* meat stock is used instead of cream and grated Comte cheese is added.

Some of the best walnuts come from the Savoie, around Grenoble, while the chestnuts of the Ardèche are renowned. The upper Rhône valley in the *département* of Drôme has thousands of acres of orchards producing the finest peaches, plums, apricots, apples and pears.

PROVENCE-ALPES-CÔTE D'AZUR

HE REGION OF Provence comprises six *départements*, Vaucluse, Bouches-du-Rhône, Var, Alpes-de-Haute-Provence, Hautes-Alpes and Alpes-Maritimes. Endless blue skies, olive groves, wild thyme and lavender fields, garlic, pine trees, parched rust-coloured soil, sea, sea, sea . . . this is Provence. It is hardly surprising that the south of France has been one of the most popular European tourist destinations for generations. Provence has one of the most beautiful stretches of coastline in the whole of the Mediterranean. It also has majestic mountains, wild gorges and cascading rivers, as well as vast forests and green, fertile valleys. Its cultural heritage is fascinating and there is a wealth of small, unspoilt villages, many in spectacular settings. Added to all this is the perennial attraction of the Mediterranean sun and the warm and benevolent climate it creates.

VAUCLUSE

THE WINES

THE VAUCLUSE IS entitled to the appellations of Côtes du Rhône, Côtes du Ventoux, Côtes du Lubéron, Côtes du Rhône Villages, Rochegude, St-Maurice-sur-Eygues, Vinsobres, Cairanne, Roaix, Rousset-les-Vignes, St-Pantaléon-les-Vignes, Sablet, Séguret, Valréas, Visan, the Crus of Rasteau, Gigondas,

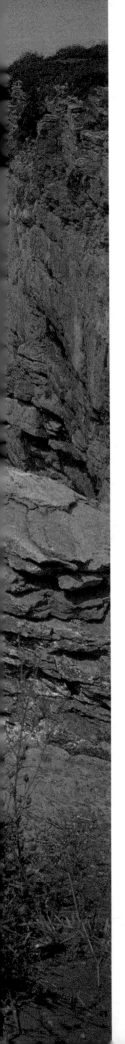

ABOVE TOP: EARLY SPRING IN VINEYARDS NEAR THE VILLAGE OF BONNIEUX IN THE LUBERON.
ABOVE: A PROVENÇAL FARMHOUSE BELOW THE MASSIF DE LA SAINTE BAUME.
OPPOSITE: CASSIS, SEEN FROM THE TOWERING CLIFFS OF CAP CANAILLE.

Vacqueyras, Beaumes-de-Venise and Châteauneuf-du-Pape and the Vins de Pays appellations of Principauté d'Orange and Vins de Pays de la Vaucluse.

The principal grape varieties permitted within the appellations are Syrah, Grenache, Carignan, Mourvèdre and Cinsaut for reds and rosés, Clairette and Bourboulenc for whites; other varieties, such as Chardonnay and Viognier, are also planted for Vins de Pays.

THE VINEYARDS

Bollène is the gateway to the vineyards of the Côtes du Rhône which fall within the Vaucluse, there is a signposted route which leads towards the important wine-village of Ste-Cécile-les-Vignes via Mondragon, where there are the ruins of a château, Sérignan-du-Comtat and Lagarde-Paréol. Here the terrain is flat and the vines stretch towards the horizon like a patterned green carpet. Ste-Cécile-les-Vignes has an attractive old quarter and many old buildings including a 300-year-old *caveau*, the eleventh-century chapel of Saint-Martin and an ancient stone bridge over the River Ouvèze.

Although there is a maze of small roads criss-crossing the vineyards and leading to innumerable small villages, the Route des Vins is extremely well sign-posted – so much so that you can virtually ignore the map and simply follow the signs. From Ste-Cécile the route leads to Cairanne, Rasteau, known for its sweet dessert wine made from Grenache, and Vaison-la-Romaine, with its Roman remains and an old village of steep cobbled streets and alleys perched on a hill above the Ouvèze.

As you travel further east a range of jagged mountains begins to loom in the distance. These are the Dentelles de Montmirail; at their foot is Gigondas. It is a handsome mountain village and produces a wonderful full-bodied, deep red wine from the Grenache, Mourvèdre and Syrah grapes that grow here. There is a small road that climbs up and through the mountain, giving spectacular views towards the western Cévennes ranges and Mont Ventoux to the east. A little north of Gigondas is Séguret, one of the many little hilltop villages in the area, perhaps more self-conscious than most, with many of the old houses having been bought and renovated by wealthy Parisians and foreigners. It remains, however, a dedicated and hard-working wine village.

A little further along the southern edge of the Dentelles de Montmirail are the wine villages of Vacqueyras and Beaumes-de-Venise. They both make good red wines, while Beaumes-de-Venise is famed for its heady Muscat, a rich, naturally sweet white wine that can be served chilled as an aperitif or more regularly with a dessert. A complete circuit of the Dentelles de Montmirail can be made by continuing round towards Malaucène and Vaison-la-Romaine.

Alternatively you can follow the signs for the Côtes du Ventoux from Malaucène. This route leads south through wonderfully scenic countryside, where the vineyards are mingled with lavender fields and the mountains are always in sight. Just outside the small walled village of Caromb is a *cave co-opérative* which also houses a small wine museum. Don't miss seeing the ancient village of Le Barroux, with its medieval walls and castle, a short distance to the north. Bédouin and Flassan are also worth visiting; the latter is a very evocative example of a Provençal village with its orangey-pink stone and red-tiled houses perched high above the surrounding countryside.

Continue through the village of Villes-sur-Auzon and then westward again via Mormoiron and Mazan to Carpentras, a bustling market town that was the medieval capital of the region until Pope Clement V decided that Avignon was more convenient. Heading towards Avignon, detour via the wine town of Bédarrides to Châteauneuf-du-Pape. All that is left of its papal château is a ruined wall and tower. Up to thirteen different grape varieties are used in the making of the village's famous rich red wine; they grow in a soil studded with round white stones, like small boulders, which store the heat of the sun and release it at night.

You must of course stop in Avignon. Its medieval Palais des Papes was the home of seven French popes; it is an imposing fortress-like structure with a strong Mediterranean character. The famous Pont d'Avignon has only four of its twenty-two arches now, but retains its chapel. Avignon holds a music and theatre festival in high summer every year, attracting world-famous performers.

Côtes du Lubéron

To the south, the countryside of the Lubéron is quintessential Provence, planted with plantations of sunflowers, lavender, fruit trees and the ubiquitous olive tree, and steep hillsides covered in pines, brush and wild herbs. It not only looks the way you imagine Provence to be; it also smells like it. Wine has been produced here since Roman times, but the vineyards have never had the same significance as those planted on the more northerly Rhône plain.

There is much to see of interest in the Lubéron, not least a twelfth-century castle at Lourmarin and a fine Renaissance château at La Tour-d'Aigues. Ansouis has a château dating from the ninth century, and Mirabeau, a medieval castle used as a location for the film of Marcel Pagnol's *Manon des Sources*.

The region is particularly rich in picturesque hill villages, such as Venasque, Bonnieux, which has two churches and a museum of bakery, and Roussillon, where ochre houses rise from a sheer sandstone cliff giving stunning views of the surrounding countryside. A short distance to the west is the artist's village of Gordes and, nearby, the ancient Village des Bories, with its perfectly preserved conical houses built from flat stones.

Don't miss the ancient villages of Menerbes and Lacoste, which is dominated by the château of the Marquis de Sade. There are oil mills at Cucuron and Oppède, and a lavender distillery can be visited at Lagarde d'Apt. Some of the best markets in Provence are held in this region: at Apt on Saturdays, Pertuis on Fridays, Cavaillon on Mondays, Gordes on Tuesdays and, perhaps the best of all, at l'Isle-sur-la-Sorgue on Sundays.

BOUCHES-DU-RHÔNE

AIX-EN-PROVENCE WAS THE capital of Provence until the Revolution, and has inherited a wealth of fine old buildings, a lovely cathedral, elegant squares, tree-lined avenues and ornate fountains. A stroll down the Cours Mirabeau under the soaring plane trees, or a lazy hour sitting at a pavement café table watching the world go by, seems to encapsulate the essence of Provençal life. The little town of St-Rémy-de-Provence, to the south of Aix, is equally charming on a smaller scale and has a pretty country market in its small square each Saturday.

Although punctuated by mountains, the landscape of Bouches-du-Rhône is largely open and exposed to the Mistral, with distinctive walls of poplar and plane trees grown to protect the crops. In addition to vineyards there are extensive orchards, producing fruit both for market and for preserving – a speciality of the region.

A view of the vineyards over the rooftops of Seguret.

contrast vividly with the rich, red-brown soil. From Pierrefeu the road leads to Cuers, which has a number of interesting old buildings, including a sixteenth-century church, as well as a *cave co-opérative* and some private *caveaux*.

After Cuers the route follows the main road, the N 97, through the wine villages of Puget-Ville with its thirteenth-century Saracen tower, Carnoules and Pignans, from which you can make a small detour to the viewpoint of Nôtre-Dame des Anges. The next village is Gonfaron, where, legend has it, a donkey once flew, and then you come to Le Luc. This colourful town on the busy N 7 is an important wine centre, and there are nine *caves* that you can visit. Also of interest are the twelfth-century clock tower and a Romanesque chapel.

The wine route now doubles back along the N 7 to the wine village of Flassans-sur-Issole, built around the ruins of an old village and dominated by a privately owned feudal castle. Here the wine road heads north again on the D 13 to Cabasse and Carcès, an old olive oil-milling town. From here a detour can be made to the famous twelfth-century Abbaye de Thoronet, a superb example of Romanesque architecture, built by the Cistercians and restored by order of Prosper Mérimée, the nineteenth-century novelist who was also Inspector-General of Historic Monuments. Just before Carcès the road hugs the shore of the Lac de Carcès, an artificial lake that supplies water to many of the coastal resorts. This is excellent countryside for picnicking. Nearby are the jagged red cliffs and quarries of the bauxite mines, which lend a rather surrealist air to the landscape.

From Carcès the route continues west to Montfort-sur-Argens, almost as noteworthy for being the home of Louis-Joseph Lambart, the man who invented reinforced concrete, as for its Templar castle and twelfth-century church. Just off the route the tiny village of Correns, set in a peaceful vine-clad valley beside the little River Argens. The main route continues north to Cotignac, set at the foot of a high, sheer cliff under a ruined watchtower. Sitting at an outdoor café shaded by enormous plane trees on Cotignac's broad main street, you can really absorb the Provençal atmosphere. There are caves cut into the cliffs, an eleventh-century priory church and the remains of an oil mill. You can also visit the Chapel of Nôtre-Dame de Grâce, a famous sanctuary since the time of Louis XIII, set on a hill opposite the village; it can be reached by a small road near the bridge.

From Cotignac the Route des Vins goes east along the D 50. The narrow country roads are lined with dry-stone walls, which are also used to terrace the vineyards and olive groves. Here, with wild flowers and herbs in full bloom and the air heady with their fragrance, everything seems absolutely perfect. The next place you come to is the hill town of Entrecasteaux, which is dominated by an eleventh-century château with a garden designed by Le Notre. It is privately owned but can be visited, and there is a chapel and two old churches built above it. As you drive towards St-Antonin-du-Var, look back at the village – it is very dramatic against the steep wooded hillsides.

The route continues towards Draguignan via the village of Lorgues, where there are many interesting old buildings including a Saracen gate, ancient ramparts and towers and an old oil mill now used as an art gallery. You can make several excursions from here. Go to Flayosc to see a typical village of the region; its village square is shaded by plane trees and there is an ancient fountain, which is quintessentially Provençal. Visit Villecroze (to the north-west along the D 10), a high mountain village, for its wine and for the spectacular view over the surounding landscape. And walk up the narrow winding streets of nearby Tourtour, which is at an altitude of 1,630 metres, and enjoy the views; some of its old towers and fortified gateways survive, and there is a private château.

The shady streets and squares of old Draguignan contain some fine old buildings including an Ursuline convent, which houses the town's museum and library, a Roman gate and a sixteenth-century clock tower. Outside the town you can visit several medieval hill villages, including Callas, Bargemon, Seillans, Fayence and Callian. Seillans has a Saracen gate and an eleventh-century feudal castle perched high up above its tiny houses.

Continue south on the D 4 through the villages of St-Paul-en-Forêt and Bagnols-en-Forêt, which, as their names suggest, are set deep in the cork forest that borders the mountains of the Esterel. There are many good picnic spots on the first part of the drive through forested hillsides; then, as it winds round the sides of the mountains, the road becomes more austere and mountainous with panoramic views of the valleys below. At Bagnols-en-Forêt you rejoin the main wine route to Trans-en-Provence and La Motte along the D 47. This too is a ruggedly beautiful road through forests and mountains. At one point, where the road runs right alongside a rugged, red gorge, you can see a dramatic outcrop of rocks and impressive views down into the gorge.

From Bagnols-en-Forêt the road winds down towards the coast and the town of Fréjus, the oldest Roman city in Gaul. Julius Caesar founded it, Augustus built up its harbour and Agricola was born here. There are many important Roman remains, including an amphitheatre where bullfights are held in summer, part of an aqueduct and ramparts. Fréjus was destroyed in the tenth century, but got a new lease of life 500 years later when its fine cathedral was built.

The wine road continues west along the N 7 through the wine villages of Puget-sur-Argens and Le Muy to Les Arcs, an important wine centre. Don't miss seeing the pretty old village, built on a hilltop behind the modern community, where there are winding cobbled streets, ancient gateways and an old Saracen tower. Take a short detour to Roquebrune-sur-Argens, where the biggest mulberry tree in the South of France grows. The village is situated beneath a red rock which rises from the flat coastal plain, and you can drive around it through the surrounding vineyards, or walk through its wooded slopes to a small chapel nestling in a cleft halfway up.

From Les Arcs the route continues through the small wine village of Taradeau to Vidauban, with its seventeenth-century château. The Route des Vins continues on the D 48 through the Massif des Maures; there are dramatic views at every turn as the road winds steeply through forested hillsides. The ancient hilltop villages of La Garde-Freinet and Grimaud are a delight, particularly Grimaud, a medieval walled town with a Renaissance chapel and a ruined eleventh-century castle. A short detour to the west from La Garde-Freinet takes you to the Roches Blanches, where there are superb views over the village and surrounding countryside. A second detour can be made, this time to the east, over the Col de Vignon to the village of Plan-de-la-Tour.

The sophisticated and crowded St-Tropez is the next town on the wine route. Early this century, long before Brigitte Bardot, it was a favourite summer resort of the Neo-Impressionist painters, including Bonnard and Matisse. You should visit the Cave Co-opérative du Golfe de St-Tropez, and the important *domaine* of Château de Minuty, which is nearby. Every May, St-Tropez honours its patron saint in a street procession unique to this part of France, and a wonderful spectacle. From here a small scenic road winds up into the mountains above the town through Gassin, where the sea views are awe-inspiring. The road continues to Ramatuelle, a lovely medieval hill village where a large, ancient elm tree grows in the square. Follow the route over the Col de Collebasse to La Croix-Valmer, and there will be spectacular views of the coast.

There are two options now: you can continue along the coast through the resorts of Cavalaire-sur-Mer and Rayol to Le Lavandou and Bormes-les-Mimosas, or you can return inland and follow the N 98 to Cogolin and La Môle. The first route stays close to the beautiful coastline. The walled town of Bormes-les-Mimosas is particularly pretty, built on the side of a steeply sloping hillside a few kilometres from the sea. This stretch of road will be very crowded and congested in the summer months, though, and perhaps should be avoided then.

The alternative route runs along the valley of the River Môle, whose banks are lined with tall reeds. These are cut and dried and made into clarinet reeds and pipes in Cogolin, which is also known for its carpets and silk yarn. From La Môle you can take a winding scenic road over the Col du Canadel to the sea; at the top there is a sudden, almost startling view of the sea far down below. The Route des Vins completes its circuit and returns to Toulon on the N 98, after passing through La Londe-les-Maures and Hyères.

Bandol

The AOC wines of Bandol and the Vin de Pays de Mont Caume are produced in the vineyards on the coastal plain between Bandol and La Ciotat. The vineyards extend to about 800 hectares around the villages of La Cadière-d'Azur, Le Castellet, Bandol, St-Cyr-sur-Mer, Evenos, Le Beausset and Ollioulles. The first traces of vines here date from about 600 BC, and the Romans were great admirers of the wines of Bandol. It is claimed that there are 3,000 hours of sun here each year to ripen the grapes, and the local *vignerons* say their wines benefit from the unique mixture of sun, sea and Mistral. One of the oldest appellations in France, it was granted its AOC in 1941.

The red wines, considered to be the glory of the region, are made from blends based on the Mourvèdre, which must represent at least 50 per cent of the blend – but the proportion is often much bigger; the balance can be drawn from Syrah, Grenache and other local varieties. The yield must be no more than 40 hectolitres per hectare, but in practice is often much less than this. The appellation decrees that the red wine, which has been described as a Château Rothschild of Provence, must be stored for a minimum of eighteen months before bottling. The white wine is produced mainly from a blend of Clairette and Ugni Blanc. There are co-operatives at St-Cyr-sur-Mer and La Cadière-d'Azur in addition to a large number of individual producers.

ALPES-DE-HAUTE-PROVENCE
THE VINEYARDS

A FEW KILOMETRES to the north of the confluence between the Rivers Durance and Verdon is the little walled town of Pierrevert. It lies just south-west of Manosque at the edge of the Montagne du Lubéron and just within the *département* of Alpes-de-Haute-Provence. It gives its name to a small wine-growing region with a VDQS appellation acquired in 1959, Coteaux de Pierrevert.

There are about 400 hectares of vines farmed by nearly 300 *vignerons* in the countryside around the towns of Pierrevert, Manosque, Villeneuve, Gréoux-les-Bains and Quinson. Geographically the vineyards can be considered to be an extension of those in the north-east of the Vaucluse and the north-west of the Var, but the wines are quite different.

The main production is by the co-operatives at Pierrevert and their allied *caves* at Villeneuve and Quinson. The co-operative at Manosque is at present independent but there are moves afoot for an amalgamation. At the Pierrevert co-operative the red wines are made from a blend of 50 per cent Grenache, 20 per cent Cinsaut and Syrah, and 10 per cent made up of Carignan, Auban and Mourvèdre; rosé wines from 60 per cent Grenache, 30 per cent Cinsaut and 10 per cent Syrah; and the white wine from a blend of Ugni Blanc, Grenache Blanc and Clairette.

The *cave* also produces the Vin de Pays des Alpes-de-Haute-Provence, which is essentially made from the grapes produced in excess of the maximum per hectare permitted for the Coteaux de Pierrevert. In addition to the blended wines they produce two varietal wines, not permitted in the VDQS appellation, a Cabernet Sauvignon and a Chardonnay.

There are, in addition to the co-operatives, a number of independent producers, of whom the largest is the Domaine de Regusse, with a massive 230 hectares of vines representing no less than 17 varieties. The vineyard is planted in the *garrigue* a few kilometres south-west of Pierrevert on the road to La Bastide-des-Jourdans. This very large vineyard has been established since 1971 in a region in which vines had not been previously planted. As well VDQS Coteaux de Pierrevert and AOC Côtes de Lubéron, the *domaine* produces a wide range of varietal Vins de Pays, from Syrah, Pinot Noir, Cabernet Sauvignon, Gamay, Aligoté, Muscat Blanc and Viognier, together with a Chardonnay which is aged in wood.

About 10 kilometres north of Villeneuve is the little stone village of Lurs, which crowns a steep domed hill overlooking the Durance valley and is well worth a visit. An important stronghold in the Middle Ages, it belonged to the bishops of Sisteron, who held the title of Princes of Lurs. After falling into ruins at the end of the nineteenth century, the village was rediscovered by Maximillian Vox, the author of a classification of printer's typefaces, and was gradually restored and repopulated. Entering the village through a fortified gateway beneath a clock tower, you find streets meandering between ancient stone houses covered in summer with flowers and creepers. The village is the venue for an annual conference of graphic artists.

The vineyards of the Alpes-de-Haute-Provence extend as far eastwards as Quinson, which is set in the lower gorges of the River Verdon. For those who appreciate dramatic scenery it's a region not to be missed. A road leads around the edge of the Lac de Ste Croix to the village of Moustiers-Ste-Marie, with houses tiered steeply up the sheer face of a towering twin-peaked mountain. A river rushes down through its centre, and a cross is suspended above the village from a chain linking the two peaks. This was the result of a pledge made by a knight departing for the crusades.

At the eastern end of the lake, roads lead along both sides of the upper Verdon gorges. It is undeniably one of the great scenic sights of France, but is best appreciated on weekdays and out of season as the narrow winding roads carved from the mountainside are not designed for busy traffic.

ABOVE: A VINEYARD NEAR THE VILLAGE OF GORDES.
OPPOSITE TOP: THE PERCHED VILLAGE OF GORDES.
OPPOSITE BELOW: AN AUTUMNAL VINEYARD NEAR PIERREFEU
IN THE VAR.

HAUTES-ALPES
THE VINEYARDS

THIS MOST NORTHERLY pocket of Provençal vineyards can be found in the upper Durance valley to the south of Gap. As you drive north from Sisteron along the N 85 you will see a sign saying Route des Fruits et Vins. This indicates a tour along the D 948 and 942 through the villages of Ribiers, Laragne-Montéglin, Monêtier-Allemont, Tallard, Valserres and Espinasse.

It's lovely countryside but at first there are few signs of vineyards. However, if you've ever wondered where all those French Golden Delicious apples originate, this valley is the answer. A virtual sea of orchards fills the valley floor and hillsides, with rows of trees planted and pruned as neatly as oversized vines.

The vineyards are centred around the villages of Monêtier-Allemont, Tallard, Valserres and Espinasses, where there are small co-operatives which are responsible for the majority of production. They are not always open, especially out of the holiday season, but the wines can be found in local shops.

I visited one of the few independent producers, Louis Allemand, near Espinasses. His 15 hectares of vines are planted on the steep slopes of a very beautiful part of the Durance valley, where snow-capped peaks crowd the horizon. He makes a robust red wine from a variety called Mollard, with a little Gamay and Syrah added, a rosé from 50/50 Muscat Blanc and Cinsaut vinified together, and a white from Muscat d'Or and Petit Gris. He also makes *eau de vie* from a variety of fruits, and during my visit his ancient, puffing *alambic* was busy distilling a powerful brew of *marc*.

The route north to Gap can be continued by following the D 3 at the head of the valley to the Barrage de Serre-Ponçon, where there are impressive views over the man-made lake towards the high peaks of the Savoie.

ALPES-MARITIMES
THE VINEYARDS

THERE ARE JUST two appellations and two small vineyards in the *département*. Bellet is an AOC wine produced high in the hills overlooking the valley of the Var, a short distance to the north-west of Nice around the village of St-Roman-de-Bellet. This area is virtually a suburb of the city, and the vineyard is being progressively reduced in size as the value of real estate greatly exceeds the value of the land for vine cultivation. Few *vignerons* can afford to plant new vineyards when building land is valued at 10 million francs per hectare.

I met Charles Bagnis of the Château de Crémat, who has been president of the appellation for more than 30 years and is one of the leading producers. He told me there were now just 14 producers of Bellet, with a total of only 60 hectares under cultivation out of a delimited 650 hectares. Red, rosé and white wines are produced, the latter made chiefly from Rolle, with small amounts of Chardonnay and Clairette. Folle Noir, Grenache, Cinsaut and Braquet, an Italian variety, are used for reds and rosés.

The only other delimited vineyard of Alpes-Maritimes is to be found higher up the valley of the Var near the village of Villars-sur-Var. Just one producer here, Le Clos Saint-Joseph, makes wine with the appellation of Côtes de Provence, which otherwise is allowed only in the Var and Bouches-du-Rhône. From a vineyard of just 3 hectares, Antoine Sassi produces white wine from Clairette, Ugni Blanc, Rolle and Semillon, and red from Cinsaut, Grenache and Mourvèdre. Many of his vines are over sixty years old, and the yield is less than 30 hectolitres per hectare. His wines can be found on the lists of such prestigious restaurants as Le Moulin de Mougins, L'Oasis in La Napoule, and Le Diamant Rose in La Colle-sur-Loupe.

From Villars-sur-Var you can continue westward along the valley of the Var to Puget-Théniers, the fortified village of Entrevaux and the old market town of Annot. From here one road leads north through the upper valley of the Verdon to the delightful walled village of Colmars; another heads south-west to Castellane and the Grand Canyon du Verdon.

THE CUISINE

Grapes are not the only important crop in Provence: the olive tree is almost as plentiful (there is a Route de l'Huile d'Olive), and olive oil is essential to the region's cuisine. *Aïoli*, a garlic-flavoured mayonnaise made with olive oil, is served with seafood or raw vegetables. There are wonderful vegetable stews such as *ratatouille* of aubergines, tomatoes and peppers cooked in olive oil. *Salade niçoise* is a combination of tomatoes, olives, capers, potatoes, beans, lettuce, anchovies and tuna. *Pan bagna* is a *baguette*, or bun, filled with salad, tuna, tomato and capers and dredged liberally with olive oil.

The rich, tangy sauce called *tapénade* is made with olives, capers and anchovies; it is delicious with hard-boiled eggs or spread on small pieces of toasted *baguette*. *Sauce provençale* is served with fish, meat and vegetable dishes; tomatoes, garlic and shallots are gently simmered in white wine and olive oil, and seasoned with parsley and basil. *Pissaladière* is similar to the Italian pizza: a flat bread dough covered with olives, anchovies and onions and baked in an oven. Another speciality of the region, traditionally served at Easter and Christmas, is Vin Cuit (cooked wine), made by boiling newly pressed, unfermented grape juice until it is reduced to about a third of its volume and adding a measure of *marc* or *eau de vie*.

Bouillabaisse, the great fish stew of Marseilles, is one of the most renowned dishes of Provence. There are many versions but they all should include a mixture of firm, white-fleshed fish (some regard *rascasse* as obligatory), olive oil, garlic, fennel and onions, with saffron added for flavour and colour. Then there are the *daubes*, hearty stews of lamb or beef cooked slowly with wine, garlic and tomatoes and seasoned with aromatic herbs. *Pieds et paquets* are sausage-like parcels of lambs' trotters and tripe stuffed with bacon, garlic and herbs and cooked in white wine.

For those with a sweet tooth, the world-famous Montélimar nougat is not to be missed, nor the *calissons* of Aix-en-Provence, lozenge-shaped parcels made from almonds and crystallized fruit.

CORSICA

THE ISLAND OF Corsica is France's southernmost territory, lying 170 kilometres to the south-east of Nice and just 12 kilometres from the northern tip of Sardinia. The island was first settled in the sixth century BC by Greeks from Phocaea who cultivated the eastern plain and established a trading base at Aleria. They were followed by a succession of other would-be colonizers, including the Etruscans and Romans, but it was ruled by the Genoese from the Middle Ages until 1768 when it became French, just over a year before the birth of Napoleon in Ajaccio.

It's a truly astonishing island, with one of the most beautiful coastlines to be found anywhere in the world and a dramatic landscape of rich variety: spectacular gorges, river and mountain scenery of alpine proportions, intensely scented *maquis*, dense forests of chestnut, beech and the magnificent laricio pines, ancient perched hill villages and vast beaches of white sand lapped by limpid blue water – all are to be found within an hour or so's drive.

From the UK you can fly direct to Ajaccio or Bastia during the summer, but out of season you will have to change at Nice or Paris: There are also car-carrying ferries or catamarans from Marseille and Toulon to Bastia, Calvi, Ajaccio, Propriano and Porto Vecchio.

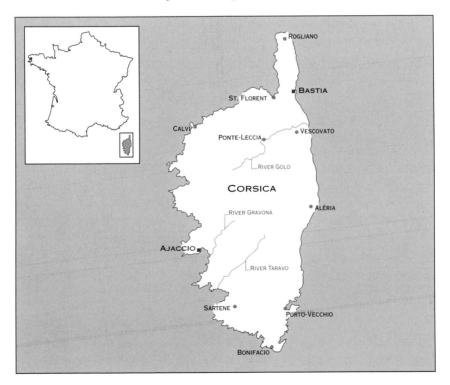

THE WINES

Corsican wines are quite different from those on mainland France. It is claimed that Corsica enjoys nearly 3,000 hours of sunshine each year, and with over twenty mountain peaks of 2,000 metres or more, a widely varied terrain and soil composition and indigenous grapes varieties not found elsewhere, the potential for making wines of great character and interest is enormous.

The first vines were planted here nearly 600 years BC; in the fourth century AD the wines of Cap Corse found their way to the popes' table, and more recent history records that Napoleon's parents owned vineyards near Ajaccio. There are three main appellations: Vins de Corse, Ajaccio and Patrimonio. Five others have Cru, or Villages, distinctions: Vin de Corse-Calvi, Figari, Porto-Vecchio, Sartène and Cap Corse, which also covers a sweet white dessert wine made from Muscat. In addition a significant quantity of Vin de Pays de l'Île de Beauté is also produced.

The three main grape varieties are the black-skinned Niellucciu and Sciacarellu, used for red and rosé wines, and Vermentinu, or Malvoisie de Corse, used for the whites. Other permitted varieties include Carcajolu, Montanaccio, Barbarossa, Aleatico, Muscat, Grenache, Carignan and Cinsaut.

THE VINEYARDS

Corsica is not a large island, measuring about 90 kilometres from east to west and 180 from north to south, but it is packed with an astonishing variety of landscape, much of which is mountainous. With the exception of the main road running the length of the east coast from Bastia to Porto-Vecchio, and some sections of the island's central route from St-Florent to Ajaccio, the roads in general are narrow and tortuously winding, and even a short distance can take some time to drive.

It's not surprising that Corsica is a favourite location for rally drivers to hone their skills. On many of the quieter mountain roads you will encounter a variety of hazards in the form of wild pigs, free-range domestic pigs, herds of shaggy-coated goats and bony cows rambling freely along the way. An unhurried journey is both the safest and by far the most enjoyable way to travel as each turn of the road brings yet another stunning view into sight. By happy coincidence a tour of the island's vineyards will also encompass much of the most spectacular scenery and interesting villages.

Ajaccio

Ajaccio is the island's capital and was founded in 1492 in the sheltered north-east corner of the Golfe d'Ajaccio. It's a lively and atmospheric place, with shops, restaurants, pavement cafés, shady squares, a casino and a daily fish market at the harbour. To the west, a road runs along the shoreline passing numerous small sandy beaches to the Pointe de la Parata, where there is a fine view of the string of small islands known as the Îles Sanguinaires.

Ajaccio is a good place to start a tour of the vineyards as it is a well-served destination for both the ferry boats and airlines as well as being the centre of one of the most important appellations.

The Ajaccio vineyards are located in four main areas which are quite widely separated. The greatest concentration of vineyards is to be found on the Montagne St Angelo, just to the north of Ajaccio and to the south of Mezzavia, including the Domaine Peraldi, one of the island's most prized vineyards.

The next most important area is in the lower valley of the River Prunelli, to the east of Ajaccio around the villages of Pisciatello and Cauro. This is where the highly regarded wines of Clos Capitoro and the Domaine Martini are produced. From Cauro the D 3 leads north-east along an ever-steepening valley with stunning views of the Prunelli gorges to the mountain town of Bastelica.

The third pocket of Ajaccio vineyards is to the south of Cauro around the villages of Cognocoli-Monticchi – where you will find the *domaine* of Alain Courrèges – Pila-Canale and Stiliccione, in the valley of Taravo. This, too, is a lovely valley surrounded by steep hillsides covered in *maquis*, which in spring are a blaze of colour with yellow broom, gorse, rock roses, helleborous, giant fennel, orchids and cyclamen. On the eastern side of the valley is the important prehistoric site of Filitosa, where there is an impressive collection of menhirs.

At the mouth of the valley is Porto-Pollo, with its fine sandy beach and several beachside restaurants. The Baie de Copabia is a short distance to the west and, for my money, one of the finest and quietest beaches on the island: a magnificent crescent of fine white sand, enclosed by steep, *maquis*-covered headlands and with a small river running across it to the limpid blue sea. To the north, on the other side of the Capo di Muro, are two more beaches worth a small detour, Portigliolo and Verghia.

The fourth and smallest area of vineyards is to be found to the north of Ajaccio in a region known as the Cinarca, a delightful pastoral landscape of steep green hillsides and plunging valleys rimmed by mountains. The vineyard of Clos d'Alzeto has 90 hectares of vines planted on the mountain slopes above the valley of the Liamone near the hamlet of Ambiegna and produces wine that is frequently singled out for acclaim. To the north, a small road follows the river through spectacular gorges high along the valley side to the old town of Vico, tucked below the 4,000-foot summit of Sposata.

Calvi

The vineyards of the Haute-Balagne, which have the Calvi appellation, can be reached by a wonderfully scenic route which follows the stunning north-western coastline for much of the way. From Vico you can follow D 70 north to Evisa, a red-roofed village set among chestnut forests. From here the road leads west through the spectacular Spelunca gorges to the pretty little resort of Porto, with its Genoese tower set on a rocky outcrop.

An essential detour from here is to the old village of Piana, set in the midst of one of Corsica's great sights, the Calanche. These rust- and rose-coloured cliffs, which are protected by UNESCO, rise from the blue waters of the Golfe de Porto in a series of towering pinnacles and sheer rock faces for several kilometres between Porto and Piana – a sight not to be missed.

From Porto the route to Calvi continues along the D 81 with stunning views of the blue sea far below from the cliff-hanging corniche. At Galéria, about halfway, a road leads up into the remote valley of the Fango, a haven for fishermen and hunters. The final leg of the journey follows an increasingly stark and rocky coastline until the headland of the Pointe de la Revellata is rounded, with a fine view of Calvi and the Haute-Balagne from the chapel of Notre-Dame de la Serra.

Calvi is a popular resort with an impressive citadel jutting out into the western corner of the wide, sand-fringed and pine-shaded bay which curves away for several kilometres. Like the vineyards of Ajaccio, those of Calvi are quite fragmented and are planted mainly in the valley of the Figarella and around the villages of Calenzana, Zilia, Feliceto and Lumio. Domaine Culombu at Lumio

ABOVE TOP: A VILLAGE IN THE HAUTE-BALAGNE NEAR CALVI.
ABOVE: THE HARBOUR AND CITADEL OF BONIFACIO.
OPPOSITE: THE VILLAGE OF NONZA ON THE WESTERN COAST OF CAP CORSE.

produces some of the best wine on the island, along with Clos Landry near Calvi
and Clos Réginu at Muro.

The Haute-Balagne has deep, fertile valleys protected by vast, soaring mountains, with tiny roads winding their way to remote hill villages while giving constant views of the distant deep-blue Mediterranean. A rewarding tour of the
region can be made by following the D 151, off the N 197 just east of Calvi,
through the villages of Calenzana, Zilia and Montemaggiore to the Col de Salvi,
from where there are sweeping views of the bay of Calvi and the numerous red-
roofed villages dotted over the mountainsides of the Balagne. From here you can
return to the coast road via the villages of Lavatoggio and Lumio, or via St
Antonino and Pigna to l'Île-Rousse. Alternatively, you can travel deeper into the
Balagne by following the D 71 to Feliceto and Belgodere, reaching the coast road
again at Lozari.

Patrimonio

Heading north-east from Lozari you pass the impressive white-sand beach of the
Anse de Peraiola. After this the D 81 leads eastwards across another of Corsica's
astonishing landscapes, the Désert des Agriates, a jagged rocky wasteland which
looks more like the surface of the moon than of Europe. As the road descends
towards the Golfe de St-Florent, the atmospheric and lively little harbour town
comes into view far below, against a backdrop of the looming mountains of Cap
Corse, the island's northern promontory.

Here the vineyards are extensive, with the valleys radiating out from St-
Florent densely planted with vines on the slopes below the steep mountainsides.
Numerous *vignerons* have roadside signs inviting you to taste and buy the wines
of Patrimonio, the first in Corsica to be granted an appellation – and some say the
best of the island. The wines of Orenga de Gaffory, Dominique Gentile, Antoine
Aréna and Domaine de Catarelli are particularly well respected in the region.

The principal wine-villages are St-Florent, Patrimonio, Farinole, Poggio
d'Oletta and Oletta. There are stunning views of the countryside and the vineyards from the road which leads up to the Col de Teghime, between Patrimonio
and Bastia, from where, on a clear day, you can see both sides of Cap Corse.
More spectacular views are to be had from the D 38, which descends from the
Col de Teghime to Oletta.

In addition to the conventional red, white and rosé wines of Patrimonio this
region also has an appellation for a sweet white dessert wine, Cap Corse, produced from the Muscat variety around the villages of Rogliano, Centuri,
Macinaggio, Luri and Morsiglia, near the northern tip of Cap Corse. The road following the western coastline of the cape provides a constant view of the huge,
sculpted, colour-flecked rocks and sheer cliffs above a purple-blue sea. The cliff-
hanging village of Nonza with its dramatic black sand beach and the pretty little
harbour of Centuri-Port are especially worth seeing. From Macinaggio a rather
less tortuous road follows the eastern coast of the cape back towards Bastia.

Côte Orientale

The bulk of Vin de Corse and l'Île de Beauté is produced from the vineyards on
the eastern plain to the south of Bastia. It's very flat and rather featureless apart
from a number of lagoons which are used to cultivate shellfish. There are,
however, some long stretches of sandy beaches, and the mountainous hinterland
has some fine scenery.

The first important wine-growing area south of Bastia is the region known as the Casinca, around the villages of Vescovato and Folelli, where the Domaine de Musoleu produces some of the best wine of the region. You can take a short drive through these villages along a small mountain road which provides sweeping views of the plain and lagoons. Take the D 37 to the west of the N 198 two kilometres after the junction with the road to Ponte Leccia. This leads first to the impressively sited village of Vescovato, with its tall multi-windowed houses set on the steep mountainside, and then, with numerous twists and turns, to Venzolasca, Penta-di-Casinca and Castellare-di-Casinca before descending again to the coast road near Folelli, where one of the numerous *cave co-opératives* of the east coast is situated.

The one major vineyard to be found in the centre of the island is the Domaine de Vico just to the north of Ponte Leccia, an important island cross-road. To get there, go west from Casamozza on the N 193. It's a good road, very scenic and takes little more than half an hour to drive from the coast. The detour is very worthwhile, not only for the excellent wine but also because the vineyard lies at the entrance to the Asco valley and its gorges, one of the loveliest on the island, with a white-water river rushing by the foot of sheer cliffs on each side. The road through the gorges continues beyond the village of Asco high into the mountains to the ski station of Haut-Asco.

Since there is little of great interest along the coast road between Folelli and Aléria, it is worth taking the very enjoyable alternative route south from Ponte Leccia, through glorious scenery, to Corte. Surrounded by snow-capped peaks, the ancient citadel has a highly impressive setting, perched on a rock above the old quarter of cobbled streets and narrow, stepped alleys. Corte is also the gateway to yet another of Corsica's great sights, the gorges of the Restonica, a deep V-shaped glacial cleft surrounded by impressive mountains of an alpine scale and appearance.

From Corte you can return to the coast road at Aléria by following the N 200 through the lovely valley of the Tavignano. There are extensive vineyards here on the coastal plain around the villages of Tallone, Aléria and Ghisonaccia further to the south. The Clos d'Orléa at Aléria is a vineyard worth seeking out.

Porto Vecchio & Figari

These two sub-appellations of Vin de Corse apply to quite small areas of vineyards around the little town of Lecci, 12 kilometres or so to the north of Porto-Vecchio and around the villages of Pianottoli and Poggiale, 20 kilometres or so to the north-west of Bonifacio. In each case there are just two producers. Porto-Vecchio has the Cave Fior di Lecci and the Domaine de Torracia – one of the island's most respected producers; while Figari has the co-operative of Omu di Cagna and the Domaine de Tanella.

Porto-Vecchio is a quite large and very popular summer resort with boutiques, restaurants, pavement cafés and a busy harbour where some of the Mediterranean's most luxurious yachts and cruisers berth. There are a number of superb beaches in the area: the Plage de Palombaggia, bordered by pine trees and edged by rose-pink rocks, is one of the lovelist – and the most popular. Further south, the picturesque Plage de la Rondinella is almost enclosed by *maquis*-covered headlands.

The port of Bonifacio lies between the two wine-growing areas and makes an ideal base from which to explore. The setting of its old town and citadel on a

ABOVE: THE GORGES DE L'ASCO NEAR PONTE-LECCIA.
OPPOSITE TOP: LES CALANCHES NEAR THE VILLAGE OF PIANA AND,
BEYOND, THE GOLFE DE PORTO.
OPPOSITE BELOW: VINEYARDS NEAR THE WINE-VILLAGE OF PATRIMONIO.

huge rock at the mouth of a deep inlet makes it one of the loveliest, and most intimate, harbours in the Mediterranean. Seen from the road which leads out to the lighthouse, the old houses are revealed to be perched precariously on the very edge of sheer white sculpted cliffs with a backdrop of distant mountains.

Sartène

The old town of Sartène lies 55 kilometres to the north-west of Bonifacio, set high on a hillside overlooking the Rizzanèse valley and looking out towards the Golfe de Valinco. The vineyards here are extensive, planted on the valley floors and mountain slopes which spread out from the town. The main areas of cultivation are along the lower reaches of the Rizzanèse valley and in the valley of the Loreto which leads south-west of Sartène to the Golfe de Murtoli.

Sartène has a *cave co-opérative*, Santa Barba, as well as six other producers. The Domaine de Fiumicicoli is one of the most highly-regarded wines of the region with two *caveaux*: one is situated 2 kilometres along the main road from Propriano to Olmeta, the other about 7 kilometres along the D 268 between Sartène and the very attractive village of Ste-Lucie-de-Tallano. The road continues to Levie and Zonza in the Alta Rocca, from where it continues to climb to another of Corsica's grand sights, the Col de Bavella, a vast amphitheatre of soaring granite spires which rise to over 5,000 feet above sea level.

The domaines of Mosconi and Fontella can be found in the lower valley of the Loreto, where a small road from Sartène follows the river to the small beach and community of Tizzano. Nearby are two important prehistoric sites, the megaliths of Cauria and the alignments of Palaggiu, where a very large number of large sculpted stones can be found standing above the *maquis*.

The popular resort of Propriano, with its large marina and numerous hotels, shops and restaurants, lies a dozen kilometres or so to the north-west of Sartène in a sheltered position on the southern shore of the Golfe de Valinco. From here a road leads out to the fine sweep of white sandy beach at Portigliolo and, at the end of the road, Campomoro.

THE CUISINE

Corsican cuisine benefits from both its French and Italian influences. There is excellent pasta, for example, and every village has its pizzeria with a wood-fired oven. The *charcuterie* is among the best to be found anywhere, and so it should be as it is produced from free-range pigs who are left to wander the hillsides and forage among the chestnut trees and *maquis*. *Coppa* is smoked cut of pork served thinly sliced, *prisuttu* a strongly flavoured dry-cured ham, and *figatelli* a sausage made from pork meat and liver. The goat's-milk cheeses are deliciously distinctive, while Brocciu is a soft creamy ewe's-milk cheese used to stuff canneloni, to fill omelettes flavoured with mint, and to make a cheesecake-style pudding called *fiadone* which is dredged with aquavit just before serving.

The fish of course is superb, with fresh trout from the mountain rivers, *langouste* from the Golfe de St-Florent, oysters from the lagoons of the eastern plain and a plentiful supply of Mediterranean fish like red mullet and sea bass along with local varieties such as *chapon* and *mustelle*.

WINE CHARACTERISTICS

THE QUALITY OF a wine, its character and appeal, can be measured by the presence and balance of certain basic elements like fruit, body, tannin, acidity, sweetness, alcohol and aroma.

A red wine needs tannin, an excess can make it tough or mouth-puckering to drink while insufficient tannin can make it seem lacking in flavour and character. Many very good red wines have a noticeably tannic taste when young which mellows and softens with age, ultimately producing a wine with more subtle and complex flavours than one which tastes pleasantly soft and fruity soon after it has been bottled.

A white wine needs a degree of acidity, an excess will make it seem astringent and sharp on the palate while insufficient acidity is likely to produce a flat or flabby wine with little character or depth of flavour.

A GUIDE TO GRAPE VARIETIES

ALICANTE BOUSCHET
A high-yielding variety grown mainly in southern France with strong colour and high alcohol potential but lacking in tannin. It is used mainly as an element of a blended red wine.

ALIGOTE
This variety is the inferior alternative to Burgundy's Chardonnay with a tendency towards high acidity. It is the traditional ingredient of Kir, an aperitif made by spiking white wine with Creme de Cassis.

ALTESSE
Also known as Roussette in the Savoie, it produces full-bodied white wines with a spicy, aromatic bouquet.

ARAMON
A traditional variety of the Languedoc, its high-yielding qualities have earned it a poor reputation for quality in favour of quantity but, as one well-known winemaker told me, it can produce good wine when driven hard.

ARBOIS
A white-skinned grape grown in the Loire region producing largely undistinguished wines and no connection with the Jura wine of that name.

ARRUFIAC
A variety used to make white wines in the Basque region.

AUXERROIS BLANC
Grown quite widely between northern Burgundy and Alsace it is a generously yielding variety with high acidity and alcohol potential making fresh, dry varietal white wines.

BAROQUE
Grown largely in south-west France, this is the variety used to make Tursan white wines and some Vins de Pays Landais. High in alcohol, it makes full-bodied country-style wines.

BOURBOULENC
A white-skinned grape cultivated largely in the Mediterranean and used largely as part of a blend for white wines.

CABERNET FRANC
This variety is widely grown in Bordeaux and has a softer taste with a more complex aroma than Cabernet Sauvignon. It is commonly used as a component of clarets and also in red wines from the Loire, like Saumur Champigny.

CABERNET SAUVIGNON
Of the black grapes from which red wines are produced, Cabernet Sauvignon is, perhaps, the one with the widest international popularity. It is thought to have derived from wild vines first grown in the Bordeaux area of France and remains the foundation of the red wines of that region.

The small, almost sloe-like, purple berries ripen late and contain generous tannin, due in part to an abundance of pips and a high proportion of pulp to juice when pressed. Although initially harsh or tough in character this grape makes a wine destined to keep and mature. Its bouquet is one of blackcurrant fruit and when aged has a fat buttery taste with masses of body and flavour.

CARIGNAN
A variety widely planted in southern France, it has a generous yield producing good colour, tannin and a high degree of alcohol. It is used mainly as an element of blended red wines.

CHARDONNAY
Probably the most popular and widely planted white-wine grape the world over. In France it is, arguably, *the* white-wine grape from which the classic Burgundies, like Montrachet and Chablis, are made. It is also the grape from which Blanc des Blancs Champagne is made.

It produces a delicately flavoured, full-bodied wine with a good balance of acidity and alcohol together with a fragrant aroma. It also has great potential to improve with maturity and lends itself well to oak ageing.

CHASSELAS
A white-skinned variety, widely grown as a desert grape but the principle variety used in the wines of Haute Savoie, such as Crepy.

CESAR
A very tannic black-skinned grape used most famously as a small proportion of a blend with Pinot Noir in the wines of Irancy.

CHENIN BLANC
Grown widely in the Loire valley, where it is used to make wines like Vouvray and Coteaux de Layon, the Chenin Blanc, or Pineau de la Loire, i found less frequently in other parts of France. A high-yielding grape, it produces a wine which c make both sweet, honeyed wines and those w are bone dry with equal success. Its bouquet often associated with citrus fruits like quince lime with hints of honey and it is also used make sparkling wines.

CINSAUT

This variety is one of the most widely planted in France, where it flourishes in the more southerly climates. It has good acidity and colour and is used often as a blend with Grenache and Carignan as well as producing varietal red wines.

CLAIRETTE BLANC

Widely planted in southern Franch this variety was traditionally used for the production of Vermouth. With a tendency towards low acidity, a fruity bouquet and a high alcohol potential, it is often used as an element in blended vins de pays and is sometimes encountered as a varietal white wine.

COLOMBARD

This is the grape from which much of the Armagnac production is distilled. It is used both as an element of blended whites and vins de cepage and is most commonly encountered in south-west France. It makes light, fresh fruity wines with a good bouquet and balance but is not a wine for keeping and is best drunk young.

COT

Also known as Malbec or Auxerrois, this variety is grown largely in south-west France and the Midi. It has relatively low acidity with a flavour some link with ripe blackberries producing soft, easy-to-drink and flavourful red wines.

COURBOU

A white-skinned variety cultivated in the Bearn and Basque region of south-west France.

DURAS

A black-skinned variety cultivated primarily in the Midi and a component of Gaillac reds.

FER SERVADOU

A red-wine grape grown largely in the Midi where it is used as an element of a blend for such wines as Madiran and Gaillac.

FOLLE BLANCHE

Grown originally to make brandy, this variety is now found largely in the western Loire where it is the main ingredient of Gros Plant Nantais, producing a light, dry wine with little body and a tendency towards high acidity.

GAMAY

Beaujolais is a wine and a region where the Gamay reigns supreme but it also accounts for a gh proportion of French red wines generally and characteristic of the young fresh fruity reds ch constitute the great fount of everyday

amay produces a light purple-tinged red wine ood fruit, acidity and bouquet but is ly low in tannin and, consequently, best

drunk young. It has a high yield and lends itself well to rapid vinification making it a popular choice for Primeurs.

GEWURTZTRAMINER

This variety is found mainly in north-east Franch where it is used to produce varietal dry white wines with a golden tint, high alcohol content, a distinctive spicy aroma and complex flavour.

GRENACHE NOIR

Widely planted in southern France it is often used to produce full-bodied fruity rosés as well as dry and quite tough reds. Most commonly used as an element of blended wines it is also encountered as a vin de cepage. Blanc and Gris versions of Grenache are also used occasionally in the Languedoc for making white and rosé wines.

GROLLEAU

Planted largely in the Loire region, this high-yielding variety is often used to produce a light, fresh-tasting Vin Gris but is also used as a component of blended red wines.

JACQUERE

A high-yielding variety producing light, dry white wines with relatively high acidity which is planted largely in the Savoie.

JURANCON NOIR

A variety used in the production of red wines and largely cultivated in south-west France.

LEN DE L'ELH

A derivation of loin de l'oeil, meaning literally and inexplicably, far from the eye. It is a mainstay of the Gaillac region and the Cotes du Tarn producing a white wine with high alcohol potential but low acidity. It is often used in a blend with Mauzac.

JURANÇON

This black grape variety is grown largely in south-west France and the Midi and is a relative of the Languedoc's Aramon variety. It produces wine with a relatively high alcohol level and is used primarily as part of a blend.

MACABEO

A white grape also known as Maccabeu, it is used principly in the most southerly part of Languedoc-Roussillon, to make a fruity, aromatic white wine which is usually quite light and dry.

MANSENG

Gros and Petit Manseng are white-skinned varieties used in the production of Jurancon wines.

MARSANNE

Widely planted in the northern Rhone valley, this high-yielding variety produces a honey-coloured white wine with a good bouquet which is best drunk young.

MAUZAC BLANC

Also known as Blanquette because of the white powder which coats the undersides of its leaves, it is planted largely in the Gaillac and Limoux regions. It produces a dry white wine with good fruit and quite high acidity. It is also used for sparkling wines, ie. Blanquette de Limoux, when it is blended with Sauvignon Blanc or Chardonnay.

MELON DE BOURGOGNE

Known more commonly as Pinot Blanc in California and Muscadet in France, this variety is grown largely in north-west France where its ability to thrive in a colder climate is an advantage. It produces very dry white wines with good alcohol levels which are best drunk young.

MERLOT

This is an important high-yield grape variety grown extensively in south-west France where it is used as an element of the blend for Clarets. It has grown enormously in popularity throughout southern France and is often used to make vins de cepage. It is valued for its fruitiness and a lack of tannin and acidity making a soft, easy-to-drink red wine.

MONDEUSE NOIR

This variety was widely planted in north-east France before phylloxera struck. Now found mainly in Savoie and Bugey, it can produce full-bodied, quite tough, varietal red wines with a distinctive character as well as being used as part of a blend.

MOURVEDRE

Found in southern France, Provence in particular, this variety is commonly used as part of a blend for red wines where its relatively high acidity, tannin and deep colour are used as a strengthening element.

MULLER THURGAU

The result of crossing Riesling and Sylvaner, this German variety, found almost exclusively in Lorraine, can produce fragrant white wines which are light, dry and fruity.

MUSCADELLE

A white-skinned variety grown largely in the Bordelais and used as part of a blend with Semillon and Sauvignon Blanc.

MUSCAT OF ALEXANDRIA

A very ancient variety used to make both sweet and dry white wines which have a distinctively grapey taste. High-yielding, and also planted for desert grapes, it is grown largely in southern Franch since it requires a hot climate. Muscat Blanc a Petit Grins is a superior variety found in

the Roussillon region where it is used as a component of Vin Doux Naturels like Banyuls as well as in the southern Rhone valley for Beaumes de Venise and Clairette de Die.

NEGRETTE

A black-skinned variety, cultivated largely in the Midi, which adds a richness of colour and flavour when used in a blend but has low acidity.

NIELLUCIO

A black-skinned grape cultivated in Corsica, notably for Patrimonio, where it produces high-quality reds for keeping.

PETIT VERDOT

A variety cultivated in the Bordelais and used as a small part of a classic blend with Merlot and Cabernet Sauvignon for long-lasting reds.

PINEAU D'AUNIS

Planted largely in the Loire region, this black-skinned variety is often used to make dry, fruity rosé wines as well as being used as an element in blended reds.

PINOT NOIR

The great red-wine grape of Burgundy is more fickle and less easily identifiable than the Cabernet Sauvignon. It is also grown widely in Alsace, Lorraine, the Savoie and Jura and is an essential ingredient of most champagnes where it is pressed swiftly to produce a colourless juice.

A low-yield grape, it produces a wine with flavours of red fruits like raspberries and plums and can mature to create highly complex tastes and bouquets with an excellent finish and considerable potential to improve with age.

Pinot Blanc, Gris and Meunier are also encountered, notably as vins de cepage in Alsace, for Cotes St Jacques and in the classic blend for Champagne, respectively.

PORTUGUESE BLEU

Grown widely in Germany and Austria, as Portugieser, this red-wine variety is found largely in the Midi. High yielding with a tendency to low tannin levels it produces fairly light wines and is used, usually, as an element of a blend.

POULSARD

A black-skinned variety which is planted in eastern France producing a light red wine with an attractive, flowery bouquet.

RIESLING

The Riesling grape originated in Germany along the banks of the Rhine and is widely grown in north-east France but is less frequently encountered elsewhere in the country. It is a k yielding grape which, like the Semillon, whe harvested late is susceptible to noble rot, en both sweet and dry wines to be made. With a good balance of acidity and alcohol it makes wines which are aromatic, fresh and clean tasting with considerable potential to improve with age.

ROLLE
A white-wine grape cultivated largely in Provence, for Bellet notably, and in Corsica to produce distinctively aromatic wines.

ROMORANTIN
A high-yielding, white-skinned variety cultivated primarily in the Loire, notably Cheverny, where it is used to make fairly lightweight wines.

ROUSSANNE
A white-wine variety grown largely in the northern Rhone valley, it produces a delicately flavoured white wine with a scented bouquet and is used both as an element of a blended wine, often with Marsanne, as well as for producing vins de cepage.

SACY
A white-skinned variety producing fresh-tasting dry wines, cultivated in the Yonne, largely for Cremant de Bourgogne, and as a key component of St Pourcain white wines.

SAVIGNIN
A variety cultivated in the Jura where it is used to produce the celebrated Vin Jaune.

SAUVIGNON BLANC
This grape produces the great French white wines of Sancerre and Pouilly Fume as well as being an important element in the white wines of Graves where it is blended with Semillon. It is widely grown in many other regions of France where it has become a popular choice for varietal vins de pays. It produces a light, fresh wine with a hint of green fruit in the bouquet and a flinty-dry flavour but has a limited potential to improve with keeping.

SCIACERELLO
A black-skinned variety cultivated in Corsica where it produces fruity, full, alcoholic reds.

SEMILLON
Widely grown in south-west France, the Semillon grape is used as a component of dry white wines, often in combination with Sauvignon Blanc. It is also ideal for the generation of botrytis cinera, the noble rot from which a highly concentrated juice is pressed to make sweet white wines like Sauternes. It produces a strongly alcoholic wine, relatively low in acidity and with a limited bouquet, having what is usually described as a grassy, lemony flavour.

SYLVANER
variety largely cultivated in Alsace where it is sed to produce lightweight white wines.

SYRAH
This is the grape which gives many of the red Rhone wines, like Hermitage, their great strength and character. It survives well on poor soil producing a good yield and has an abundance of tannin making strongly alcoholic wines with plenty of body and flavour which have the potential for high quality and improvement with keeping. It has also gained considerable popularity for varietal vins de pays rosés.

TANNAT
A variety used to make Madiran, one of the most interesting wines of south-west France, as well as red Cotes de St Mont. Strong in colour, tannin and alcohol it has a perfumed bouquet and benefits from ageing.

TERRET BOURRET
Planted widely in the Languedoc coastal region, both white and gris grapes are produced in this variety producing light, dry white wines with good acidity.

TERRET NOIR
A variety grown largely in southern France which produces a light red wine with a pleasing bouquet and some acidity. Used mainly as part of a blend.

TIBOUREN
A black grape grown mainly in southern France, notably Provence, which lends itself well to making full-bodied rosés with a distinctive bouquet.

TOKAY
The name given in Alsace to Pinot Gris.

UGNI BLANC
Also known as Italy's Trebbiano and Cognac's St Emilion, world-wide this high-yielding grape is responsible for producing more white wine than any other variety. A large proportion in France is distilled into brandy. It has a limited bouquet, high acidity but little body and is often used to provide an acidic element of a blend, although it is sometimes found as a vin de cepage.

VERMENTINO
Given the name of Rolle in Provence, it is also called Malvoisie in Corsica where it is widely cultivated for white wine production.

VIOGNIER
A variety associated primarily with the northern Rhone valley but becoming increasingly popular for vins de pays throughout southern France, albeit in small plantings. It produces a high-quality, full-bodied white wine with a very distinctive, aromatic bouquet and is nearly always used to produce vins de cepage.

INDEX